CAMBRIDGE SOUTH ASIAN STUDIES

THE STATE AND POVERTY IN INDIA

A list of the books in the series will be found at the end of the volume.

THE STATE AND POVERTY IN INDIA

THE POLITICS OF REFORM

ATUL KOHLI

*Department of Politics and
Woodrow Wilson School of Public and
International Affairs
Princeton University*

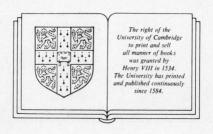

*The right of the
University of Cambridge
to print and sell
all manner of books
was granted by
Henry VIII in 1534.
The University has printed
and published continuously
since 1584.*

CAMBRIDGE UNIVERSITY PRESS

CAMBRIDGE

LONDON   NEW YORK   ROCHELLE
MELBOURNE   SYDNEY

Published by the Press Syndicate of the University of Cambridge
The Pitt Building, Trumpington Street, Cambridge CB2 IRP
32 East 57th Street, New York, NY 10022, USA
10 Stamford Road, Oakleigh, Melbourne 3166, Australia

First published 1987

Printed in Great Britain by
Redwood Burn Limited, Trowbridge, Wiltshire

British Library cataloguing in publication data
Kohli, Atul
The state and poverty in India: the politics
of reform. – (Cambridge South Asian Studies; 37)
1. Poor – India – Political aspects
2. Poor – India – History – 20th century
I. Title
362.5'8'0954   HC 440.P6

Library of Congress cataloguing in publication data
Kohli, Atul
The state and poverty in India.
(Cambridge South Asian Studies; 37)
Bibliography;
Includes index.
1. Land reform – India – States – Case studies.
2. Manpower policy – India – States – Case studies.
3. Rural poor – Government policy – India – States – Case studies.
4. Income distribution – Government policy – States – Case studies.
5. Political parties – India – States – Cases studies.
6. India – Rural conditions – Case studies.
I. Title.
II. Series.
HD 133.I4K65 1985   333.3'1'54   85-25554

ISBN 0 521 32008 9

TP

CONTENTS

LIST OF TABLES AND FIGURES

Tables

Figures

ACKNOWLEDGEMENTS

This book was researched and written during a period of four years, the final version being completed in the spring of 1984. A number of institutions supported the project. My first research trip to India in 1979 was funded by the Social Sciences and the Humanities Research Council of Canada and The Institute for the Study of World Politics, New York City. This project might have never been initiated but for the early risk these institutions were willing to take. The Michigan State University supported my travel and stay in India in 1981. The trip in 1983 was undertaken in conjunction with another project; that was funded by the Smithsonian Institute. And the last visit to India in the summer of 1984 was supported by Princeton University.

The Centre for the Study of Developing Societies, Delhi, was a much-needed base for research in India. I owe thanks to the respective directors of the Centre — Rajni Kothari, Rameshwar Roy, and Bashiruddin Ahmed — for providing an intellectually stimulating and hospitable environment whenever I was in New Delhi. Binoy Chowdhry and D. Bandopadhyaya in West Bengal, and Devraj Urs in Karnataka facilitated my field'research by providing jeep transportation, government accommodations, and important contacts in the rural areas.

The comments of several individuals have helped improve this book. Those who read the whole manuscript and commented on it generously included Paul Brass, Pranab Bardhan, Reinhard Bendix, Jyoti Dasgupta, Marie Gottschalk and William Kornhauser. Parts were read by Henry Bienen, Gary Bonham, Don Crone, Michael Bratton, David Gordon, Marcus Franda, Francine Frankel, Stephen Haggard, James Manor, and Bhabani Sengupta. Anonymous reviewers of the manuscript have also been extraordinarily helpful. I have not incorporated all the criticisms made by these insightful readers. The book is, however, much richer for their help.

Three different universities provided the support necessary for the writing of this book. I was a doctoral student at the Department of Political Science, University of California, Berkeley, when this project was initiated. The book was stimulated by and remains a product of the intellectual environment at Berkeley. Michigan State University generously provided free time to write the book. Evette Chavez of Michigan State University typed an earlier version of it. Lastly, research support from Princeton University has enabled me to complete it. Ashok Subramanium helped complete the footnotes, references, and index. Robert Kimmerle edited my rough writing style into a more polished form, and Edna Lloyd typed the final manuscript.

The acknowledgements would not be complete without thanking some very special people. Elliott Tepper of Carleton University, Ottawa, Canada, was my teacher during the undergraduate years. He helped spark a wide array of intellectual interests. Some of them have matured in this book. Jyoti Dasgupta always maintained his confidence in me during graduate school. I hope I have met his expectations. My dear friends Gary Bonham and Chris Paige provided that all-encompassing support which only close friends of the same graduate class understand. The love of my parents, brother, and sister, which was always there, was of special importance because it had nothing to do with whether I wrote this book or not. And finally, the book is dedicated to Dijana Plestina for the years spent together in Ottawa and Berkeley.

Princeton   *Atul Kohli*
December 1984

Introduction

I met a Sculptor in your land.
He carved heads in stone.
A small head had enormous round
eyes and almost no face.
That is poverty, he said.
>   Rama Krishnan Jaina
>   (Indian poet)

Three decades of planned economic development have failed to improve the living conditions of India's poor. This persistence of poverty is clearly manifest in the continuance of low percapita income. It is nevertheless clear by now that higher growth rates, and therefore higher percapita income, are not sufficient to improve the lot of the poor. New wealth has not "trickled down." The solutions to the problem of India's poverty will thus not emerge from higher rates of economic growth alone; if they emerge at all, they are likely to involve conscious state intervention aimed at reconciling growth with distribution. The analytical issue this raises goes beyond the often-discussed question of suitable development strategies. The more fundamental issue concerns the role of public authorities in economic development: what type of regimes are most likely to pursue a successful redistributive strategy aimed at alleviating the worst of India's poverty?

This volume is a study of redistributive intervention in a developing society. The impact of authority structures and regime types on patterns of socio-economic development has not received the scholarly attention it deserves. An earlier generation of development scholars tended to investigate political phenomena in isolation from their economic context. The study of poverty, for example, would rarely have been considered a legitimate area of enquiry for a political scientist in the 1960s. The more recent neo-Marxist scholarship, by contrast, tends to reduce political analysis to economic forces. Scholars in the so-called dependency perspective would seldom be attracted to analyze the state's redistributive role within capitalist development. Important exceptions to these dominant analytical tendencies have recently emerged.[1] Systematic

---

1. The relevant bodies of literature are reviewed in greater detail in Chapter 1 below. For one of the many cases arguing the need to synthesize the study of political and economic variables in developmental context, see James Coleman, "The resurrection of political economy," in Norman Uphoff and Warren F. Ilchman (eds., *The political*

1

analysis of the state's role in economic development has, however, only begun.

This study was designed to contribute to this emerging trend. To avoid the analytical pitfalls of both the modernization and neo-Marxist perspectives, and to follow the lead of others, I have adopted an alternative standpoint: the state's developmental role in the capitalist Third World is important and involves elements of both choice and constraint. Under what conditions is a Third World regime likely to possess a degree of autonomy from social constraints so as to facilitate economic gains for the lower classes? I hope to contribute to an understanding of this general question by analyzing empirical materials from one significant case, namely, the case of India.

The State and Poverty in India

The study of the state's role in India's poverty problems is significant for several reasons. First and foremost is the continuing magnitude of the Indian problem: over 200 million people in that nation are living in conditions of abject poverty. In spite of three decades of democratically-guided economic development, the living conditions of a large mass of humanity have not improved.[2] Why? And, more important, under what conditions is India's poverty likely to be alleviated? Discussions of these issues have in the past tended to adhere to one of two positions: (1) that poverty will only be alleviated in the long run as national wealth grows or

economy of development: theoretical and empirical contributions (University of California Press: Berkeley and Los Angeles, 1973), pp. 30-9. Dependency literature has been cogently summarized and criticized by Tony Smith, "The underdevelopment of development literature," *World Politics*, 31, 2 (January 1979), 247-88. For an example of the new literature consciously seeking to move beyond the "liberal" and "Marxist" debates, see Alfred Stepan, *The state and society: Peru in comparative perspective* (Princeton University Press: Princeton, New Jersey, 1978), esp. pp. 3-45.

2. The literature on the size and trends of rural poverty in India is sizable and controversial. For a sampling, see V. M. Dandekar and N. Rath, "Poverty in India: dimension and trends," *Economic and Political Weekly*, 6, 1 (January 2, 1971), 25-48, and 6, 2 (January 9, 1971), 106-46; P. K. Bardhan, "On the incidence of poverty in rural India in the sixties," in P. K. Bardhan and T. N. Srinivasan (eds.), *Poverty and income distribution in India* (Statistical Publishing Society: Calcutta, 1974), pp. 264-80; B. S. Minhas, "Rural poverty, land distribution and development strategy: facts," *ibid.* pp. 252-63; Montek Ahluwalia, "Rural poverty and agricultural performance in India," *Journal of Development Studies,* 14, 3 (April 1978), 298-324; and Pranab K. Bardhan, "Poverty and 'trickle-down' in rural India: a quantitative analysis," (mimeo, 1982), to be published in a forthcoming volume of essays in honor of Dharm Veera, ed., John Mellor. To get a sense of the diversity in the policy-oriented literature, see V. M. Dandekar and N. Rath, "Poverty in India"; B. S. Minhas, *Planning and the poor* (S. Chand and Company Ltd: New Delhi, 1974); P. K. Bardhan, "India," in Holis Chenery *et al., Redistribution with growth* (Oxford University Press: London, 1974), pp. 255-61; and Raj Krishna, "The next phase in rural development," *Voluntary Action,* 20, 7 (July 1978), 38.

(2) that revolutionary change will remain a prerequisite for meaningful redistribution. The more sophisticated policy-oriented literature, proposing "policy packages" to alleviate poverty,[3] has often suffered from political naivete based on the belief that failure to adopt appropriate policies can be blamed on the absence of "political will," as if leaders were free to bring about anything they wished. The alternative line of analysis pursued here focuses on the conditions that broaden the state's reformist scope within a democratic–capitalist model of development. Systematic analysis of this issue requires a focus on the state and societal interactions in the process of planned capitalist development.

It is important to note at the outset that a judgement of India's poverty as a significant problem is not merely an imposed scholarly judgement on observed phenomena. Poverty has long been considered a significant political issue within India. Gandhi and Nehru, for example, were, at least ideologically, always committed to the cause of the poor. Indira Gandhi also made *garibi hatao* ("eradicate poverty") a central slogan in her mobilization strategy. India's Planning Commission, as well as several international organizations that are in a position to influence India's policy thinking, have of late tended to treat poverty as a basic problem. The recognition that there is considerable, stubborn poverty in the country and that this requires state intervention is thus part and parcel of contemporary India's political idiom.

A focus on the state's role in Indian poverty problems is made still more meaningful by the fact that the country's leadership has utilized the state machinery to affect the living conditions of the rural poor. Land reforms, for example, have been continuously on India's political agenda. India's regime authorities also took a series of steps in the 1970s to involve the poor peasants in the "green revolution," and to improve employment and wage conditions for the landless agricultural laborers. An investigation of regime efforts in these three policy areas — land reforms, attempts to include the smaller farmers in the process of economic growth, and wage and employment schemes for the landless — provide empirical materials for analyzing the distributive role of the Indian state.

The federal nature of the Indian polity allows for a disaggregated and comparative analysis within India. Below the federal government, the state (or provincial) governments in India play a significant role in the for-

---

3. Two examples of this are Chenery *et al.*, *Redistribution with growth;* and the World Bank, *The assault on world poverty: problems of rural development, education and health* (The Johns Hopkins University Press: Baltimore, 1975). To be fair, there was some attempt made in this policy literature to take account of political variables. For example, see C.L.G. Bell, "The political framework," in Chenery *et al.*, *Redistribution with growth.*

mulation and the execution of agrarian policies. Variations in the nature of political rule at the state level can lead to differential effectiveness in the pursuit of anti-poverty programs. A comparative political analysis of Indian states, which are often governed by different political parties, allows one to isolate the significance of regime type in the alleviation of rural poverty from "above." I investigate the distributive attempts of three different regimes within India: the Communist Party of India, Marxist (CPM) regime in West Bengal (1977-83); the Congress (I) government under Devraj Urs in Karnataka (1974-80); and the Janata party rule in Uttar Pradesh (1977-80).

These three states — West Bengal, Karnataka, and Uttar Pradesh — provide some similarities and some differences regarding regime ideology and organization on the one hand, and the effectiveness of the anti-poverty programs on the other. With populations of approximately 45, 30, and 90 million respectively, these Indian states could easily be viewed as some of the larger Third World countries. This is not to suggest that these units are comparable to three sovereign nations. They are rather three states within a federal unit. They nevertheless approximate to the *ceteris paribus* assumption often made, and necessary for comparative studies, better than most independent countries. Ruled by different political parties within a federal polity, they provide a unique opportunity to raise and answer the following comparative question: what difference does the varying pattern of political rule, within more or less similar social–structural conditions, make for the effectiveness of redistributive policies? Can one type of regime pursue, i.e., legislate and implement, such anti-poverty programs as land reforms, small-farmer schemes, or wage- and employment-generation projects for the landless more effectively than other types of regimes? If so, what are the defining features of these regimes and what accounts for their relative success?

This, then, is a study of state intervention for alleviating the poverty of India's lower rural classes. The role of the Indian central government as well as that of the provincial governments in West Bengal, Karnataka, and Uttar Pradesh have been investigated comparatively in three policy areas: land reforms, support of small farmers, and attempts to improve the wage and employment prospects of the landless. The study is designed not only as an investigation of political performance, but also as an explication of the planned redistributive role of varying regimes within the context of societal constraints.

All political attempts to improve lower-class economic conditions affect the distribution of valued social goods. From an analytical standpoint, therefore, the study of the Indian state's redistributive intervention directs attention to theoretical issues concerning the relationship of authority structures to society. Given a constitutional, democratic regime and an economy based on private ownership of the means of production, how much autonomy do regime authorities possess for deliberate redistribution? Through what mechanisms do social groups enforce the pursuit of specific public policies, and what explains the variation in regime autonomy from the dominant classes? Can political authorities utilize the machinery of a democratic regime to counteract the vested social interests so as to reform the social order? If so, to what extent and under what political and organizational conditions? If not, why not, and again under what conditions? The empirical investigation of the distributive role of the Indian state then allows one to shed some light on the more general contemporary debates concerning state autonomy, or the interaction of politics and class force in the process of societal change.[4]

The Study

The empirical materials for this study were collected mainly during two field trips to India in 1978-9, and 1981. It will become clear in due course that West Bengal materials are crucial for this study. As a consequence,

4. The general issue of the relationship of democratic political power and social classes has of late been addressed primarily by the scholars in the Marxist tradition. For example, see Nicos Poulantzas, *State, power and socialism* (Schocken Books: New York, 1980); and Claus Offe, "Political authority and class structure," *International Journal of Sociology*, 2, 1 (1972), 73-108. Among non-Marxist scholars, the same set of issues concerning the prospect of reducing social inequalities by the use of the power of a democratic state has been recently readdressed and reassessed in Robert Dahl, "Pluralism revisited," *Comparative Politics*, 10, 2 (January 1978), 191-203. Dahl now seems to be in agreement (see p. 199) with the Marxist scholars, at least on the conclusion, that such prospects are not very bright. In empirically oriented studies, however, the debate over the prospects of social reform in a democracy continues to arrive at varying conclusions. For a recent review of this literature, see Jose M. Maravall, "The limits of reformism," *British Journal of Sociology*, 30, 3 (September 1979), 267-90. Other studies that address similar issues, primarily in the Third World context, include the classic discussion on "reform mongering" by Albert Hirschman, *Journeys toward progress: studies of economic policy-making in Latin America* (Twentieth Century Fund: New York, 1963), pp. 251-98. For an analysis of the cases of individual countries around this theme, see Brian Loveman, *Chile: the legacy of Hispanic capitalism* (Oxford University Press: New York, 1979); Stepan, *The state and society*, ch. 5; Nora Hamilton, *The limits of state autonomy: post-revolutionary Mexico* (Princeton University Press: Princeton, New Jersey, 1982); John Waterbury, *The Egypt of Nasser and Sadat: the political economy of two regimes* (Princeton University Press: Princeton, New Jersey, 1983); and Jyotindra Das Gupta, *Authority, priority, and human development* (Oxford University Press: New Delhi, 1981). This, of course, is only a sampling of the more recent literature. The question "is there a democratic road to socialism?" however the word socialism is interpreted, is as old as Marx and historically includes vociferous debates among such thinkers as Kautsky, Bernstein, Lenin, Luxembourg, Gramsci, and Oscar Lange. For an analysis of some aspects of these debates, see Peter Gay, *The dilemma of democratic socialism*, 1st edn. (Collier Books: New York, 1962).

West Bengal received greater research attention than the other areas. Research efforts were then more or less equally divided between New Delhi, Karnataka, and U.P. Aside from the use of such printed materials as government documents (published and unpublished) and newspapers (in English as well as in the vernacular), information was collected mainly through structured and unstructured interviews with the relevant members of both the state and civil society. Those interviewed included political leaders, government bureaucrats, intellectuals, social workers, and common citizens — rich and poor — who are likely to be affected directly by these efforts. Additionally, a formal survey aimed at assessing the impact of governmental programs was carried out in West Bengal in 1983, and a trip in the summer of 1984 facilitated a few important interviews in U.P.

During the fieldwork, I was often uncomfortably conscious of the gap between my eclectic research methods and the sequence suggested by textbooks: generate theory, derive hypothesis, specify research methods, collect data, and present conclusions. This sequence may be useful for testing ideas, but I found it far too constricting for discovering the "why" and "how" of a relatively unexplored intellectual terrain. While the research and conclusions are thus presented here in their textbook version, that is not how I arrived at them. The method of presentation has been easy to reorganize. How I actually arrived upon the "story" was far more haphazard and complex. I sympathize with Peter Evans when he finds much in common between his "messy and eclectic" research style and the methods of Dashiel Hammett's "Continental Op:"

What he soon discovers is that the "reality" that anyone involved will swear to is in fact itself a construction, a fabrication, a fiction, a faked and alternate reality — and that it has been gotten together long before he arrived on the scene. And the Op's work therefore is to deconstruct, decompose, deplot and defictionalize that "reality" and to construct or reconstruct out of it a true fiction, i.e., an account of what "really" happened... What one both begins and ends with, then, is a story, a narrative, a coherent yet questionable account of the world.[5]

This is not to suggest that the "story" or the argument presented here is not supported with evidence, or that the evidence is not reproducible. Rather, it is to suggest that the method of discovering an argument is not nearly as precise as its presentation may suggest.

The poverty of Indian villages touched me deeply. Therefore, a question repeatedly arose during this research on poverty: who is to blame? This normative question is of considerable consequence, because it

---

5. Quoted in Peter Evans, *Dependent development: the alliance of multinational, state, and local capital in Brazil* (Princeton University Press: Princeton, New Jersey, 1979), p.7.

affects one's analytical disposition, and it is easier raised than answered. As a result of a research technique using extended interviews, there was a sense of empathy for those being interviewed; it was hard not to conclude that there are few culprits in societies. The villains and the heroes, the exploiters and the exploited, all have their social roles and apparently understandable reasons for doing what they do. If the motivations of social actors are understood, sooner or later their actions appear to be legitimate. Yet patterned social actions, under the Indian conditions at least, cumulatively tend to perpetuate privileged life-styles for some, while relegating many to the bottom of the socio-economic ladder, beholden for the crumbs of valued societal goods. This gap between focusing on the motivations behind social actions on the one hand, and assessing seemingly objective reality against cherished values on the other, posed a constant dilemma for the interpretation of collected information.

As a methodological orientation, I decided that the consequences of social action are more important than the motivations behind them. My reasoning in reaching this conclusion — though considerable misgivings remain — was as follows: even the worst of social evils is committed while societal actors have convinced themselves of their own virtues in the light of some value system. Accordingly, motivations are a poor guide for assessing actions. The judgements — which become a part of analysis whether one holds given social arrangements to be desirable, merely understandable, or reprehensible — are better derived from the consequences of patterned actions than from the motivations behind actions. Given this intellectual position, and given an attachment to liberal values, the systematic perpetuation of poverty for over 200 million people raises serious questions about the adequacy of India's political–economic development. ·

The research sites within India were chosen in a controlled manner with the aim of getting some degree of representation into the sample of a one-man survey team. The three states were chosen because they represent a continuum of maximum to minimum governmental efforts in mitigating rural poverty: the two extremes are the Communist government of West Bengal, representing the maximum effort, and the Janata government in U.P., representing the minimum effort. Karnataka under Devraj Urs falls between these two on the continuum. Within each state, districts, blocks, and villages were chosen in a similar manner so as to capture aspects of variation of which there was some prior knowledge. In each area the attempt was to travel the length — from the center to the periphery — of those political institutions which are utilized by political authorities to intervene on behalf of the poor. In some parts of the country, these were primarily political parties; in others, the established bureaucracy; and in yet others, *ad hoc* arrangements designed specifically for individual tasks. The focus was as much on the patterns of interaction between social forces and political institutions as it was on the institutional design. The intellectual aim of the investigation was to compare and isolate the conditions under which political intervention on behalf of the poor was likely to be successful.

The Argument

If questions concerning the efficacy of differing regimes for redistributive capitalist development are at the core of this study, a summary of the overall argument that has emerged with reference to India can be outlined.

The failure to mitigate even the worst of India's poverty is a consequence of the institutionalized patterns of domination within India. Over the last three decades India has been ruled by an alliance of a nationalist political elite with entrepreneurial classes capable of stimulating economic growth. The nationalist political elite have wielded power through a dominant party in control of a democratic regime. This regime has not had the political or the organizational capacity to implement redistributive goals. This failure to pursue the regime's own professed goals is best understood as a type of regime weakness, because it represents the failure to make the state's legitimate authority binding. The political features which contribute to regime weakness will be discussed in due course. As coercion and economic incentives are two important resources available to all regimes for facilitating socio-economic development, a regime incapable of imposing authority typically provides economic incentives to propertied groups to buttress its own political support and at the same time to stimulate productive activities. Favorable economic incentives provided by the state have thus become the basis of the ruling alliance between political authorities and the more dynamic, propertied classes within India.

The resulting pattern of development has generated moderate economic growth, but very little distribution of this growth. Profits have accrued to a small minority in the industrial and agricultural sectors, upper-middle classes and professionals have benefited from association with an expanding state, and labor absorption in the economy has not been very significant. These conditions, combined with population growth, have led to an undramatic conclusion: the poverty problem has continued unabated. Economic growth and democratic arrangements have buttressed the legitimacy of political authorities, while providing economic rewards to the upper and the upper-middle classes. Social groups left out of this arrangement — as much as half of India's population — have mostly remained unmobilized and have therefore not posed a significant political threat. To the extent that the excluded groups have opposed the dominant alliance, they have been confronted with one or more of the three available strategies: rhetorical promises, some genuine concessions, and repressive exclusion from politics.

Given these broad trends, has there been and does there remain any scope for political intervention on behalf of the poor? An alliance of a nationalist elite with the entrepreneurial classes as a basis of development does not automatically preclude redistributive concessions. While the balance here is clearly in favor of the propertied classes, lower-class gains remain a function of the pattern of state intervention in the economy. The pattern of state intervention is, in turn, largely determined by the ideology, organization, and class basis of the regime that controls state power. As the ideology, organization, and pattern of class alliances underlying a regime can vary within a democratic–capitalist model of development, so can regime capacities to facilitate lower-class redistributive gains. The Congress-dominated democratic regime in India has been short on redistributive capacities. Does this suggest that the democratic–capitalist model itself is responsible, or are the redistributive failures rooted in the more specific patterns of Congress-propertied class alliance? The empirical materials presented here tread a line between these two positions, taking the constraints of democratic capitalism seriously, and yet delineating the element of choice facilitated by regime types.

The range of redistributive choices available within the constraints of democratic capitalism are delineated here through a comparative analysis of regional materials from within India. West Bengal, ruled by a party that is communist in name and organization but "social democratic" in ideology and practice, highlights the redistributive possibilities within India's contemporary democracy and capitalism. The communist government of West Bengal has undertaken some successful reforms aimed at altering the socio-economic conditions of the rural poor, especially the sharecroppers. If sustained, these efforts promise to have a significant long-term impact on the living conditions of the lower agrarian groups in Bengal. In Karnataka, by comparison, the Congress (I) government under Devraj Urs was able to bring about some changes affecting the conditions, not of generalized poverty or of a specific "target group" as a whole, but of select lower groups, especially some tenant farmers. The short experience of the Janata government in Uttar Pradesh, however, stands in a marked contrast to both of these cases and probably represents the general tendency of other Indian states more accurately than either West Bengal or Karnataka. It represents probably the worst of democracy and emerging capitalism within a factionalized, hierarchical, low-income society. Here the guidelines of the central government for redistributive programs were ignored; few, if any, autonomous redistributive actions were initiated by the provincial government; and a case could be made that there was an attempt by the political authorities to consciously deny the existence of massive poverty as a political problem.

The three Indian states, then, highlight a small but significant range of redistributive options possible within similar social-structural constraints. The core task of this study is to explain the conditions which maximize these small but significant redistributive possibilities. If deliberate alleviation of poverty within a democratic–capitalist developmental model is a valued goal, it is precisely the small gains that are of consequence. These are the only types of gains that are likely to be achieved in India. What at one point in time appears to be merely a small redistributive gain can, if sustained, accumulate to bring about significant improvements in lower-class living conditions.

Variations in regional distributive outcomes, it is argued here, are a function of the regime controlling political power. Regime type, in turn — at least in the case of India — closely reflects the nature of the ruling political party. The ideology, organization, and class alliances underlying a party-dominated regime are then of considerable consequence for the redistributive performance of that regime.

More specifically, comparative research here leads to the conclusion that, under the conditions of the Indian political economy — electoral–constitutional rule and a private-enterprise economy — a regime capable of introducing elements of redistribution into the developmental process tends to display the following characteristics: a coherent leadership; an ideological and organizational commitment to exclude the propertied interests from direct participation in the process of governance; a pragmatic attitude toward facilitating a non-threatening as well as a predictable political atmosphere for the propertied, entrepreneurial classes; and an organizational arrangement that is simultaneously centralized and decentralized.

The communist government of West Bengal, more social–democratic than communist in practice, possesses most of these attributes. This pattern of rule results from the existence of a relatively well institutionalized, dominant political party, and it is here that impressive beginnings have been made towards eradicating rural poverty. The Urs regime in Karnataka possessed some of the attributes but was lacking in two important dimensions: in direct governance, it was closely linked to many of the propertied interests in the area; and, organizationally, its redistributive capacities were dependent on *ad hoc* arrangements. The consequence was partial and temporary success. By contrast, the Janata government in Uttar Pradesh possessed virtually none of these characteristics. As a consequence, the lower agrarian classes did not benefit from state intervention in the economy and society.

The regime attributes specified above seem to be of considerable significance in explaining varying reformist capacities. These regime attributes make the institutional penetration of the society possible, while facilitating a degree of regime autonomy from the propertied classes. The organizational characteristics of such regimes create a degree of separation between political and social power. This margin of autonomous political power can be utilized to manipulate state intervention in the interest of the lower classes. Regime variations are, therefore, decisive in understanding the prospects of reforming poverty conditions from above. Such other variables as the nature of the bureaucracy and the level of the politicization of the lower classes were found to be of some significance. Nevertheless, it seems to be regime attributes that account for a modicum of redistributive effectiveness, the attributes being ideology, organization, and the class basis of the power-holders.

If poverty in India is to be eradicated by state intervention within the framework of democratic politics and a largely capitalist economy, it is my argument that the regime most likely to accomplish this would be a well-organized, left-of-center regime. This regime must be led by a coherent leadership committed to the interests of the lower classes; and it must translate this commitment into an organizational arrangement capable of penetrating the countryside without being co-opted by the propertied interests. At the same time, this regime must be flexible enough to offer the growth-providers of the society — the propertied classes — political space and predictability, enabling them to pursue economic activities for profit. Only such a regime is capable of utilizing the quintessential resource of state power — binding authority — in the interests of the lower classes without totally alienating the upper classes. Such a regime faces the constant danger of being undermined by both the upper and the lower classes. It nevertheless offers social democrats the opportunity to trade with the propertied their right to reasonable profits for a stable democratic rule, aimed at incremental redistribution within the framework of a privately owned economy.

To specify the type of regime that can eradicate poverty within the framework of democracy and capitalism is, of course, not to suggest that such a regime is likely to come to power in India in the near future. The utility of the argument presented here for future predictions is largely negative, and the overall prognosis pessimistic. State intervention for wealth redistribution is heavily constrained within the framework of democratic capitalism. Short of a revolution, redistribution is likely to be accomplished in India only if the type of well-organized, left-of-center regime specified above emerges dominant within India. Because the political trends in India are certainly not moving toward organized social democracy, this study leads one to conclude that neither the main Congress party, nor the various opposition parties now being carved out of the old Jan Sangh and the Lok Dal, are likely to make a significant dent in India's rural poverty. The ideology, the organization, and the class alliances of these parties make the prospects of mitigating poverty under their rule rather bleak.

What the Study is Not About

Every adopted perspective must of necessity lead to a neglect of other significant considerations. The focus on the state's redistributive intervention in India is no exception. Because a study of this nature might be expected to focus on certain issues that I have not covered, I wish to specify these issues at the outset. This is partly as a defense and an explanation of what I have ignored, and partly to inform readers of issues that will not be included in this study.

First, I do not concentrate on the issue of economic growth. This omission can be a significant one for several reasons. A respected body of literature continues to consider poverty as essentially a function of levels and rates of economic development. Even the Indian experience, especially of such "green revolution" areas as Punjab, can be interpreted to support this position. While much could be said about the analytical and empirical validity of such arguments — and I will discuss them in passing below (see especially Appendix II) — my reason for ignoring the issue of growth is fairly simple: three decades of slow but steady economic growth have failed to alleviate India's poverty. The statistical evidence for this macro-fact is unequivocal. This fact could lead to a case for yet higher economic growth. The failure of "trickle-down," however, also shifts attention to the state's redistributive capacities. After three decades of experience, the burden of proving the proposition that higher growth rates will automatically alleviate poverty in the near future, now more than ever, rests squarely on the shoulders of the believers in "trickle-down."

The neglect of growth considerations can be serious in another related sense: if redistribution is at the expense of economic growth, then the long-term gains for the poor are likely to be neutralized. I have accounted for this consideration in a cursory manner. I have not gone much beyond checking for the most obvious inverse relationship between rural redistributive policies and agricultural production. As this study analyzes neither agriculture growth nor the consequences of growth on poverty, some subtle but significant consequences of state intervention on poverty, mediated by the process of economic growth, may well be ignored here. I leave the analysis of these ignored considerations to others.

The reader should also be aware that though I undertake a comparative analysis of policy performance in three Indian states, this volume is not a study of politics in these three states. The difference is an important one. I analyze three Indian states with a single theme in mind: how do regime variations affect the implementation of poverty programs? This necessarily leads me to a selective focus on the political economy of all three states. Specialists of individual states may feel that state-level analysis is relatively superficial as both intra-state variations and themes other than those linking regime type to policy outcomes are neglected. These omissions flow from the general plan of the study. If state-level specialists, however, do find that the analysis of "their" state is plausible, then that would not only partially exonerate the selective focus but, more importantly, would justify the core task of this study: the comparative analysis of state-level materials around a unifying theme.

Lastly, as the focus here is on the policy consequences of regime variation, the issue of social determinants of regime variations is neglected. This neglect is partly inevitable and partly an analytical choice. It is inevitable in the sense that the chain of causation stemming from the phenomena to be explained can stretch back continually. One has to cut into the chain of causation somewhere to undertake manageable research. Given this inevitability, where one cuts into the causal chain is then a matter of analytical judgement. I have chosen to focus on the role of the state in society rather than on social determinants of the state's role, not because I think the latter is unimportant, but mainly because I think the former has been neglected in recent scholarship. As a consequence, societal variables are often missing in this analysis; there is little below, for example, on the debates about peasant societies and economies, modes of production or caste and class variations among Indian regions. I leave it to others to delineate how variations in such conditions affect rural poverty or the patterns of authority formation.

Given the above omissions, this study attempts to isolate the significance of regime variation for the effectiveness of redistributive policies. If I convince the readers of one or more of the following points, the purpose of the study has been served: (1) the focus on state intervention helps reorient Indian empirical materials in an interesting way, leading to new insights linking Indian politics and economy, (2) comparative analysis of Indian states or provinces is a promising research strategy for isolating the significance of political autonomy, and (3) well-organized, left-of-center regimes are best suited to facilitate deliberate redistribution within India.

The Organization

The study is organized as follows. The first chapter is aimed at delineating the theoretical orientation underlying this study. Because the study of state intervention in the process of development has not been a central focus in comparative Third World studies, I use this chapter to develop a state-oriented theoretical frame of reference suited to reorient some Indian empirical materials. I discuss the concepts of state and regime, and argue that regime types condition economic development in general and distributional outcomes specifically. I also suggest why some of the existing treatments linking political conditions to issues of redistribution and poverty — in a general developmental setting and in India — are inadequate.

The second chapter interprets, historically, the interaction of the Congress regime and India's social classes in the process of reformist development. Here I develop the argument summarized above, namely, that the failure to eradicate poverty in India has resulted from an alliance of domination between a weakly organized nationalist political elite and the commercially oriented propertied groups. Specialists on India's political and economic development may not find this chapter very useful. Given the broad interpretative scope of the chapter, those who have their own well developed interpretations will probably disagree with a number of points, or may find it too compressed and therefore underdocumented. If the account is deemed plausible, however, it will serve the purpose of an overview consistent with the theoretical themes of this study.

In Chapters 3, 4, and 5, the core empirical chapters, the role of the three state governments in poverty reform is analyzed. It is here that, proceeding comparatively, I delineate the factors that seem to account for the variation in regime capacities for redistributive development.

The concluding chapter resummarizes some of the central themes of the argument. I also comment on the significance of this study for cases other than that of contemporary India. Given that the focus here is on state intervention aimed at facilitating distribution in a democratic–capitalist model of development, I briefly examine some comparable cases. The central comparative themes are (1) whether deliberate redistributive gains for the lower classes are possible within the framework of democracy and capitalism and, if they are, then (2) how important is the nature of the regime directing state intervention for effective redistribution.

1

The State and Redistributive Reforms

This study analyzes the conditions under which public authorities of a developing society can effectively pursue redistributive reforms. Empirical investigation of politically directed socio-economic change requires a prior discussion of several conceptual and theoretical issues. How does one systematically think of political actors as constituting a potentially significant force capable of reforming civil society from above? The section to follow on the one hand, presents state institutions as not entirely determined or controlled by society, and on the other, delineates the factors enhancing or enforcing the state's autonomy from society. Also, how does one conceptualize variations in authority structures and relate these to varying capacities to pursue reforms? Some ideas are developed here by first considering the varying regime types governing developing capitalist states, and then by discussing specific arguments over the capacities of a democratic Third World regime for poverty reforms. By discussing these issues I hope to accomplish two theoretical tasks in this chapter: to develop a state-oriented frame of reference directing attention to the centrality of the state's role in economic development; and to derive some specific hypotheses that link democratic-regime types to redistributive outcomes and set the stage for the discussion of Indian empirical materials.

The State, State Autonomy, and Regimes

The concept of the state has re-emerged as a significant one in comparative political–sociological studies. If a few years back Alfred Stepan had trouble finding major writings discussing the state, today one could easily fill a shelf with books having the word "state" in their titles.[1] As this study of Indian empirical materials is conceived to be a part of the ongoing reas-

1. Reference is to Stepan, *The state and society*, p. 3. For a sampling of the new, state-oriented literature, in addition to Alfred Stepan's book, see Theda Skocpol, *States and social revolutions: a comparative analysis of France, Russia and China* (Cambridge University Press: Cambridge–New York, 1979); Eric Nordlinger, *On the autonomy of the democratic state* (Harvard University Press: Cambridge, Mass., 1981); Hamilton, *The limits of state autonomy;* David Collier (ed.), *The new authoritarianism in Latin America* (Princeton University Press: Princeton, New Jersey, 1979); Jyotindra Dasgupta,

sessment in comparative politics, these intellectual trends are clearly welcome. They nevertheless also require caution. In a subfield where the life cycle of "paradigmatic revolutions" tends to be about a decade, one can be sure that today's intellectual challenge will appear tomorrow to be yesterday's passing fad. To an extent this is both healthy and inevitable. And yet it is important to insulate oneself partially from the vagaries of intellectual fashions. Prior to an argument for a state-oriented focus, therefore, it is important to highlight what is really new and what is not so new in the statist world view adopted here.

The new state-oriented literature alleges that liberal, structural–functionalist, and Marxist frameworks are inadequate for state studies because they tend to reduce politics to societal variables. These prevailing analytical orientations lead to a focus on social determinants — class forces, cultural orientations, interest-group pressures, levels of economic development, and individual psychology — of the political process, while detracting attention from the significant role of the state in controlling, molding, and even transforming social structures and processes. What is therefore needed, the argument continues, is to move away from a society-centered frame of reference, and toward a state-oriented world view emphasizing the architectural role of the state in society.[2]

While I agree with the thrust of this argument — and that is why I have adopted a state-oriented focus — the allegations need to be qualified at the very outset. With reference to the body of theoretical literature of immediate interest here, would it really be fair to argue that modernization and neo-Marxist approaches to comparative development have in the past ignored the role of the state? Clearly, numerous scholarly works would not fit this allegation. While the concept of the state may not have been used frequently in the last few decades, the more general point concerning the significance of political authorities and authority structures for development has certainly not bypassed discerning modernization scholars. The early studies of modernizing elites, Third World intellectuals, and military rulers tended to be implicitly, if not explicitly, concerned about the consequences of elite actions — "state intervention" in modern

Authority and development; Evans, *Dependent development*; and Stephen R. Graubard (ed.), *The state* (W.W. Norton and Company, Inc.: New York, 1979). Two new books which have come to my attention only after this book was largely completed are Peter Evans, Dietrich Rueschemeyer, and Theda Skocpol (eds.), *Bringing the state back in* [Cambridge University Press: New York (forthcoming)]; and Martin Carnoy, *The state and political theory* (Princeton University Press: Princeton, New Jersey, 1984).

2. While all the references cited in footnote 1 tend to share this general assumption, for its most explicit statement see Stepan, *The state and society*, pp. 3-45; and Nordlinger, *Democratic state, passim*.

terminology — in developing countries.[3] David Apter's comparative analysis of "modernizing regimes" and Richard Lowenthal's explicit discussion of "the role of the state in economic development" addressed the issue of how variations in authority structures effect socio-economic outcomes.[4] Samuel Huntington's work can also be read as highlighting the significance of state stability and order for development.[5] And country-level studies often sought to delineate the significance of political institutions and actions for economic change.[6]

Within the neo-Marxist literature the issue of the state has received even more attention. As a matter of fact, it could be argued that the current concern with the state, especially when juxtaposed with Marxist formulations of the state, has its intellectual origins in recent Western European Marxist debates.[7] The better scholars in Latin America's dependency tradition have also sought to accommodate the significance of the state within a general neo-Marxist orientation. For example, we may note O'Donnell's focus on the causes and consequences of Latin American authoritarianism,[8] Cardoso's emphasis on populist regimes as harbingers of early Latin American industrialization,[9] and Peter Evans' conceptualization of the state as a significant actor in the alliance for "dependent development."[10] These studies partially exonerate the Marxist-inspired Third World scholarship from a blanket charge of reductionist political analysis.

3. For a sampling of this literature, see the articles in Part IV entitled, "The modernizers," in Jason L. Finkle and Richard W. Gable (eds.), *Political development and social change* (John Wiley and Sons, Inc.: New York, 1971), pp. 233-52. For a recent review of the role of the military, see Henry Bienen, "Armed forces and national modernization: continuing the debate," *Comparative Politics*, 16, 1 (October 1983), 1-16.
4. See David Apter, *The politics of modernization* (The University of Chicago Press: Chicago, 1965), esp. chs. 6, 7, and 10; and Richard Lowenthal, "The nature of underdevelopment and the role of the state," in Richard Lowenthal (ed.), *Model or ally? the communist powers and the developing countries* (Oxford University Press: New York, 1976), pp. 11-46
5. Samuel Huntington, *Political order in changing societies* (Yale University Press: New Haven, Connecticut, 1968), *passim*.
6. For example, see Henry Bienen, *Tanzania: party transformation and economic development* (Princeton University Press: Princeton, New Jersey, 1967); and Thomas Skidmore, *Politics in Brazil, 1930-1964: an experiment in democracy* (Oxford University Press: New York, 1967).
7. For a review of these debates see Erik Olin Wright, D.A. Gold, and C.Y.H. Lo, "Recent developments in Marxist theories of the capitalist states," *Monthly Review*, 27, 5 (October 1975), 29-43; 27, 6 (November 1975), 36-51.
8. Guillermo O'Donnell, *Modernization and bureaucratic authoritarianism: studies in South American politics*, Politics of modernization series, 9 (University of California Press: Berkeley, 1973); also see Collier (ed.), *The new authoritarianism*.
9. Fernando Cardoso and Enzo Faletto, *Dependency and development in Latin America* (University of California Press: Berkeley, 1979).
10. Evans, *Dependent development*.

Similar important exceptions exist within the literature on India inspired by the modernization and the neo-Marxist frameworks. The opening line of Rajni Kothari's classic "modernization" study of Indian politics is telling: "If 'modernization' is the central tendency of our times, it is 'politicization' that provides its driving force."[11] Clearly the significance of politics as a "driving force" of social change has not bypassed the author. Marxist scholars of South Asia such as Hamza Alavi recognized the significance of "state autonomy" prior to its fashionable resurgence in North American scholarship.[12] And even Barrington Moore, in spite of his focus on agrarian classes, spends a large part of his chapter on India discussing first Gandhi and then Nehru's policies and programs, i.e., discussing the actions of political authorities in society.[13] Other prominent scholars of India such as Reinhard Bendix, Lloyd and Susanne Rudolph, Baldev Raj Nayar, and Francine Frankel have, moreover, self-consciously avoided the rigidities of modernization and neo-Marxist frameworks in order to delineate the role of political authorities in socio-economic change.[14]

Citation of these important exceptions to the reductionist problem in comparative political analysis serves several purposes. First, it gives intellectual credit where it is due. Second, the exceptions underline the point that the role of the state in developing societies has not been and does not have to be ignored by scholars committed to perspectives emphasizing the primacy of societal variables. The significant issue, therefore, is not one of recognizing the significance of state intervention in the process of development. The more important point concerns how this intervention is understood and explained. And this leads to the third and main reason to cite at the outset scholarly works sensitive to political variables, namely, to juxtapose statist assumptions with prevailing theoretical tendencies, and thus to delineate and underline what is really new in orienting empirical materials around a state focus.

The case for a statist orientation initially rests on the following assertions: state intervention is an important variable for the study of political

---

11. Rajni Kothari, *Politics in India* (Little Brown and Company: Boston, 1970), p.1.
12. Hamza Alavi, "The state in post-colonial societies," *New Left Review*, 74 (July–August 1972), 59-82.
13. Barrington Moore Jr, *Social origins of dictatorship and democracy: lord and peasant in the making of the modern world* (Beacon Press: Boston, 1966), esp. pp. 370-412.
14. Reinhard Bendix, *Nation-building and citizenship: studies of our changing social order*, enlarged edn (University of California Press: Berkeley, 1977), ch. 7; Lloyd I. Rudolph and Susanne Hoeber Rudolph, *The modernity of tradition: political development in India* (The University of Chicago Press: Chicago, 1967); Baldev Raj Nayar, *The modernization imperative and Indian planning* (Vikas: New Delhi, 1972); and Francine Frankel, *India's political economy 1947-1977* (Princeton University Press: Princeton, New Jersey, 1978).

and social change; the logic of state action in society cannot be fully explained by reference to social conditions; political actions, especially patterns of state intervention, partly reflect political interests and goals; and political interest and goals are not always synonymous with the interests and goals of social actors. Dissatisfaction with both modernization and dependency perspectives from a statist standpoint, therefore, is not because they necessarily lead to a neglect of the role of the state. As the examples cited above highlight, such a claim would be patently false. The problem is rather that the core theoretical logic of both modernization and neo-Marxist scholars tends towards reductionism. Politics is reduced to society. The understanding of how and why the state intervenes is thus inadequate as long as it remains tied primarily to the conditions of the society and the economy.

Within the modernization perspective, for example, significant state intervention is seen as being rooted in "abnormal" or "perverted" patterns of social change. Deriving from the Durkheimian concern with "social solidarity," the functions of state organization are conceived to have the character of a "last resort." "Development" is often assumed to be imminent, in the sense that once constraints upon it are removed, entrepreneurial energies are unleashed, leading to self-sustained economic growth. In the case of late developers, however, given the concentrated nature of the development process, rates of "integration" do not always keep up with those of "differentiation." Social solidarity is then threatened. The state intervenes to maintain stability and continues to do so until some form of "value consensus" is re-established.[15]

State intervention is in the above account treated as a consequence of abnormal and somewhat perverted socio-economic development — perverted in comparison with historical examples of early industrializers — rather than as a relatively autonomous force initiating such a development. Important elements of this core reductionist logic then remain significant even in the most politically oriented scholarship emerging from this intellectual tradition, namely, in the works of Samuel Huntington. After all, political stability for Huntington remains largely a function of social conditions — a function of the gap between social mobilization (differentiation) and institutionalization (integration).[16] That these are not only intellectual problems of the past is highlighted by the fact that a very

15. For one of the most succinct statements of this widely shared perspective, see Neil Smelser, "Mechanisms of change and adjustment to change," in Bert F. Hoselitz and Wilbert E. Moore (eds.), *Industrialization and society* (UNESCO and Mouton: The Hague, 1963), pp. 32-54.
16. Huntington, *Political order*, esp. ch. 1.

similar logic has recently been adopted by Harry Eckstein to refocus attention on the issue of the state and state intervention.[17]

Marxist and neo-Marxist logic for the explication of the "political" is of course similarly reductionist. It is to the credit of Marxist-inspired scholarship that the significant role of the state in development has been widely recognized. Varying explanations of this role, however, share one blind spot in common: the role must reflect interests and goals, not of the political elite, but of specifiable economic actors. If the state exhibits "relative autonomy," this must be a consequence of a "Bonapartist" condition, whereby the social situation does not make the establishment of a clear class hegemony possible, and political authorities emerge as significant mediators.[18] If the state does not clearly pursue policies favoring capitalism, this must be a consequence of some peculiarity of the class structure of a developing society, such as its being dominated by "petty bourgeois" or other "intermediate classes."[19] If the state adopts policies further enmeshing domestic economies in the world economy, this must reflect the fact that the class balance is altering in favor of those representing the interests of world capitalism.[20] And changes in political organization, especially towards authoritarianism, must result from shifting economic "needs" to sustain and reproduce capitalism.[21]

I do not wish to dispute the accuracy of any of these specific propositions. The point I am concerned with is a more general one. At a specific level, important and profound insights concerning politics in developing countries have been occasionally generated by scholars working in both the modernization and the neo-Marxist traditions. More generally, however, there are limits to how far one can strain the logic of social determinism in political analysis. Many issues of state intervention for development are simply better analyzed by abandoning the analytical commitment to a social logic of politics and admitting that political structures and process result from a partially autonomous logic — a political logic that is not reducible to or derivable from social variables. This does not imply

17. Harry Eckstein, "On the 'science' of the state," in Graubard (ed.) *The state*, esp. pp. 15-16.
18. For a development of such an argument with reference to South Asia, see Alavi, "The state in post-colonial societies."
19. A general statement along these lines has been made by Michael Kalecki, *Selected essays on the economic growth of the socialist and the mixed economy* (Cambridge University Press: Cambridge, 1972), vol. II, ch. 15. For an application of this idea to India, see K.N. Raj, "The politics and economics of intermediate regimes," *Economic and Political Weekly*, 8, 27 (July 7, 1973), 1189-98.
20. This is of course a central idea in the "dependency" literature on Latin America. For example, see Fernando Cardoso, "Associated-dependent development: theoretical and practical implications," in Alfred Stepan (ed.), *Authoritarian Brazil: origins, policies and future* (Yale University Press: New Haven, 1973), pp. 142-78.
21. See O'Donnell, *Bureaucratic authoritarianism*.

embracing a political determinism in exchange for a social one; it rather suggests conceptualizing the state and society as being in mutual interaction. A state–society focus then enables one to analyze the role of the state in development partially as being conditioned by socio-economic conditions and partially as reflecting autonomous choices made by political authorities. At least, this is the theoretical focus I have adopted in this study. The empirical analysis will buttress the claim that such a general perspective is a useful one.

How does one systematically conceptualize the role of the state in a developing society? An adequate framework would not only draw attention to the state as an actor, but would also situate this role within social conditions. The latter implies that empirical analysis of the state, in addition to emphasizing the state's autonomous role, needs to be located in some "theory of society." Whether one conceives of a specific society in terms of a Marxist, a structural–functionalist, or some other frame of reference is of course an issue on which many do not agree. As this is, however, primarily a study of the dynamics of state intervention, I will not take sides in the elaborate debates about how to conceptualize Third World social structures. While tempting, such a discussion would only detract from the main issue at hand, namely, the issue of state intervention. Suffice it to note here that I consider both economic and non-economic social groups as significant elements in civil society for political analysis. Within the Indian context this implies treating class structure and class groupings as well as caste and regional–ethnic identities as significant political variables.[22] My interpretation of the controversial concept of class is elaborated in Appendix I.

To develop the main theoretical ideas relevant for this study, I will commence the discussion by delineating the concepts of state, state autonomy, and regime type. Following Alfred Stepan and Theda Skocpol, I conceive of the state as a set of administrative and coercive institutions headed by an executive authority.[23] This common view of the state is not only consistent with the widely accepted Weberian position but also helps focus attention on those elements of the state — coercion, institutional identity, and leadership authority — that enable political actors to play a significant role in civil society. If one contrasts this conceptualization with that offered in another important and recent formulation by

22. For a recent, general statement along these lines, see M.S.A. Rao, "Concepts of caste, class and ethnicity," 1983, mimeo. A revised version of this will eventually be published in Francine Frankel and M.S.A. Rao (eds.), *Caste, class and dominance: patterns of politico-economic change in modern India.*
23. Stepan, *The state and society*, esp. pp. xi–xiv; and Skocpol, *States and social revolutions*, p. 29.

Eric Nordlinger, several potentially controversial and significant issues emerge.[24]

First, Nordlinger argues that to think of the state as an "institutional arrangement" is to reify the problem at hand; in his view it is preferable to conceive of the state in terms of individuals occupying public offices.[25] While it is important to be wary of the problem of reification, Nordlinger's formulation is not really convincing. It leads us to think of the state as little more than a collection of individuals with distinctive preferences and roles — the public, as distinct from the private roles. While this is seemingly sensitive to empirical concerns (one can identify individual political actors), the issue of role differentiation — how public and private roles are distinguishable and yet linked — is no less of an analytical pitfall than defining the state institutions from other social institutions. Moreover, focusing on public officials draws attention away from the historically evolved, collective, and corporate relationships of many states with their respective societies. And this is not only an issue for non-democratic societies. Even in party-dominated democratic governments (e.g., Britain), decisions often reflect party and therefore institutional, rather than individual, goals. While it is probably always useful to focus on important leaders as crucial individual actors influencing the way the state acts upon society, other constituent units of the state — the government, the civil bureaucracy and the armed forces — are best thought of as organizations and institutions, rather than as mere collections of public officials with distinctive preferences.

Nordlinger's focus on public officials is still more problematic, as it detracts analytical attention from the quintessential political resource — coercion — the successful control of which ultimately enables state authorities to impose their preferences upon societies. The tendency of some scholars to shy away from the issue of state domination of society is of course an old one; earlier, we may recall, it had led Parsons to translate Weber's concept of "domination" as "imperative coordination."[26] Similar analytical preferences are somewhat surprising today in the new attempts to restore the centrality of the state. This may in part result from the different empirical referents of scholars, e.g., advanced, democratic societies versus developing countries. I suspect, however, that whether one approaches the issue of the state from a former attachment to a pluralist perspective, a Marxist perspective, or some type of elite-theory perspective will nevertheless continue to influence and maybe even divide scholars on the question of how to conceptualize the state, state autonomy, and the role of the state in society.

24. Nordlinger, *Democratic state*, esp. ch. 1.   25. *Ibid.* p. 9.
26. For a discussion of this problem, see Reinhard Bendix, *Max Weber: an intellectual portrait* (Anchor Books, Doubleday and Company, 1962), ch. 9, esp. p. 292, n. 16.

The state, to my mind, then, is best thought of as a set of administrative and coercive institutions headed by an executive authority, defining, at minimum, the territorial boundaries within which societies conceiving of themselves as a nation or competing nations exist. This view, like that of Nordlinger, Skocpol, and others, but unlike Weber, does not insist that control over coercion is either complete — centralized — or necessarily legitimate. Degrees of centralization and legitimacy are better thought of as variables, the significance of which is captured at a lower level of generality, namely by focusing on the regime types wielding state power. To this issue I will return below.

In order to minimize the problem of reifying the state, several important points need to be kept in mind. While the concept of the state is clearly an abstraction, aimed at analytically distinguishing the structure and the dynamics of political rule from that of civil society, it also refers to empirically identifiable institutions. When one talks of the state, therefore, one generally refers to the government, the bureaucracy and the armed forces as having a collective interest, a unified goal, and a specifiable role *vis-à-vis* civil society. The state's interests and goals may or may not be coterminous with those of social actors. That is an empirical question and does not concern us for the moment. What concerns us is that it is empirically meaningful to discuss the role of the state in society because it refers to the role of identifiable political institutions and actors. Moreover, there is no reason to assume that the state normally acts as a collectivity. As soon as one moves away from the most general considerations, it is immediately clear that governments and bureaucracies are often in disagreement concerning their appropriate jurisdictions over and actions in civil society. Reification of the state is therefore minimized by keeping in mind that the concept of the state refers to identifiable institutions, and that state actors do not always work as a cohesive force *vis-à-vis* civil society.

So far I have discussed the concept of the state in isolation from its social context. This is to stress the general point that irrespective of the type of society and economy — agrarian or industrial, capitalist or communist, developed or underdeveloped — all modern states share some features. The control of an executive authority over the means of administration and coercion gives the state in all societies considerable potential to mold socio-economic change. To be more specific, however, one needs to discuss types of states. This immediately necessitates situating the state within its social and historical context. A discussion of the state in the Third World, for example, requires the specifying of state features in relation to Third World societies.

Modern states differ from each other primarily along two related yet

State's relationship to productive property	State's teleological commitment	
	ultimate goal directed	*managerial*
State ownership	most communist states	(some historical monarchies; future communist states?)
Private ownership	most third world states	most western democratic states

distinct criteria: the relationship of a state of productive property; and the degree to which a state is teleological in relation to the society. Dichotomizing these two continuous variables for simplification gives us a 2 × 2 matrix, which can be used as a starting-point to discuss what is distinctive about the state in the Third World.

According to the matrix, most Third World states can be characterized as having a teleological orientation — an orientation to "develop" their societies — and by the fact that productive resources within their boundaries are owned by private actors. Because both of these characteristics are historically acquired, understanding them requires a brief historical excursion.

Third World countries are those that have historically lacked political cohesion and economic dynamism. As a consequence, they fell prey to colonialism. The social and political traits of these "underdeveloped countries" are not now, and never have been, traditional in the sense of resembling the pre-industrial-structures of the West. Their failure at development was also not simply due to their consolidation as peripheries into a world system. Rather, the absence of development within them was historically rooted in their distinctive social and political traits. Not only did these areas, in contrast to Western Europe, fail to develop a strong commercial impulse, but also, in contrast to such cases as Russia, they were unable to resist the onslaught of colonialism. These twin societal and political failures in turn resulted from two interrelated historical conditions: brittle state structures that were overcentralized or fragmented, and control of economic resources by non-productive groups. While the further causes of this failure are rooted in individual histories, weak states and stagnant economies were no match for those who were politically unified and economically and technologically more advanced.

Once imposed on these polities, colonialism further stifled their developmental prospects. The structuring of raw materials to create export economies; the consolidation of non-productive, dominant classes; the creation of state structures designed mainly for preserving law and order and appropriating surplus; and the non-developmental use of available surplus — either for the maintenance of colonial rule or as direct appropriation — all contributed to the absence of economic growth and industrialization, and to the formation of political economies that would eventually be incapable of sustaining self-generated development. These, however, were not the only consequences of colonialism. By providing the rudiments of a modern state structure and by facilitating the rise of a nationalist elite, who in time would lead oppositional movements, colonialism also laid the foundations upon which later attempts at politically directed development would be built. Colonialism, therefore, not only reinforced the existing tendencies towards the non-developmental use of economic surplus, but also initiated its own demise by generating new political forces that would eventually alter this situation by capturing and using state power.

Colonialism thus bequeathed a twin historical legacy: the absence of socio-structural dynamism on the one hand, and on the other hand the consequent emergence of political forces aimed not only at the creation of sovereign states, but also at remedying the absence of this dynamism. This historical legacy provides a point of departure for understanding the role of the state in the Third World. The absence of socially rooted dynamism has combined with colonialism to leave Third World countries "underdeveloped." The consciousness of having been left behind and the simultaneous commitment to state intervention for social change have emerged simultaneously in the developing countries. Third World political authorities view their society as in need of basic change. Their society is deemed to be inadequate and as a consequence must be altered and "developed."

From the onset of state sovereignty, therefore, Third World state authorities are committed to planned socio-economic change. This goal of "deliberate development" of one form or another is, moreover, widely accepted as legitimate by the politically relevant strata. It is in this sense that Third World states can be characterized as teleological — as having a *telos*, an ultimate end, namely, the end of "development" or "modernization" or, even more vaguely, "being as good as others in the world system." Whatever the specific content of these goals, their widespread acceptance puts Third World states — like the communist states — in a leading role *vis-à-vis* their respective societies. Established as well as opposition elites within the Third World tend to view their societies as deficient — backward or underdeveloped — and in need of politically guided emancipation. Empirically, therefore, the role of state intervention in Third World societies tends to be rather large, and normatively, this is often viewed as legitimate, stemming from the teleological nature of these states.

If socio-economic development is a political goal, Third World states seldom have full control of their society's productive resources, enabling them to pursue this goal directly. Except in a few communist cases, productive resources are under the control of private actors — national or foreign. There is nothing new about this situation; it continues from the colonial and, in some cases, even pre-colonial pasts. What is important to note here, however, is the fact that the existence of a private-property economy is not only a societal characteristic; it is also a political trait. Private property has a profound influence on the defining of the scope and the limits of state intervention in society. This influences the nature of the state itself. While Marxist scholars may carry the societal determination of the state too far, it can hardly be denied that state capacities in communist and capitalist settings differ sharply and that this is at least in part rooted in the state–property nexus. The state's relationship to productive property therefore needs to be built into an understanding of the nature and the role of any state. What is central to an understanding of non-communist Third World states is, then, the inherent tension between the state's commitment to "develop" and "transform" social structures on the one hand, and on the other hand the private control of productive resources, limiting the scope of state intervention.

The characterization of Third World states by focusing on their teleological orientation and on their relationship to the means of production is, of course, only an "ideal typical" characterization. Some Third World states are clearly more committed to "development" than others. States having their own goals for society are nevertheless distinguishable from states mediating and molding — managing — social demands. I would argue that most Third World state authorities have their own goals for their respective societies. Similarly, even many non-communist Third World states control considerable parts of their economies. Again, however, on a continuum of state to private ownership of productive property, most non-communist Third World states are closer to the latter end. In an ideal–typical manner then, we may characterize many Third World states as developmental–capitalist states: developmental because of the state's commitment to this goal, and capitalist because this goal must be achieved by intervening in an increasingly capitalist economy — an economy based on private ownership of the means of production. The focus on the developmental and the capitalist element of Third World states thus not only enables us to distinguish these states as a group from communist and advanced capitalist states, but also helps to direct our attention to a somewhat neglected but crucial issue in Third World studies: the varying capacity of states to mobilize and control social actors as an explanation of varying developmental outcomes.

Having said something about the state in general and Third World states specifically, it is important to address the issue of state autonomy and regime variations within the Third World. "State autonomy" as a concept describes a relationship — the state's relationship with society — and is most clearly comprehended by focusing on the state's capacity to restructure social relations and mobilize societal resources. As this is a concept that makes sense primarily in terms of the consequences of its presence — state autonomy is what it does — there is a real danger of treating state autonomy as an explanatory variable, while the proposed relationships may simply be true by definition. It is important, therefore, to define when a state will be deemed autonomous and to identify the resources and conditions that enhance or shrink a state's autonomy *vis-à-vis* society.

The clearest cases of state autonomy from society are revolutionary communist states. While we are not primarily interested in these cases in this study, a brief look at them may help clarify some of the issues involved. After successful social revolutions, communist parties in control of the state have typically utilized their newly won powers to eliminate private property. Once in control of property, communist leaders have further utilized their democratic–centralist party structures to simultaneously mobilize and control social forces for accomplishing ideologically defined goals. While societies with communist states have seldom proven to be totally malleable, communist states nevertheless represent the clearest cases of politically determined socio-economic change: i.e., of autonomous state power being used to transform social structures fundamentally.

State autonomy from society thus refers to a macro-political–sociological condition whereby state authorities can (1) insulate themselves from social demands in general, but specifically from the demands of propertied classes, and (2) utilize state power to consciously alter socio-economic relations. An autonomous state thus contrasts with a reflexive or a captured state, where state actions are largely controlled by social forces. Patterns of leadership and ideology, and the organization of state power, as well as control over productive property, are some of the important varying conditions and resources that affect the state's capacity to act autonomously *vis-à-vis* society. As these variables are all continuous and vary in degree, so does state autonomy. Of course, in contrast to communist cases, state autonomy in class societies is always a relative matter. Marxist scholars correctly insist on this limiting condition by only discussing the "relative autonomy" of the "capitalist state." Nevertheless, a focus on limits can underestimate both the range and the significance of the state autonomy that does exist in class societies in general, and in Third World cases specifically.

State autonomy from social forces is clearest in cases where the state acts against the interests of propertied classes. Within the capitalist Third World, the few cases of successful land redistribution or property nationalization highlight this type of autonomous political intervention. The rarity of such examples, however, also suggests that state autonomy in this maximum sense is hardly a norm. The more common instances of state autonomy within the capitalist Third World are similar to those that Nordlinger, in another context, brilliantly analyzes as "type II" and "type III" state autonomy.[27] These are instances in which state actors either first mold societal preferences to minimize later opposition to political initiatives, or take the lead in initiating socio-economic changes that no groups in society may be actively demanding or opposing. It is possible to argue that the entire process of politically-guided, deliberate development within the contemporary Third World can be interpreted as autonomous state action of these two types.

If "development" is interpreted in this manner, it is less of a demand from Third World societies and more of a political goal which state authorities wish to impose upon their societies. "Impose" may be too strong a word in the absence of any clear evidence of mass opposition to the state's developmental goals, particularly in light of the fact that the pursuit of such a goal may well benefit society as a whole; it nevertheless serves to highlight the fact that fundamental socio-economic changes are set into motion within the Third World primarily as a consequence of politically defined goals and decisions. A state-oriented focus is therefore important for interpreting some of the patterns of change within the Third World.

If the concept of state autonomy is to help explain state capacities to mold social change, what factors help explain variations in state autonomy itself? As has been implicit in the discussion above, part of the answer lies in the historically derived basic variations in the nature of the state itself: communist states have a greater degree of autonomy *vis-à-vis* their societies than do developmental–capitalist states. This variation, in turn, results in part from the nature of the leadership, the ideology, and the organization of state power, and in part from the state's subsequent relationship to private property. What is interesting here is that similar factors also help explain the issue we are primarily concerned with, namely, the varying degrees of state autonomy within a specific capitalist Third World case. State autonomy within a capitalist setting is largely a function of the type of regime wielding state power. To develop this idea further, however, requires a discussion of varying regime types that con-

27. Nordlinger, *Democratic state*, chs. 3 and 4.

trol state power within the Third World. As the leadership, ideology, organization, and class alliances underlying specific regimes vary, so does the capacity of political authorities to define and implement state goals.

Prior to delineating the major dimensions on which developmental regimes vary, two prefatory comments should be noted. First, irrespective of the regime type, new regimes generally possess a greater capacity to redefine old goals and to implement new ones than do established regimes. This is because regime change momentarily frees the state from established social entanglements and offers the leaders an opportunity to redefine coalitions, alliances, goals, and policies. Of course, all new regimes do not undertake such a redefinition. Some use up their newly won energies primarily on settling political conflict and consolidating rule; others waste their power resources in their unwillingness to take risks; and yet others implement new development strategies emphasizing such significant goals as high growth or property redistribution.

The second preliminary issue can be posed as a question: what are the distinctions between the concept of the state and the concept of the regime? While the distinctions are fuzzy, and therefore any attempts to delineate them vulnerable to criticism, they are nevertheless real and, one might say, crucial. The main point here is that regimes can come and go but the basic state type does not alter easily. Democratic or authoritarian regimes, for example, are both variations on the theme of how authority relations are structured within the framework of a capitalist state. Regime changes are not likely to alter the two fundamental characteristics of Third World states — they seek development and this development is based on private property. While a communist revolution may alter the latter, even such a revolution is not likely to alter the teleological character of these states. For those who have been "left behind" in the world system, irrespective of regime type, the state's commitment to lead the society to a "developed stage" is likely to remain central.

From an analytical standpoint, therefore, the concepts of the state and the regime attempt to capture the distinction between the longer-lasting features — the "deep structure" — and the relatively changeable aspects of how public authority is structured in relation to society. Empirically, the concept of regime draws attention to how political rule is organized (e.g., patterns of legislative–executive relations) and the relationship of the rulers to the ruled (e.g., involving democratic participation or not). While regime types within the capitalist Third World vary widely, three important dimensions of variation can be delineated in a general way: the degree of institutionalization, the degree of nationalism, and the degree of democratic participation. Each of these needs to be discussed.

First, regime institutionalization consists of two components: organizational continuity and class valuation. Continuity itself reflects the capacity of political organizations to survive in the face of the demands and tasks they must perform. As Huntington suggested in his important formulation, this in turn reflects the adaptability, complexity, and coherence of public organizations.[28] What Huntington had not suggested, however, was that the demands on and the tasks performed by regimes are seldom devoid of class issues. Different social classes value a given political order to different degrees. Class valuation is therefore also an important component of institutionalized regimes. If organizational continuity is achieved with minimal overt use of force, this reflects the fact that organizations have proven to be efficacious and have come to be valued, albeit to different degrees by different social classes, by society as a whole. This we recognize as the process of institutionalization. On the other hand, if overt use of force is necessary to perpetuate the dominant political organizations, this more often than not demonstrates that there is a breakdown in elite consensus and that organizational arrangements are being sustained in the face of opposition, often involving the lower classes.

Organizational continuity and class valuation as defining components, then, help us delineate the institutionalization dimension. At one end of the dimension are regimes marked by an absence of institutionalization — there is an organizational breakdown in which the issue of class valuation is not even relevant. At the other end are regimes where continuity is sustained with minimal use of force. This rare Third World condition of institutionalized regimes reflects a marriage of adaptable and complex and coherent organizations with a minimum degree of legitimacy bestowed by all social classes. Most Third World regimes, however, tend to fall between these two stools. These are cases of coerced institutional maintenance where organizational continuity is sustained by force. This force is usually tolerated if not demanded by the upper classes, but generally runs contrary to the interests and wishes of the lower classes.

Secondly, state consolidation within the Third World has been accompanied by regimes with varying degrees and types of nationalism. This variation has resulted from several historical conditions: the nature of the colonial rule (e.g., direct versus indirect); the nature of the power transition from colonialism to sovereignty (e.g., prolonged and confrontational versus short and negotiated); the leadership and ideology of the nationalist movement (e.g., reformist versus revolutionary) and the social basis of the nationalist movement (mass-based or based on a narrow elite). Varying nationalist legacies, resulting from this historical

---

28. Huntington, *Political order*, esp. pp. 12-23.

diversity, in turn not only have consequences for the patterns of regime formation, but also influence the policy proclivities and preferences of the new regime authorities.

For example, wherever the struggle for state sovereignty was prolonged, mass-based, and led by relatively cohesive nationalist movements, regime authorities are likely to be sensitive to issues of economic self-reliance. Dependence on foreign aid and investment here will be viewed with suspicion. Development strategies are then likely to be along a more nationalist and less dependent capitalist option. Contrasting cases are those where consolidation of a sovereign state was accomplished without any real nationalistic mass mobilization. In this case, not only is there a weak basis of a national consensus in the civil society, resulting in weak institutions and periodic military regimes, but also regime authorities are more inclined to involve foreign economic actors in national development. Regime variation along the nationalist dimension, in sum, helps distinguish regimes that value national sovereignty as a significant goal — nationalist regimes — from dependent regimes, such as those that seek incorporation into the world system as a desirable option. Economic dependencies are themselves, therefore, partly a result of political choices made by regime authorities at crucial historical junctures.

Thirdly, the variation in degrees of democratic participation results in part from the nature of the inherited political institutions and in part from the variations in the social and economic structure, including the impact of the levels of development already achieved. Open polities within the Third World, rare as they are, do share enough structural characteristics to be grouped together. These characteristics include demand-oriented political participation by various interest groups, including labor; the incapacity of such regimes to impose lower levels of consumption forcibly on society; the periodic need of the regime to secure legitimacy and thus to make policy concessions to competing societal contenders; and the penetration of state institutions by the more powerful within the society. These political characteristics not only constrain state autonomy in relation to society, but also influence economic activities in an identifiable manner. I will return to this issue below.

The opposite of the open or democratic polities, namely, closed or authoritarian polities, are not homogenous enough to be categorized as a meaningful type. The Saudi Arabian monarchy, Khomeni's Iran, Uganda under Amin, and Brazil under a military junta are all authoritarian, but hardly share enough political characteristics worth generalizing. Authoritarian regimes, therefore, have to be further categorized into types of authoritarian regimes prior to meaningful theorizing.[29] As authoritarian regimes are not the focus of this study, however, I will not pursue their discussion any further.

The three dimensions in which Third World regimes commonly vary — institutionalization, nationalism, and participation — help us, in combination, delineate three of the important regime types commonly found within the capitalist Third World: fragmented, nationalist–democratic and authoritarian–dependent. This is not a typology of Third World regimes, in that it leaves out such other possible combinations as democratic–dependent and authoritarian–nationalist; it also leaves out regimes that vary in dimensions other than those specified in the discussion above. The attempt here is not to be all-inclusive. It is rather to capture and categorize the more salient elements of the political variation found within the Third World, in order to set the stage for the analysis of some of their developmental consequences.

Regime Types and Economic Development

The specific task of this study is to analyze the impact of regime variations on distributional outcomes in India. So far the general discussion has focused on the concepts of the state, state autonomy, and regime types. This discussion has been structured in a manner that will lead to a conceptualization of authority structures as a potentially significant force in socio-economic development. Continuing the discussion in a descending order of abstraction — from the most general towards the specific — I will briefly address the "middle range" issue of how variations in regime type generally condition economic development.

Fragmented regimes are those where authority structures have failed to gel. These fragmented or unstable cases can be roughly viewed as belonging to one of two subtypes. The first set of cases are those where from the very onset of political independence, there was a failure to achieve political cohesion (e.g., Uganda, Angola, and Bangladesh). This failure is in turn rooted in fragmented social structures — where fragmentation has at least in part been manipulated and exacerbated by former colonial rulers — and/or the absence of prolonged nationalist movements preceding the establishment of state sovereignty. The former makes coalition formation for the establishment of cohesive rule difficult, and the latter — as nationalism provides a rare ideological force enabling political cohesion even in fragmented societies — only re-enforces the basis of

29. I have extended this discussion elsewhere. See Atul Kohli, "The state, economic growth and income-distribution in the Third World," paper presented to the International Studies Association meetings, East Lansing, Michigan (November 3-5, 1983).

instability. The second set of unstable cases are those where a coalition of national political forces undermines the established and often externally supported dictatorial regime, but fails to replace it with a cohesive alternative (e.g., Iran, Nicaragua, and El Salvador). The failure of political institutionalization of either type not only minimizes state autonomy from society, and therefore state capacities to pursue politically defined economic goals, but also leads to unpredictability in the socio-economic environment. These conditions have identifiable developmental consequences.

Regimes struggling to maintain a modicum of stability are in no position to formulate and implement coherent development policies. Regime weakness, moreover, encourages the precipitation of latent social conflicts. Political and social instability in turn discourages both domestic and foreign private investment. As a consequence, neither the state nor private enterprise undertakes new and sustained economic activity. It can thus be hypothesized that little or even negative economic growth will occur under conditions of political instability and social conflict. It is not surprising to note that Uganda, Angola, and Mozambique have experienced negative growth rates throughout their unstable decade of the 1970s and that the national wealth of Iran and El Salvador has declined over the last few unstable years. This is, of course, not to suggest, or even to imply, that instability is evil and that stability is preferable at all costs. On the contrary, instability may in some cases be a necessary prelude to the emergence of more desirable political–economic arrangements. In most cases, however, the breakdown of dominant political institutions is followed by harsh rule of one form or another. Whatever the normative implications of stability versus instability then, it is clear that Huntington's old hypothesis continues to be a challenging one: regime cohesion is a necessary prerequisite for sustained economic development.[30]

Nationalist–democratic regimes (e.g., in India, Malaysia, Sri Lanka, and Zimbabwe) are generally born out of prolonged nationalist movements made reformist by the constraints of dominant social classes and colonialism. Nationalism provides the force and the glue for the mobilization of various social classes into an anti-colonial political struggle. The impact of colonialism is in turn manifest, not only in ensuring that the nationalist movement does not become revolutionary and communist (this often minimized the costs of decolonization), but also in leaving behind basic democratic institutions. While the nationalist element generally enhances state autonomy from economic forces — especially economic forces under foreign control — the democratic element of the

---

30. Huntington, *Political order, passim.*

regime tends to tie the state to organized social interests. Over time, therefore, as anti-colonial nationalism falls into the background and interest groups compete for state resources, the autonomy of states governed by nationalist–democratic regimes typically declines.

Development strategies adopted by nationalist–democratic regimes are based on the following premises: as national sovereignty is valued, attempts are made to minimize foreign dependencies; a developmental alliance between the regime and national capital forms the state's core "pact of domination"; but in order to sustain a somewhat open polity, redistributive goals are held to be of legitimate political concern.

Nationalist–democratic regimes, then, attempt to reconcile the goals of national sovereignty, economic growth, and a modicum of redistribution in their overall development. A singular emphasis on the pursuit of any one of these three goals generally endangers the other goals. For example, nationalization or severe restrictions on new foreign investment endangers economic growth; an exclusive policy emphasis on growth hampers the goals of both redistribution and sovereignty; and too much emphasis on redistribution encourages consumption and discourages savings, capital formation, private investment, and economic growth. Compromise among the competing goals is thus of the essence in nationalist–democratic settings. While some progress on all three goals is possible, in most cases the performance is skewed in one direction or another.

For example, democratic politics, moderate to impressive growth rates, and some income redistribution — especially along ethnic lines — have been reconciled in Malaysia within the framework of regional co-operation.[31] Zimbabwe also appears to be moving in this direction.[32] India's democratic regime, discussed in much greater detail below, has been able to stimulate only moderate to low growth rates. While external dependencies have been minimized, neither "trickle-down" nor effective redistribution has alleviated mass poverty.[33] The case of Chile under Allende, in contrast to all of the above, highlights how a sharp move towards maximizing national sovereignty and redistributive goals can undermine the whole precarious balance of nationalist–democratic regimes.[34] I will return in the concluding chapter to the question of why degrees of regime cohesion appear to be an important variable explaining variations within the nationalist–democratic cases.

31. See Donald R. Snodgrass, *Inequality and economic development in Malaysia* (Oxford University Press: Kaula Lumpur, 1980).
32. See Michael Bratton, "Development in Zimbabwe: strategy and tactics," *Journal of Modern African Studies*, 19, 3 (September 1981), 447-75.
33. See Frankel, *India's political economy,* for a general argument along this line. For statistical evidence on this, see Ahluwalia, "Rural poverty", and Bardhan, "Poverty and 'trickle-down.' "
34. See Loveman, *Chile,* chs. 8-10.

Authoritarian–dependent regimes (e.g., in Brazil, the Philippines, South Korea, and Chile) are generally born out of the breakdown of the more democratic developmental experiments. Slow economic growth rates and demands for nationalization and redistribution often accompany development within nationalist–democratic settings. If these issues arise in countries where the political–institutional framework is basically weak, the characteristic response has been authoritarian intervention in the interest of the upper classes. The successful installation of authoritarian–dependent regimes presupposes some need for them. These may be the perceived needs of the leadership to stimulate higher economic growth or to discipline the labor force. Regime installation also presumes a capacity to impose such an arrangement, utilizing the strong coercive arm of the state. These regimes thus characteristically come into being in the more "advanced" Third World countries, where both the economy and state structures have developed at least to an intermediate stage. Such regimes typically, in the short run, enhance the state's autonomy *vis-à-vis* society. The new political situation thus enables the state authorities to forge new ruling coalitions with propertied classes, to exclude the access of others to the state while promising them some economic benefits, and to exclude yet others (generally the lower classes) from both political participation and economic benefits. This situation of flux, and therefore flexibility, often results in the adoption of new policies, with important consequences for economic development.

The high-growth oriented authoritarian–dependent regimes typically attempt to (1) exclude the lower classes, especially the working classes, from both political participation and a proportional share of economic rewards; and (2) create a policy framework to encourage domestic and foreign private investment. The most "successful" authoritarian–dependent regimes, therefore, generate developmental patterns that tie the domestic economy intricately to the world capitalist economy and are accompanied by high economic growth rates and increasingly skewed patterns of income distribution.[35]

Authoritarian–dependent regimes, however, like those that are nationalist–democratic, face their own internal contradictions. The core dilemma continues to be regime legitimacy: how to institutionalize state power without giving a modicum of participatory rights to the majority. Political conflicts, moreover, penetrate the supposedly apolitical ruling centers and threaten to politicize the military. Additionally, in the

---

35. For statistical evidence linking regime types and income distribution, see Atul Kohli, Michael F. Altfeld, Saideh Lotfian, and Russel Mardon, "Inequality in the Third World: an assessment of competing explanations," *Comparative Political Studies*, 17, 3 (October 1984), 283-318.

economic sphere, skewed income distribution limits the size of the internal market and becomes a constraint on economic growth. The externalization of the economy also generates its own problems, such as an increased foreign debt, which is a further growth-bottleneck. Both political and economic problems thus generate pressures to move towards political democratization, income redistribution, and a degree of economic self-reliance. In other words, there are pressures to move towards a more nationalist–democratic model. Just as the failures of reformism, then, have often paved the way for the emergence of authoritarian–exclusionary regimes, the developmental contradictions of the latter model create forces that push regime authorities to adopt a more reformist approach.

This cursory discussion is aimed only at enhancing the plausibility of the more general assertion: regime types affect a state's capacity to act upon society and can thus be associated with patterns of development. While it would be interesting to discuss further the typical origins and the developmental dynamics created by each of these regime types, that is not the task of this study. I am concerned only with the distributional dynamics within the nationalist–democratic case of India. However, the reasons for moving from a general discussion towards a more specific one are (1) to clarify the concepts of state, state autonomy, and regime type used in this study; and (2) to underline the point that the state orientation adopted here is applicable to cases of development other than India.

Democratic Development and Redistributive Reforms

If political conditions indeed influence patterns of economic development, under what conditions are effective redistributive reforms likely to be pursued? Can democratically elected regime authorities reform the social order within a capitalist model of development? Answers to this question are likely to be controversial and to be rooted in one's normative views on and theoretical assumptions about the nature of democratic–capitalist development. I will in this section review some of the prevailing positions on this subject as a vehicle for developing my own hypothetical ideas to be examined empirically in the following chapters.

Two serious political–economy hypotheses on reformism — the "urban bias" and the "organize the poor" hypotheses — require discussion. Prior to that, however, several other related sets of ideas, which are not entertained here at length, but which can nevertheless yield plausible propositions, deserve mention in passing. These ideas are not considered here in any detail mainly because they tend to misunderstand the dynamics and the significance of state-initiated social reforms within democratic–capitalist development.

The first of these views comes from maintaining that social stratification, income distribution, and poverty conditions tend to alter only with the overall economic development of a society. While challenged frequently, this somewhat evolutionary and developmental perspective on socio-economic change has a powerful hold on scholarly imagination. It derives its inspiration from the historical experiences of Western societies. And its adoption leads one to conceive of poverty amelioration within the contemporary Third World essentially as a long-range process. According to this view, as economies continue to develop, income distribution is likely to worsen in the early stages and improve with maturing industrialization, and the living conditions of the lowest groups are likely to improve steadily only as the overall percapita incomes improve.[36]

I have discussed elsewhere these views and their empirical inadequacy for explaining some contemporary Third World patterns.[37] The main points developed in this other study can be restated briefly. First, the fact that communist countries have achieved quite different income distribution and poverty profiles in comparison to capitalist countries at similar levels of development strongly suggests that there are no general laws relating levels of development to levels of welfare. Second, changes in income distribution and in welfare levels within the contemporary Third World vary a fair amount, and these variations are not a simple function of levels of development. And third, whether income distribution worsens or improves in the contemporary Third World is best explained with reference to the pattern of state intervention in the economy.

Evolutionary and developmental views on contemporary Third World poverty are thus inadequate because they are ahistorical — they assume that the contemporary Third World will develop along the Western path — and because they refuse to recognize the significance of state intervention to alter any "inevitable" laws of economic development. As Adelman and Robinson have also concluded, adopted development strategies appear to have considerable bearing on the welfare of the poor in developing countries. [38] Adopted strategies and policies in turn draw attention to the issue of political choice. The range of choice available to political authorities is a further function of the degree of state autonomy from society, or the structure of state power in relation to society.

Certain Marxist scholars and practitioners also deny the significance of "bourgeois reformism." With the stress on class determination of the political process, redistributive state intervention is in such views held to be either impossible or a meaningless palliative aimed only at co-opting

36. For a discussion of these views, see *ibid.*
37. *Ibid.*
38. I. Adelman and S. Robinson, *Income distribution policy in developing countries: a case study of Korea* (Stanford University Press: Stanford, California, 1978).

potential class conflict.[39] Socialist revolutions are then conceived to be a prerequisite to any meaningful redistribution. Those subscribing to this world view can draw evidence both from the persistence of widespread poverty in much of the capitalist Third World and the asserted absence of the same in such cases as China and Cuba. This perspective, like the developmental one, has a widespread appeal as it simultaneously explains certain current conditions and points towards their future solution. As Albert Hirschman has eloquently explained:

... the revolutionary who is out to ridicule the peaceful reformer has an easy task indeed. He will show that a basic transformation of existing power relationships is a prerequisite to adopting and enforcing any measure that threatens the interests and privileges of ruling classes.... The idea of revolution as a prerequisite to any progress draws immense strength from the very limited human ability to visualize change and from the fact that it makes only minimal demands on that ability. All we are asked to imagine by the revolutionary is the tumbling down of the old regime in a total upheaval which will give birth to the new order.[40]

There are a number of well-known problems with this revolutionary standpoint. They require but the briefest reiteration. First, from an empirical standpoint, there are important exceptions within the capitalist Third World where redistributive intervention has been successful and/or welfare policies have been effectively pursued. Also there is room to dispute the extent of welfare and egalitarian achievements in such cases as China and Cuba.[41] Related to this, and from a normative perspective, welfare achievements in socialist cases have not been without other costs.[42] And third, there is an important analytical problem: the revolutionary perspective overemphasizes class constraints at the expense of the role of the state in mediating and structuring class relations.

To state the above is not to deny the significant insights generated by both the developmental and the Marxist perspectives on the problems of Third World poverty. The developmental view sensitizes us to the overwhelming fact that there are serious limits on poverty eradication within

39. For example, see Dilip Hiro, *Inside India today* (Monthly Review Press: New York, 1976), esp. ch. 8.
40. Albert Hirschman, *Journeys toward progress: studies of economic policy-making in Latin America* (Twentieth Century Fund: New York, 1963), pp. 252 and 254. While I accept Hirschman's critique of the "revolutionary" perspective, it will become clear in due course that I do not subscribe to the concept of "reform mongering" in his sense of that word.
41. For example, see the two articles by Edward B. Vermeer: "Income differentials in rural China," *China Quarterly,* 89 (March 1982), 1-33; and "Social welfare provisions and the limits of inequality in contemporary China," *Asian Survey,* 19, 9 (September 1979), 856-80.
42. For a discussion along these lines, see Peter Berger, *Pyramids of sacrifice: political ethics and social change* (Doubleday: New York, 1976), esp. chs. 3, 4 and 5.

the framework of a low-income economy. Similarly, the Marxist framework highlights the limits on redistribution within a non-revolutionary society. What both perspectives nevertheless neglect is the scope of deliberate reform within the broad limits of a low-income, class society. While I take the constraints on the state's reformist intervention seriously, I nevertheless hope to demonstrate empirically a range of reformist options possible within a democratic–capitalist model of development. Theoretically, therefore, I do not find that either level of development or class variables fully explain developmental outcomes. Variations in authority structures and related variations in the pattern of state intervention are also a crucial variable influencing lower-class welfare.

That poverty conditions can and ought to be deliberately influenced came to be widely recognized during the 1970s. Important international organizations, such as the World Bank, argued that eradication of poverty ought to be an important development goal.[43] Reform-oriented development economists put forward varying policy prescriptions for reconciling "growth with distribution" within the capitalist Third World. Elaborate arguments were put forward urging Third World leaders to adopt a more "employment oriented," "rural oriented," or "basic-needs oriented" strategy of economic development.[44]

From the standpoint of the present study, this literature, in recommending "growth with distribution," was clearly moving in the right direction. It recognized that growth goals were not sufficient to alleviate poverty and that policy reorientation was required. It did not, however, go far enough. Having recognized the significance of policies for developmental outcomes, it stopped short of asking the next question: under what political conditions can redistributive policies be adopted? Are regime changes likely to be a prerequisite of significant policy change? There was a tendency in this economic-policy literature to assume that if alerted to alternatives, Third World leaders might modify their policies, leading to a better balance between growth and equity considerations. But what if the leaders to whom the advice is given are themselves an obstacle to policy changes?[45] The refusal to recognize that policies reflect concrete social and political interests, then, led to unrealistic expectations concerning the prospects of alleviating Third World poverty by mere policy advice. It is no surprise that the first flush of enthusiasm for "growth

---

43. See the World Bank, *Assault on world poverty*.
44. For example, see Holis Chenery *et al.*, *Redistribution with growth*.
45. For a trenchant critique of some of the economic-development literature from this standpoint, see Keith Griffin, *The political economy of agrarian change: an essay on the green revolution*, 1st edn (Harvard University Press: Cambridge, Massachusetts, 1974), esp. ch. 7.

with redistribution" has faded within the international development establishment.[46]

So far I have commented on several sets of general ideas concerning poverty and the mal-distribution of income in the Third World. I have not found these to be satisfactory for guiding my study, as either they do not admit the scope of state intervention for social reforms or they fail to highlight the political conditions necessary for such reformist intervention. I would now like to discuss two other and, in my view, more relevant propositions: the "urban bias" and the "organize the poor" propositions. These have emerged from the India literature. They are of considerable importance for this study, not because I agree with them or because they help orient the following empirical materials, but because they help focus discussion on the political determinants of distributional outcomes.

Michael Lipton's well-known "urban bias" hypothesis suggests that a root cause of Third World poverty is the concentration of urban interests and orientations within the political structures of these countries. Development policies emerging from these power centers consistently tend to favor the urban over the rural sectors. This favoritism is manifest in the fact that larger shares of public investment are allocated for industrialization than for agricultural development, and in the fact that urban areas enjoy favorable terms of trade, as well as easier access to many services such as credit, schooling, and health. This urban policy bias enhances urban productivities, incomes, and levels of living at the expense of the same in the rural areas. Since the bulk of the Third World poor live in rural areas, it is hardly a surprise that the pro-urban development pursued so far has failed to reach these people. Eradication of poverty in this view would thus require a political and policy shift in favor of the agrarian interests.[47]

While one could quibble with Lipton over such empirical issues as who is favored by the terms of trade in a country such as India, the strengths and the weaknesses of the argument lie elsewhere. The argument shifts

46. Instead of arguing for a direct attack on poverty, for example, the World Bank now conceives of poverty amelioration as a function of higher growth rates. Discussing the purposes of economic development, the 1981 Bank report still argues that "the most urgent of them is to further the struggle against poverty." However, rapid economic growth, judged to be attainable, will now provide the resources necessary to tackle poverty. See the World Bank, *World development report, 1981* (Oxford University Press: New York, 1981), p. 119.

47. Michael Lipton had first put forward this argument as a critique of Indian planning. See his article, "Strategy for agriculture: urban bias and rural planning," in Paul Streeten and Michael Lipton (eds.), *The crisis of Indian planning: economic planning in the 1960's* (Oxford University Press: London, 1968), p. 142. Later Lipton generalized this argument. See Michael Lipton, *Why poor people stay poor: urban bias in world development* (Harvard University Press: Cambridge, Massachusetts, 1977).

attention away from class issues (propertied rich versus the propertyless poor) toward sectoral ones (urban versus rural). This is useful in so far as it reminds us that many class realignments, especially in the so-called communist countries, have not necessarily benefited the rural poor. And when they have, as in the case of China, the benefits have been a function of considerable public investment in the rural areas. As long as the majority of the poor are in the rural areas, therefore, improvements in their living conditions are likely to remain a function of their having access to more productive work. And it is not unreasonable to argue that such access is likely to be greater with long-term, public-investment shifts favoring the agricultural sector.

But what about the issues of the rich versus the poor within the agrarian sector? What is to ensure that the fruits of greater public investment in the agricultural sector will not be monopolized by the agrarian rich? Why should the rural poor necessarily benefit? Are we to continue to believe in the miracles of "trickle-down"? Do we have any convincing evidence to suggest that the "green revolution" has benefited the rural poor? If not, what redistributive intervention will be necessary to ensure that new agrarian wealth reaches the agrarian poor? The empirical evidence in at least one of the cases examined below further highlights how the passing of political power to propertied agrarian groups has not brought benefits to the rural poor.

While the rural–urban cleavage is, therefore, not an unimportant focus for poverty studies, it nevertheless cannot fully replace the matter of inequitable gains along class lines. Whenever issues of poverty and poverty reform are dealt with, and especially in a democratic–capitalist setting, a central concern is always likely to be the distribution of economic resources among the rich and the poor, and the potential role of the state in altering this pattern of distribution. This focuses analytical attention on the nature of the state itself and upon the political preconditions necessary for successful redistributive reforms.

A number of scholarly treatments of India's poverty have in recent years thus emphasized the need to "organize the poor" as a vehicle for altering the political and policy balance in favor of the poor. Francine Frankel's major study of the Indian political economy traces the failure to eradicate India's rural poverty back to the failures to implement redistributive land reforms. And in her view this political failure, in turn, reflects the narrow social base of state power. She argues that the future solutions to poverty problems are likely to emerge through widening the social base of state power: i.e., by organizing the poor and by further democratizing the political structures.[48] Both Marcus Franda and Raj

48. Frankel, *India's political economy,* esp. conclusion.

Krishna have also made similar arguments in their recent works.[49] And even India's Planning Commission under the Janata government (1977-80) put this forward as its official position.[50]

The optimism about reform in this view stems not only from the possibility of enlightened policies, but also from a faith in democratic, pluralist politics. As the lower classes get organized, the argument goes, they gain political significance. Democratic politics allow political inputs from competing social interests. As the power base of the state is widened, so are the policy outputs, increasingly reflecting a reformist orientation aimed at benefiting the lower classes. Democratic politics and the organization of the lower classes are thus the prescriptions for reformist development. As this perspective is widely shared, my disagreement with it must involve a somewhat lengthy discussion.[51]

The analytic correlate of this world view is that it conceives the outputs of the political process to be largely determined by the leadership and the underlying economic interest groups. It follows that, if one set of interests predominates at one time, another set can at least compete with the first at a later date. Because franchise and organization are the processes whereby economic interests are converted into political power, there is reason to feel optimistic that the interests of the lower classes, once organized, can be transformed into a significant political force.

What this widely shared perspective on politics fails to recognize is that inequalities of power are not merely a consequence of the degree of organization. Rather, they are prior to the political — that is, they are rooted in the social organization itself. They are very much a function of the position various social groups occupy in the organization of production. Within a society's division of labor some manage, control, or own the means of economic production of a society. Others serve, obey, or — as they own little else — sell their labor for survival and continuity, while obeying the rules of selling and buying. Those at the top of this class hierarchy are intrinsically more powerful than those below. This inequality of social power is, moreover, often reproduced within the dominant political institutions. Class inequalities, therefore, can never be reversed within the framework of a stable, developmental–capitalist state. They can at best be mitigated.

49. See Marcus Franda, *India's rural development: an assessment of alternatives* (Indiana University Press: Bloomington, Indiana, 1980), conclusion; and Raj Krishna, "The next phase."
50. Government of India, *Draft five year plan, 1978-83* (Planning Commission: New Delhi, 1978), p. 15.
51. The following discussion builds on an article I had written in 1980. See Atul Kohli, "Democracy, economic growth, and inequality in India's development," *World Politics*, 32, 4 (July 1980), esp. pp. 631-5.

Viewed from a perspective that holds class constraints to be serious, though not determining, the prospects for generating effective lower-class power in a stable democracy require exceptional political circumstances. These have to do with the emergence of disciplined left-of-center parties as ruling parties. Such parties, and not merely the organization of the poor, enable a degree of separation between social and political power. This degree of state autonomy can then be used to implement redistributive reforms. But this is jumping way ahead in the argument. A prior case must be made for why and how the "organize the poor" perspective fails to comprehend the seriousness of class constraints on redistributive politics. If one traces the steps through which political inputs are transformed into outputs, one is struck by the layers of obstacles faced by any attempt at converting the majority interests into redistributive policies. Some of these layers can be delineated in a general way.

First, a community of shared economic interests has to be perceived by the members of the lower classes. Here there are objective and subjective constraints. Objectively, there is in no society one single "exploited class." There are only vaguely specifiable lower classes. The interests of various groups within them are not identical. To the extent that, at a macro-level, one can discuss lower- versus upper-class interests, the entire socialization apparatus of a hierarchical society tends to detract attention from the recognition of the cleavage. Representatives of the upper classes penetrate and often control religious, educational, and informational institutions. The value system generated and/or sustained by these institutions leads to the creation of an ideological obstacle within the political process. This type of thinking tends to neutralize what should come naturally to citizens belonging to the lower classes — consciousness of shared economic interests. If effective, it can also lead to the creation of a belief structure specifying that the interests of the lower classes are best served by pursuing common endeavors with the upper classes, such as increasing production and maintaining systemic stability.

A second obstacle emerges when individuals with common interests have to be organized into unions to pursue economic gains, or into parties to wage a political and economic struggle. For the organizers, there are a number of discouraging elements: minimal economic rewards, scarcity of resources to pursue the tasks of organization, and prospects of being socially punished in either a subtle or an overt manner. These factors tend to reduce the pool of potential organizers of the lower classes. Likewise, even if those who have to be organized perceive a community of interests, they do not always follow their perceptions with predictable political behavior. Not only can other values compete with economic ones in the choice of association, but economic dependency and the fear of reprisal can act as factors inhibiting association for economic gains. Cumulatively, the factors stacked against organizers and organized create conditions in which the task of mobilizing the lower classes is an arduous one. Furthermore, even if the efforts succeed, organization itself is a two-edged sword. On the one hand, it transforms atomized interests into a potential social and political force; on the other, it opens up the possibility of co-opting or compromising the interests of the organized *en masse*.

Within a democratic polity this potential political force, once organized, needs to be converted into electoral power. Here again, the limited resource base of the lower classes, as well as their limited access to the informational institutions of society, either put them at a permanent disadvantage *vis-à-vis* the upper classes or lead them to make significant compromises with others higher up in the social hierarchy. Furthermore, because lower-class parties generally enter the political arena as latecomers, they have to fight established beliefs concerning the legitimate mode of politics and the appropriate role of the state in social life. Since these established values were institutionalized while the interests of the upper classes were dominant, the struggle to create legitimacy without significant compromises is an uphill battle for the lower-class parties. Even if they achieve success in the electoral process, they often face another obstacle in the structure of the government itself. The ineffectiveness of parliaments as policy-making bodies is an example: in democratic polities, it is not uncommon for some higher authority to usurp power when faced by parliaments whose sentiments favor the lower classes.

If, despite the ideological, organizational, electoral, and governmental obstacles, those representing lower-class interests manage to gain control in important policy-making bodies, it is still not the end of their struggle — policies have to be implemented. Established bureaucracies are not only incremental and therefore by nature resistant to sweeping social change but, since they have usually been designed by the upper classes or by colonial rulers, they are biased against the lower strata. Implementation of redistributive policies through established bureaucracies is, therefore, an inherently difficult task, and the same holds true for the creation of new, competing structures.

Finally, if the implementation of redistributive policies gets under way, the short-term consequences are, as a rule, disruptive of stability and production efficiency. This is due partly to the reorganization of the production process that such changes often involve, and partly to the fears of and blackmail by the upper classes, as manifested in the flight of capital, the hoarding of goods, and minimal new investments. At the same time, the more extreme elements, encouraged by the growing strength of the lower classes, tend to go too far. Illegal confiscation of property, lockouts, and other activities disruptive to property and production may take place. As a consequence, generally speaking, production goes down, and goods are often scarce in the markets. Meanwhile, lower-class expectations rise and explosive inflationary tendencies build up. In other words, the rise of left-of-center regimes and the implementation of redistributive policies can lead to a problem of law and order. The failure to absorb the consequences of change within a democratic framework tends to undermine the legitimacy of regimes that favor the lower classes. Ironically, therefore, what starts out as a battle to organize the lower classes into an effective political force can lead to their disenchantment with their own representatives. They may even vote them out of office in an attempt to regain a modicum of predictability and stability.

For reasons like these, one cannot feel very optimistic about the possibilities of converting lower-class interests into effective redistributive policies within a stable, democratic framework. The prospects of transforming plurality of numbers into real economic gains for the poor are made very slim by layers of obstacles at the ideological, organizational, electoral, governmental, and bureaucratic levels. Substantial success, if achieved, tends to undermine the stability of democratic polity. Therefore, in a stable system, a modicum of success is achieved only through considerable compromises in the goals.

Am I suggesting the impossibility of reform within the democratic–capitalist framework? No! The point of the above discussion is rather that political attempts at reform are constrained by the class structure. The failure to comprehend these constraints can only lead to unrealistic expectations. Moreover, there is no built-in, evolutionary tendency in democratic polities towards the broadening of political power among competing social groups.[52] Significant political power passing into the hands of the lower classes is a possible scenario, but a rare scenario that has to be consciously contrived. It requires rule by parties which are specifically designed to institutionalize — ideologically and organizationally — the power of the lower classes within the democratic political process.

If the "organize the poor" perspective argues for some form of popular social democracy as a political precondition for poverty reforms, by contrast, the argument of this study can be best thought of as a case for a disciplined social democracy. The specifics of the argument will eventually emerge with reference to the empirical materials and are summarized in

---

52. Even Robert Dahl has reached this conclusion lately. See Dahl, "Pluralism revisited," p. 199.

the introduction and the concluding chapters. What is important to note here is the distinction between these two positions. The distinction is not over the preferred outcomes, but over the analysis of the preconditions leading to successful poverty reform. What is crucial for implementing reforms — and I will demonstrate this with reference to empirical materials — is not merely a shift in the social basis of power, but a change in the design of state institutions. Mobilizing hitherto excluded groups into the political arena is by itself an invitation to political instability and reaction. Disciplined political parties are thus crucial for controlled mobilization. Disciplined left-of-center parties are, moreover, crucial for the controlled mobilization of the lower classes and for institutionalizing reformist goals within the state. Such parties also create a partial insulation of the state from society, making reformist intervention possible. Regime organization and ideology, and not the social basis of power alone, are thus considered to be important variables in this study for implementing poverty reforms.

Analysis of the political preconditions for social reforms is inherently difficult and controversial. What one scholar may consider to be social reform may well be thought of by others as insignificant co-optation or excessive state intervention. The prospects of implementing reform can, moreover, always be thought of as simultaneously limited and yet not non-existent. This ambivalence can easily lead to either undue optimism or undue pessimism. While the latter tendency often stems from an excessive analytical concern with structural constraints, the former as often results from an undue focus on processes of choice. As is clear from the brief review above, some of the existing scholarly treatments tend to underestimate the possibility of state-initiated reforms, and others fail to highlight the social–structural constraints upon such reforms. I hope to tread a line between these two positions by (1) focusing on the state as a location of a society's crucial choice and constraint mechanisms and (2) conceptualizing regime organization and ideology as the important variables enhancing the state's autonomy in initiating social reforms.

Some theoretical and conceptual issues having been discussed, as well as the relevant works of several other scholars, the argument to be explored below empirically can now be summarized in the form of several generalizable but hypothetical assertions:

1. State intervention for social reform necessarily involves regime
authorities in social conflict over valued economic resources.

In order to pursue reform, regime authorities can go for two broad sets of available options: redistribution of existing resources; and/or alteration of the pattern of distribution of newly created resources. While the former poses greater problems for a reform-oriented leadership, both options tend to evoke upper-class opposition: both options are perceived to involve a redistribution of societal resources. If reformist authorities pursue the radical option of redistribution of existing resources, this typically takes the form of land redistribution or selected nationalization of commerce and industry. That this would immediately involve the regime in conflict with the members of the landed or the urban upper classes is so obvious that it does not require elaboration. What is not so obvious, however, is that the attempts to alter the distribution of future resources also have similar, though somewhat less intense, consequences.

The attempts to redistribute newly created resources can take the form of direct or indirect regime intervention. Direct intervention typically leads the state to increase public revenues through taxation and rechannel them into activities of direct benefit to the lower classes. Taxation, in turn, involves the regime in conflicting social issues: who will pay and how much? The issue of how the public revenues will be used is also fraught with controversy. Any attempt to alter the existing pattern of public expenditure, such as moving expenditures away from production subsidies towards public works aimed at employment creation, often invokes the wrath of influential interests benefiting from state subsidies. The rechannelling of only the increments in public revenue to the benefit of the lower classes is somewhat easier. However, not only would this require an effective regime apparatus that is capable of collecting taxes and is not easily manipulated by those who are socially influential, but the range of redistributive political actions possible with these limited resources would be rather small.

The indirect attempts at the redistribution of new resources involve manipulation of the policy process aimed at benefiting the lower groups. Rural credit and agricultural pricing policies are two common examples. Because the total credit resources are always limited, attempts to rechannel credit to smaller farmers by policy measures either fail, or invoke the hostility of the upper classes, or both. Similarly, the attempts to remove price supports so that landless laborers and others who are net consumers may benefit, hurt the interests of the producers and are not treated by them as politically neutral actions. Once again, therefore, the attempts to manipulate the policy process to benefit the lower classes bring back political tremors of dissatisfaction from the socially influential.

2. A common response of a Third World democratic regime anticipating or
experiencing opposition to reforms is to adopt a rhetoric of reform, while
eschewing any serious attempts to take such actions.

Given the fact that the state's reformist intervention is generally opposed
by the dominant social classes, most Third World regimes eschew such
efforts. While the case I want to make in this study is the opposite one,
namely, that state-initiated reforms are possible, a realistic understanding
of the conditions under which such reformist interaction is likely to succeed can only be achieved by realizing that the state's incapacity to
counter dominant social interests constitutes a normal state of affairs.

Authoritarian regimes often attempt to prevent the emergence of, or
deny the significance of, redistributive issues as politically significant.
Democratic Third World regimes, by contrast, find themselves needing
to maintain redistributive commitments. This need results from several
interrelated aspects of democratic politics: the need for broad-based
regime legitimacy; the need to incorporate the demands of newly emerging interest groups; and the dynamics of electoral competition, leading
competing leaders or parties to vie for the numerically significant lower-
class support. If these dynamics of democracy lead to adoption of reformist ideologies, class constraints on the political process make it difficult to
implement redistributive reforms. The emergence of simultaneous tendencies to maintain reformist rhetoric while eschewing any significant
redistribution is thus rooted in democratic–capitalist development. This
tension cannot, of course, be maintained permanently; over time, either
some reforms must be implemented or democracy must be curtailed.

3. Regimes pursuing successful redistributive reforms must have both
a reason and the capacity to do so. The reasons generally emerge when the
interests of the rulers in maintaining or enhancing their power position are
coterminous with the pursuit of reforms. And the capacity to pursue
reforms varies with the degree of ideological and organizational coherence
of the regime.

Political leaders aim to gain, maintain, and if possible enhance their
power position. Under certain circumstances their political goals become
coterminous with the pursuit of social reforms. The most common of
these circumstances is when counter-elites — the outsiders in political
competition — challenge established elites by mobilizing hitherto neglected social groups into the political arena. Established elites will also
then occasionally respond to such challenges by courting the same neglected groups. In either case, excluded or neglected groups are periodi-

cally mobilized by competing elites. This mobilization usually involves promises of socio-economic rewards in exchange for political support. Social reforms in democratic–capitalist settings are thus generally pursued as a consequence of competitive political mobilization.

While many Third World leaders would thus have reason to pursue social reform, only a few possess the political capacity to carry it through. Competitive mobilization and promises of social reform create conditions within which lower-class expectations are raised and upper classes tend to be cautious of and hostile towards the leadership. To stabilize this changed situation, therefore, regime authorities must first possess the simultaneous capacity to assuage the suspicions of the propertied by acting "responsibly," and "control" lower-class demands by stressing the need for incremental reforms. Within the constraints of this difficult juggling act, the regime then must also possess the organizational capacity to carry through reforms, even if they are only incremental. This generally requires the capacity to reach the poor directly, without the programs and benefits being captured by others in the social hierarchy. This in turn often means working, not only with established bureaucracies, who have their own well-established agendas, but also through alternative organizations designed to respond readily to regime goals.

A capacity to carry through social reforms thus puts a high premium on the ideological coherence and organizational discipline of the regime. Ideological coherence enables leaders to lay out their programs clearly, including the limits of their reformist intent; appear in control; and create a predictable environment, and thus appease the propertied. Organizational discipline also has some crucial functions. First, it enables leaders to impose an element of control on regime supporters expecting and demanding rapid redistribution. And, second, it generates capacities to translate the regime's reformist goals into grassroots action through a disciplined political organization. Ideological and organizational coherence are thus crucial variables enhancing a regime's reformist capacities.

4. Disciplined left-of-center parties are the most likely agents of systematic social reform within a democratic–capitalist model of development.

Disciplined left-of-center parties in power tend to have both reasons and the capacity to pursue social reforms. Such parties gain power in a democratic setting, if they gain power at all, by repeated promises of a better deal for the lower classes. Party ideology, regime legitimacy, and the need to sustain support will thus push the leadership towards undertaking redistributive reforms. There will, of course, be counter-pressures from the propertied classes. An attempt to incorporate these counter-demands is likely to slow the reformist thrust.

Party discipline then becomes crucial for the successful management of pressures for and against redistributive policies. Moderation of the redistributive thrust in the face of opposition is likely to generate dissatisfaction among party members and supporters. Discipline becomes crucial for maintaining coherent policy positions on the one hand and sustaining support on the other. Moreover, disciplined party organization is even more important for pursuing incremental reforms. This is especially true if reforms cannot simply be implemented by pursuing legislation. If the arm of the law is short, as it tends to be in most Third World countries, and reforms involve such actions as land redistribution, which are often seen as a redistributive policy measure in pre-industrial societies, then a disciplined party's capacity to penetrate society without being captured by the socially influential becomes a crucial variable for implementing regime goals in the outer reaches of society. Party organization enhances state autonomy from society, enabling a degree of separation between social and political power. This degree of political autonomy can in turn be used to pursue incremental redistribution within the constraints of a democratic–capitalist model of development.

The empirical study that follows is aimed at a detailed investigation of these hypothesized generalizations. In the chapter immediately following this one, I undertake a historical analysis of the development of the Indian state and the patterns of regime intervention for India's development. This will, I hope, highlight the plausibility of the related propositions 1 and 2 above, namely, that it is normal for democratic, developmental regimes to espouse a reformist rhetoric while eschewing any serious redistributive measures. Having analyzed this larger picture, I will investigate the distributional impact of regime variations by analyzing more recent regional materials from India. Here the core propositions of this study, namely, the specific political conditions under which redistributive reforms do or do not succeed, are highlighted by a comparative analysis of three of India's important states.

2

Democracy and Development in India: an Interpretation

India has now undergone three decades of politically guided development. Shorn of many complexities, the record is clear. Democracy has survived. Industry and agriculture have both grown at moderate rates. Redistributive efforts have, however, not been very successful. As much as 40 percent of the population continues to live in conditions of absolute poverty. Why has a democratically planned economy, committed to "socialism," failed to improve, even moderately, the living conditions of the lower classes? An adequate analysis of this issue is a necessary first step in exploring the scope and the limitations of distributive possibilities within contemporary India.

This chapter does not present new empirical materials. It rather reinterprets some of the major themes in India's political economy so as to focus attention on the political roots of redistributive failures in India. It is argued here that the failure of the Indian state to facilitate social reforms has resulted from a tacit ruling alliance between a loosely organized, ruling nationalist elite and those property owners who are in a position to stimulate economic growth. The loose and heterogeneous nature of the ruling coalition has made it difficult for the political authorities to intervene in a rigid, hierarchical society so as to benefit the poor. Political and social-structural characteristics are thus both crucial for understanding redistributive outcomes in India. As social-structural constraints are not likely to vary significantly in the short run, poverty conditions will only alter with changing regime types and policies.

The reformist role of the Indian state can be conveniently divided into four historical periods. One must first go back to India's nationalist movement. It was during this period that the incipient state in the form of the Indian National Congress (INC) was already acquiring some of its important future characteristics. The second period is the Nehru period. While the rhetoric of socialism was much in evidence during Nehru's time, the role of the political authorities was mainly twofold: consolidation of the new state; and planned public investments in support of a largely capitalist pattern of industrialization. This was followed by the "green revolution" under Shastri and Indira Gandhi. The earlier logic of state support for private enterprise was now expanded beyond urban industry

51

and commerce to include the agrarian sector. The resulting commercialization of the agrarian sector has led to the present or fourth stage: the consolidation of an alliance between the state and private enterprise on the one hand, and the emergence of the twin crises of authority and distribution on the other. The latter has also been accompanied by the emergence of varying regional experiments in structuring authority as well as in attempted redistribution.

It is in the present differentiated context that the issue of the types of authority structures suitable for handling distributional problems is of considerable significance. A sweeping historical interpretation of the overall Indian picture, then, provides important background for the later investigation of the more recent experiences of three of India's important states.

State Formation: The Nationalist Movement

India's nationalist movement represents a more complex political history than needs to be analyzed here.[1] An important focus from the perspective of this study is the early manifestation of a recurring tension in the Indian political economy: an ideological orientation favoring some type of socialism and the pursuit of political actions largely supportive of the commercially oriented, propertied classes. This tension came to characterize India's nationalist movement early under the leadership of Gandhi. It simultaneously became embedded in the Indian National Congress. As the Congress was to eventually become a crucial political force molding the nature and the role of the new Indian state, it is important to analyze the origins of this continuing gap in India between ideological commitments and political practice.

As is well known to specialists, India's nationalist movement took a decisive turn in the 1920s. The INC under Gandhi's leaderhip was transformed from a narrow elite movement, aimed at reforming colonial practices, to a full-blown mass movement. This movement incorporated the support of various social classes. And it demanded *swaraj* — i.e., self-rule

1. Standard works on the Indian nationalist movement include R. C. Majumdar, *History of the freedom movement in India* (3 vols., Firma K. L. Mukhopadhyay: Calcutta, 1962-3); P. B. Sitaramayya, *The nationalist movement in India* (National Information and Publications: Bombay, 1950); A. R. Desai, *Social background of Indian nationalism*, 4th edn. (Popular Prakashan: Bombay, 1966); Percival Spear, *A history of India*, vol. II (Penguin Books: Baltimore, 1965); and Francis Hutchins, *India's revolution: Gandhi and the Quit India movement* (Harvard University Press: Cambridge, Massachusetts, 1973). Also useful here are the writings of Gandhi and Nehru. See Mohandas Gandhi, *An autobiography: the story of my experiments with truth*, trans. from original in Gujarati by Mahadev Desai (Navjivan Publishing House: Ahmedabad, 1957); and Jawaharlal Nehru, *The discovery of India* (Doubleday: New York, 1960).

for India. The mass character of the movement was evident both in the changing leadership ideology and in the nature of the social support. Gandhi, for example, considered the task of carving out a new India intricately linked to the task of improving the lot of the Indian poor. He argued that "the independence movement is essentially for the poorest of the land." For Nehru, the INC similarly represented a movement committed not only to "the freedom of India" but also to "national unity ...and the raising of the depressed classes." These ideological commitments further corresponded with the changing social basis of the Congress. If, prior to Gandhi, the INC had been "limited in franchise and restricted to the upper classes," under his influence "the peasants rolled in." Henceforth the new Congress "began to assume the look of a vast agrarian organization with a strong sprinkling of the middle classes."[3]

In spite of this mass character evident in the ideology and the following, the Congress leadership remained conservative in political practice. It eschewed any actions that might enhance or precipitate class hostilities. This conservatism was manifest both in Gandhi's strategy of political mobilization and in the policy positions adopted by the Congress leadership. Without doubt there was only limited class conflict in both the countryside and the cities in India at that time.[4] Gandhi, however, resolutely sought to put a lid on such social conflict rather than use it for mobilization. This was just as evident in Gandhi's emphasis on the reconciliation of landlord–peasant conflicts in Champaran, as it was in his "trusteeship" doctrine developed to promote co-operation between industrialists and labor.[5] The Congress as a party in the central legislature also often demanded and succeeded in securing governmental aid for the Indian industrialists.[6] Even with reference to future policy issues, the National Planning Committee under Nehru — a forerunner to the Planning Commission — committed itself to the goal of industrialization in which private industry would play an important role.[7] The goal was quite consistent with the needs of the Indian industrialists. The implications of such a strategy for the welfare of the lower classes were, however, never spelled out.

How does one explain this early manifestation of a recurring gap in India between ideological orientation and political practice? One simple mode of explaining away the issue would be to argue that, as a principle of analysis, what leaders say should not be taken all that seriously. View-

---

2. Nehru, *Discovery*, p. 277.   3. *Ibid.* p. 277.
4. For a discussion of the limited extent of class conflict in India, see Moore, *Social origins*, esp. pp. 378-85.
5. For a detailed analysis of this, see Frankel, *India's political economy*, pp. 28-71.
6. See Nehru, *Discovery*, p. 324.   7. *Ibid.* pp. 317-23.

ed from this perspective, the mass orientation of Gandhi and Nehru was a poor guide to their real commitments in the first place. Vocal commitments, it could be argued, served functions other than specifying policy preferences: they were also aimed at mobilization and at legitimizing the role of these leaders as national political leaders.

This perspective should not be overlooked. There is, nevertheless, a twofold problem with this mode of argumentation. First, leadership commitments have concrete political consequences. Commitments made at one time not only become yardsticks for measuring performance, but also contribute to the mobilization of hitherto excluded social groups. The ideological orientation of a leadership, moreover, defines the range of acceptable political issues in a polity. Even if commitments are not translated into corresponding actions, therefore, they have to be taken seriously as a part of any political analysis. Second, if leadership utterances are not a guide to commitments, then what is? Would one be willing to argue on an *a priori* basis that the intentions and the role of leadership are not important? Or to make the circular argument that only actions reveal commitment? If not, one is left with little choice but first to take leadership goals seriously and then to analyze the relationship of goals to actual outcomes. The problem of the early gap between ideology and practice in Indian politics is thus a real one requiring explanation.

Two less-than-satisfactory explanations of this gap need to be discussed at the outset. It has been argued, for example, that the failure to translate reformist commitments into meaningful reforms reflected the leadership's distaste for violence and forced change. Because class mobilization or redistributive intervention might have resulted in violence, democratically inclined leaders eschewed any such attempts from above. The unfortunate neglect of the lower classes has therefore resulted, not so much from collusion of interests, as from a marked ideological preference of the leaders for non-violent and incremental change. Francine Frankel thus makes Gandhi's predilection toward non-violence, and his belief that an attack on the propertied classes would retard rather than facilitate national and political development in India, central to her explanation of why India's nationalist movement eschewed a serious redistributive program.[8] This perspective could be further extended. It could be argued that, for Nehru, support of commercial and industrial groups was not so much a contradiction of but rather a means of "raising the depressed classes." A belief that the conditions of the lower classes could be reformed by the democratic guidance of capitalism thus precluded the need for coercion.

8. See Frankel, *India's political economy,* p. 44.

This focus on leadership faithfully describes the role and orientation of Gandhi and Nehru. It nevertheless barely touches the surface of why the emergent nationalist political forces in India tended to side with the propertied at the expense of the propertyless. To understand the latter, the issue has to be framed differently: why did the moderate leadership of Gandhi and Nehru, and not a more radical one, gain control of India's nationalist movement? The answer would immediately reveal the relatively cohesive nature of India's class structure as significant. Because of the absence of any significant social polarization in India at that time it was not likely that sharply radical and redistributive ideologies would catch the imagination of the masses.[9] An incremental, non-violent approach that chose class conciliation rather than class conflict as its *modus operandi* was therefore, if not destined at least more likely to succeed in India — if for no reason other than the lack of real alternatives. Furthermore, to the extent that the radical forces were occasionally successful in the mobilization efforts, these forces were far more likely to fall prey to repression by the British rulers than were Gandhi and his followers.[10] Aside from the leadership orientation, then, the social and colonial matrix was of considerable significance in molding the shape of India's nationalist movement.

An alternative explanation for the reluctance of the political authorities to attack the propertied would focus on the class content of the nationalist movement. Social historians in the Marxist vein have thus described the INC essentially as a "bourgeois movement."[11] A political movement having been reduced to a class movement, the problem of why leaders end up serving some interests and not others is seen as self-evident. The appeal of this argument is that it provides a logical explanation for what otherwise appears to be a mysterious collusion between political authorities and business interests. It is nevertheless difficult to support with historical evidence.

The concept of a "bourgeois movement" ought to refer to the phenomenon of a rising social class — a class engaged in the capitalist mode of production — organized in a more or less conscious manner to make political demands. Bourgeois movements of this type historically accompanied the "great transformation" of some Western European countries from agrarian to industrial political economies. Colonial India, however, never witnessed any such phenomenon. Neither on quantitative nor on qualitative grounds can anything in the India of the first half of

---

9. See Moore, *Social origins*, ch. 6, sections 3 and 6.
10. For evidence on this, see Gene Overstreet and Marshal Windmiller, *Communism in India* (University of California Press: Berkeley, 1959), chs. 3 and 7.
11. For example, see Moore, *Social origins*, ch. 6, esp. pp. 353-70.

this century be conceptualized as a rising bourgeois class. Even as late as 1948-9, the national share of the income originating in privately owned manufacturing was as low as 6.6 percent.[12]

This is not to suggest that there were no significant private industrialists and new commercial actors on the economic scene. It is rather to suggest that these new economic participants would not easily qualify as a rising new class. Furthermore, it is important to remember that the support of industrial and commercial groups for Indian nationalists was based on the fact of the nationalists favoring protectionism and state intervention.[13] This mercantilist preference is characteristic of a weak bourgeoisie and contrasts with the demands of an ascending new class for free trade and minimal state intervention. Had there been a rising bourgeoisie, pursuing agricultural and industrial production, the entire problem of the minimal economic dynamism in India would have been qualitatively different. In the absence of a significant bourgeoisie, then, it is difficult to understand how a phenomenon as significant as the nationalist movement can be treated as a mere reflection of a relatively insignificant shift in class forces.

India's nationalist movement is thus best conceptualized in its textbook version — as a quintessential political movement. The primary goal of the movement was political: achievement of state sovereignty for a people conceived to be a nation. The leadership of the movement originated from various backgrounds, but consisted mainly of professionals (lawyers, doctors, social workers) turned full-time politicians.[14] This varied leadership was bound together by anti-colonial sentiments on the one hand and by the interest of acquiring political power on the other. Nationalism further served as the basis for mobilizing support from all social classes. Important leaders such as Gandhi were therefore able to carve out a relatively cohesive political movement from heterogeneous social material, held together by the force of leadership and the ideology of nationalism, aimed at ousting the British and establishing a sovereign India.

If this textbook analysis is adequate as a beginning, it does not yet explain the socialist ideology and the conservative practice of the INC. The socialistic orientation of the INC is, however, not difficult to understand. It is readily traceable to the formative experiences of important leaders. Gandhi, for example, had been deeply touched by India's downtrodden upon his return to the country. Over the years sympathy for the poor

12. Government of India, *First five year plan* (Planning Commission, New Delhi, 1953), p. 420.   13. See Desai, *Indian nationalism,* pp. 200-8.
14. See B. B. Misra, *The Indian middle classes: their growth in modern times* (Oxford University Press: New York, 1961), chs. 11 and 12; and Desai, *Indian nationalism,* pp. 196-200 and 307-81.

became integral to his political outlook.[15] Nehru and others had similarly been influenced by various currents of socialism, especially Fabianism and other left-of-center strains within the British labor movement.[16] As Gandhi's and Nehru's positions became stronger within India's nationalist movement, the INC took on these leaders' preferred ideologies.

There is no reason to doubt that the sympathies of Gandhi and Nehru for the poor were genuine. The real historical puzzle, then, is not the socialist inclinations of the leadership but rather their incapacity to translate these political preferences into a concrete outcome. Why did these leaders fail to mold the nationalist movement in a manner likely to facilitate redistributive outcomes? Most answers would focus on the social–structural constraints. That would, however, constitute only one half of the answer. Constraints are always a relative matter; they are constraints only in relation to the forces attempting to overcome them. The other half of the answer, then, has to do with the weakness of India's nationalist movement as a political force, i.e., as a force capable of confronting societal constraints.

A weak political movement can be described as one incapable of translating its multiple goals into a concrete outcome. This weakness is especially manifest in the political incapacity to challenge the dominant classes to fulfill the commitments to the lower classes. The ideology and the organization of a weak nationalist movement precludes the use of an essential political resource, compulsion, either to resist concerted opposition from strategic social groups or to implement its redistributive goals. The leaders of such movements, therefore, do not possess the organizational capacity either to cope with social constraints or to transform social relations from above. As a consequence, compromise in general, but specifically compromise with powerful social interests, is the appropriate strategy for political survival and success. It is this type of political weakness of the Indian nationalist movement, rather than its class content alone, that helps explain the consistent tendency of the leadership to compromise with the propertied.

The ideology of the nationalist movement was inclusive, i.e., it assigned all social classes a role in the process of national regeneration. Except for occasional outbursts against the "feudal" elements in collusion with the British, the Congress leadership made promises to be guardians of the interests of the propertied and the propertyless alike. While in the short run this strategy broadened the INC's political base, it also opened it to penetration by various social forces. Individuals and groups even

15. See Nehru, *Discovery*, p. 274-83.
16. See Michael Brecher, *Nehru: a political biography* (Oxford University Press: New York, 1959); esp. chs. 3, 5 and 9.

vaguely sympathetic to the goal of *swaraj* and willing to sport *khadi* (hand-spun cotton) could join the Congress. This open recruitment policy discriminated neither against class nor against ideological lines. The INC as a consequence grew into a loose and amorphous organization, lacking the mechanisms to facilitate organizational loyalty or discipline. Factional conflicts over policies were often barely kept under control by the force of leadership and by the collective interest in maintaining a unified opposition to the British.

The INC, therefore, increasingly became a political organization characterized by an inclusive ideology, open recruitment, and a weak internal control structure. These characteristics made the INC into a weak political force suitable for accomplishing only a limited range of goals. More specifically, this organizational form proved eminently suitable for "unifying" Indians from various walks of life into a nationalist political force. Later it would also contribute to the political integration of India. Against this, however, one must note that the same characteristics diluted the capacities of the INC as a tool of social transformation. Enmeshed into the existing social structure, the INC was incapable of generating an autonomous political force to confront and reform this social structure. The INC was not designed to challenge the dominant social interests and therefore did not prove useful in doing so.

The latter assertion rests on certain theoretical presuppositions that need to be restated. Social inequalities are rooted in the structure of a society. Political leaders occasionally attempt to modify these inequalities by planned state intervention. This, however, requires a political force consciously designed to neutralize inherent social inequalities. Propertied classes, for example, are powerful members of a society. If some redistribution of material resources is to result, this social power needs to be balanced by political forces. State intervention in the interests of the lower classes is in turn generated by building a lower-class bias into the dominant political institutions of a society. This further requires that exclusive leadership ideologies, a selective recruitment pattern, and strong internal-control structures are combined to design a disciplined organizational weapon, which not only directs the authoritative use of political power, but also is capable of institutionalizing reformist politics within the state. This general argument will become clear as the study proceeds. Suffice it to note here that the failure to incorporate lower-class bias institutionally within the state generally leads to the propertied classes benefitting disproportionately from state intervention.

It was the weakness of the INC as a political force from the beginning, rather than the mere ideological preferences of its leaders or the class content of the nationalist movement, that inclined India's emerging leaders to compromise with the propertied interests. There was no conscious intent here to politically further the interests of the privileged. That was, nevertheless, the consequence. The relationship between intent and consequence is seldom a straightforward one; it was no different in India. The primary aim of the leadership was to secure national independence, and the leadership carved out a successful political movement to achieve this goal. The organizational form of the movement, however, made political survival and success dependent on the support of propertied and propertyless alike. The movement was thus never designed as a radical nationalist movement capable of simultaneously confronting the Indian propertied classes and the British rulers. While accomplishing its primary political goal — achievement of state sovereignty — the new Indian leadership found it expedient to compromise with the powerful members of society.

If the political weakness is held responsible for the upper-class bias of the INC, a question arises: what forces gave this ideological and organizational form to India's nationalist movement? One only has to look at such attempts as the efforts of Mao in China to combine disciplined organization with nationalism to realize that there is nothing intrinsic about nationalist movements compromising with social forces. What, then, were the forces at work in the Indian society which molded the emerging political institutions to take the route of class compromise rather than confrontation? Three sets of variables, which comprise too complex a historical issue to be analyzed fully here, can be identified as having molded India's emerging political institutions: social–structural conditions, the impact of colonialism, and the role of the political leadership and traditions.

As noted earlier, the class cohesiveness of India's traditional social structure created formidable obstacles to the growth of revolutionary movements and organizations. India being largely a pre-commercial agrarian society, landlord–peasant relationships in India were characterized more by vertical dependencies and less by horizontal cleavages. The landlord–peasant ties, to use Barrington Moore's terminology, were "strong."[17] At the core of these strong ties was the sheer material dependence of the landless on property owners. These material dependencies were buttressed not only by the personalistic ties of the pre-commercial, village communities, but also by religious values and the caste system legitimizing rigid stratification. The propertyless agrarian groups were furthermore divided among themselves by the virtue of caste, locality, and linguistic regions. Cleavages along all lines other than class created

17. See Moore, *Social origins*, pp. 330-41.

obstacles for the politicization of rural social classes. As a consequence, India's peasantry did not really offer a volatile social base from which revolutionary organizations could flourish. Leaders committed to channeling nationalist sentiments into the creation of a militant political force were at a distinct disadvantage. Social–structural conditions provided a fertile ground for those who sought to mobilize communities as a whole against the outsiders rather than mobilizing one segment of the community against another.

To the extent that radicals on the left and on the right were occasionally successful in carving out some support from the lower classes, they were far more susceptible to repression from the British rulers than the Congress leaders. This is not to suggest that Congress leaders were not persecuted. Rather, the constancy with which the militant movements were kept illegal contrasted with the legal participation of the INC in both elections and provincial governments under British supervision. In other words, the colonial forces offered greater political space for the growth of moderate and democratic movements than for the radical and disciplined ones.

Along with the constraints generated by the social–structural and the colonial framework, independent political forces were also at work. Important leaders like Gandhi were not only helped by circumstances. They further molded the movement in their own image. Gandhi's commitment to non-violence must remain one of the elements in understanding the absence of radical tendencies in Indian nationalism. Furthermore, the democratic traditions inherited from the British, participation in elections by many of the politicized Indians, and the commitment of Nehru to democracy all contributed to a reformist political orientation.

The impact of social, colonial, and political conditions was cumulative and was in the direction of making the INC a political organization suited for certain tasks and not for others. The ideology and the organization of the INC fostered non-violence, non-co-operation with the British, open membership, weak internal control, and multiple class goals. This approach proved eminently suitable for mobilizing Indians from various social backgrounds into a political force aimed at securing sovereign state power. The same organizational form was, however, singularly unsuited for generating autonomous political power. Enmeshed in society, the movement was incapable of formulating and implementing goals independent of those of the powerful in the society. India's nationalist movement thus came to be simultaneously characterized by a considerable capacity to mobilize various social groups into a consensual organization, but an incapacity to translate the leadership's socialistic commitments into corresponding actions. Because India's nationalist movement represented the new Indian state in the making, these twin tendencies of radical ideology but conservative practice were embedded early in India's political life.

State Consolidation: The Nehru Years

India emerged from colonial rule under the auspices of the Indian National Congress. As the INC transformed itself from an anti-colonial movement to a ruling party, some of its acquired characteristics became more pronounced. Most significant of these was the tendency of the Congress leadership to work through rather than against powerful social interests. In spite of vocal commitments to create "socialism," therefore, the Nehru years resulted primarily in the consolidation of newly won state power and in the initiation of industrialization by public support of the private sector. The lower classes did not gain much from this pattern of political intervention. The nationalist leadership, industrial and commercial classes, and the professional and bureaucratic groups were, however, all able to enhance their political and economic interests.

This specific pattern of state intervention resulted from the needs of a nationalist–reformist leadership to preserve political power while presiding over a state increasingly captured by the socially powerful. The legitimacy of the new rulers was bound up with their promises to help India "step out from the old to the new." And yet the tools available to the leadership for facilitating this socio-economic transformation were few. Economic incentives and political compulsion are two mechanisms utilized by most states to introduce socio-economic change from above. The INC was, however, already weak in its capacity to utilize the state's legitimate power as a means of social transformation. The compromises reached by the new leadership in the creation of a consolidated polity further weakened the interventionist capacities of the new Indian state. These are discussed below. As state autonomy was reduced, the only alternative for initiating economic change was state support for private enterprise. Intrinsically, of course, there is nothing wrong with this mode of planned economic development. In the face of minimal political capacities to implement redistributive change, however, the fruits of this pattern of economic development were monopolized by the already-privileged. While the state-and-entrepreneurial links in this period are clearest in the issue area of planned industrialization, the incapacity of the state to confront the propertied is evidenced in the failure of land reforms.

The New State

The new Indian state emerged from colonialism with a considerable degree of legitimacy. Nehru and others in charge of the INC were perceived to be the unquestioned leaders of the new nation. As Nehru consolidated his position in the early years, his brand of socialism became virtually the national ruling ideology. The precise content of this socialism was never clear. At the very least, however, it involved a commitment to state intervention in the economy aimed at industrialization, economic growth, and a modicum of income redistribution. That leadership ideology was an important input into policy-making highlighted the degree of state autonomy that existed in India at that time. The failure to implement redistributive policies, conversely, drew attention to the factors limiting the Indian state's capacity to confront the upper classes.

Political changes following independence had an adverse impact on the capacities of the new Indian state for planned social reform. Three issues were to prove especially significant: the failure to reform a colonial bureaucracy; the constitutional protection for private property as well as the limitations on the jurisdiction of the central government; and, in the face of widening suffrage, the growing dependence of the Congress party on local notables for securing rural electoral support. The cumulative impact of these changes was to reduce the state's autonomy further and thus to restrict severely the redistributive abilities of all the major organs of the state, namely, the dominant party, the central government, and the bureaucracy.

The debate on bureaucratic reforms centered on the issue of the efficacy of a colonial bureaucracy for new tasks of economic development. Would an elite civil service, trained as non-specialists for maintaining order and appropriating "surplus" (revenue collection), adapt to new developmental tasks? Would the members of the Indian Civil Service (ICS), who studied Shakespeare, played golf, wore British hats, and took orders from no one but their British superiors, now serve the *khadi*-clad Congress leaders sympathetic to the cause of the Indian downtrodden? While some sections within the Congress had their doubts, the more conservative leaders, such as Patel, argued successfully for leaving the civil service intact. At stake for the conservatives were not only the privilege of the ICS but, more important, the stability of the fragile new Indian state. Faced with the refugee problem and other problems of partition, the assimilation of the princely states, and a border war with Pakistan, the new government met with heavy demands. An experienced core of civil servants was accordingly felt to be indispensable for the day-to-day run ning of a government under a relatively inexperienced political leadership.[18]

If political consolidation and stability were the immediate goals, these were probably well served by leaving an efficacious bureaucracy intact. This role of the ICS, and later the Indian Administrative Services (IAS), has been widely recognized and needs no further investigation here. What bears reiteration, however, is the fact that, for every goal accomplished, others get neglected. And those accomplished and those neglected often reflect leadership priorities. Indian leaders chose political stability as a primary goal. This choice relegated the concern over the state as a tool of social reform to a secondary status.

Constitutional provisions further restricted the scope of state intervention for social reform. Rights to private property were inserted into the constitution as "fundamental rights." While essential for creating a legal framework of a private-enterprise economy, these provisions restricted other governmental programs. The attempts to expropriate private property to facilitate redistribution were either not likely to be significant or, if significant, were doomed to end up in lengthy litigation claiming violation of constitutional rights. What was equally significant was the constitutional limitations on the power of the central government over the rural sector. State governments were assigned the primary responsibility over agricultural policies and reforms. This was of considerable consequence. Local landed interests were powerful in state governments, and this constitutional division of power was to become a permanent obstacle to land redistribution. As Francine Frankel has convincingly argued, these constitutional provisions resulted from the concerted role of conservative Congress leaders in alliance with propertied groups. Once instituted, however, these political arrangements put severe limits on the prospects of "sweeping changes of the social order by actions from above." [19]

The changes in the Congress party further tied dominant political forces to the socially powerful. With universal suffrage, the rural poor emerged as an important political resource. Embedded in pre-commercial social structures, however, the majority of these rural poor had not yet been released as independent political actors. Their corporate social existence molded their political behavior. This implied that the landlords or other local notables often controlled the votes of their poor depen-

18. Two good general treatments of the civil service in India are C. P. Bhambri, *Bureaucracy and politics in India* (Vikas Publications: Delhi, 1971); and Stanley Heginbotham, *Cultures in conflict: the four faces of Indian bureaucracy* (Columbia University Press: New York, 1975). For the more specific discussion of the post-independence debates over the future of the ICS, see Frankel, *India's political economy*, p. 80.

19. *Ibid.* p. 81.

dents. These dominant individuals were willing to trade votes for appropriate rewards from the political leaders. The Congress leaders built their rural electoral support on such vertical dependencies. The resulting patronage networks, so characteristic of the Congress party, intricately enmeshed the Congress-dominated Indian state into society. Important scholars of Indian politics have lauded the consensus-building role of such "aggregating mechanisms."[20] And once again there is no need to deny this significant outcome. What deserves to be noted, however, is that these party–class linkages increasingly made the Congress more a part of a tacit alliance of domination than a potential force for social transformation. Not only was the deliberate politicization of the Indian lower classes thus set back, but the capacity of the Congress to force changes upon the propertied was further diminished.

The major organs of the state — the ruling party, the central government, and the bureaucracy — all became restricted in their capacity to intervene on behalf of the lower classes. This class bias of the state reflected, first, the penchant of Congress for political expediency over a commitment to structural change, and second, the incapacity of the INC as an autonomous political force to confront powerful social interests. Political interests and the organizational weakness of the dominant political party were thus responsible for the limited autonomy of the new Indian state. This state was increasingly incapable of extricating itself from the grip of the propertied groups and consequently could not utilize legitimate compulsion as a tool of social reform. In the absence of forced change from above, the only alternative for India's new leadership was to attempt to release the economic dynamism of the society by the public support of private profitability.

Planned Industrialization

As a national leader Nehru was committed to the goal of creating a "modern" and "socialist" India. Nothing expressed this commitment better than the active role of the state in encouraging heavy or "basic" industry. After all, this is how Soviet "socialism" was interpreted and admired by many Indians. In retrospect, it is clear that state participation in the industrialization of India had little to do with socialism. On the contrary, it provided the base and support necessary for a state-supported, capitalist

20. For example, see Kothari, *Politics in India,* chs. 5 and 6; a similar theme, emphasizing the "adaptive" quality of the Congress party, runs through Myron Weiner, *Party building in a new nation: the Indian National Congress* (University of Chicago Press: Chicago, 1967), esp. chs. 1 and 22. Weiner, however, does qualify his discussion (see ch. 23) by suggesting that what may be functional for winning elections may well be dysfunctional for generating socio-economic change.

pattern of industrial development. Planned industrialization thus expressed both the dominant political and the dominant economic interests. It buttressed the legitimacy of a new state, the *raison d'être* of which was the creation of a "New India." An industrial infrastructure, moreover, helped consolidate India as a militarily viable state in the international arena. The interests of the state and of the state authorities were thus both served. As state support for basic industries created new opportunities for private entrepreneurs, private interests were also served by state intervention.

The role of the state in industrialization in any setting can follow one of three broad possibilities: (1) minimal state intervention as a framework for maximizing the role of private enterprise; (2) indirect state participation in support of private enterprise, involving some state ownership and planning; and (3) direct state participation as an alternative to private enterprise, involving considerable state ownership and public investment. Each of these are not so much options as they are alternative paths reflecting concrete historical circumstances. The first of these is viable under conditions of a rising and strong capitalism, while the last requires the existence of a strong and autonomous state that has the willingness and capability to utilize compulsion as a tool of social transformation. Neither of these conditions existed in India.

India after independence had weak capitalism as well as a weak and increasingly "captured" state. As a consequence, the second option of a mixed economy, though by no means inevitable, emerged as an alternative suited to the political and economic circumstances of India. State involvement aimed at developing a capitalist economy therefore reflected neither "creeping socialism," nor behind-the-scenes bourgeois control of political power. It rather reflected a tacit but mutually beneficial alliance of domination between political and economic forces, neither of which was strong enough to mold the process of social change in line with its own interests and ideals.

The pattern of state investments and involvement in the economy further reveals the nature of the alliance between a weak developmental state and weak capitalism. Emergent from colonialism, Indian capitalism needed public support in many areas before it could become a viable instrument of economic change. First, the creation of a national market required not only political consolidation, but also transportation and communication networks linking the various regions into a single market. Second, energy resources such as electricity were essential for private manufacturing to flourish. Third, basic inputs such as steel, cement, and various minerals at politically supported prices would stimulate private investment. Fourth, government support in securing loans, insurance,

Table 2.1 *Public Outlays[1] in the First Three Plans*

Sector	First five-year plan (%)	Second five-year plan (%)	Third five-year plan (%)
Industrial, mining, and power	18.7	27.4	33
Transportation and communication	23.6	28.9	20
Agriculture (including irrigation)	32.1	21.9	27
Services (including education and health)	22.6	19.7	16
Miscellaneous	3	2.1	4
Total	100	100	100

[1] As outlays include the salaries of personnel, they are not exactly equal to "investment," though they are broadly indicative of it.

Source: Government of India, Planning Commission, *Third five year plan* (New Delhi, 1960), Appendix B.

market research, and occasionally even prices, if not essential, was certainly helpful for capitalist development. And lastly, a predictable political atmosphere in which the state would protect the principle of production-for-profit was essential for capitalism to develop.

In all of these areas, Indian capitalism was not strong enough to take a dynamic, leading role. The new state took all of these initiatives to promote India's capitalism. For example, the pattern of public investment in the first three plans (see Table 2.1) reveals that the bulk of the public investment was in precisely the above stated areas: transportation, communication, power, and basic industrial inputs.[21] If we add to this the favorable legal and constitutional framework, as well as the services, the subsidies, and the tax breaks provided by the state for capitalism, it is clear that the political authorities in India laid the groundwork necessary for capitalist industrialization.

If capitalism gained support from public authorities, the latter were no slaves to the former. The entire dynamism towards "development," manifest in the five-year plans, was at the behest of the new nationalist leadership. Both the ideology and the legitimacy of the new rulers required political actions aimed at facilitating planned socio-economic change. In the absence of a strong and autonomous state, however, the leadership was not in a position to squeeze some or all segments of society to generate surplus for much larger public investments. To use

21. For a discussion of India's early planning efforts, see A. H. Hanson, *The process of planning: a study of India's five year plans, 1950-1964* (Oxford University Press: London, 1966); Gunnar Myrdal, *Asian drama: an enquiry into the poverty of nations* (3 vols., Pantheon: New York, 1968), Part IV and ch. 25; and John Mellor, *The new economics of growth: a strategy for India and the developing world* (Cornell University Press: Ithaca, New York, 1976), esp. chs. 5 and 6.

Nordlinger's terminology, the Indian state possessed "type II" and "type III" state autonomy, but was weak on "type I."[22] While the motive behind the goal of "development" was thus political, the political means for accomplishing it were absent. As a consequence, the new state allied with emerging capitalism to facilitate industrial development. Whatever the long-range problems of this tacit alliance, in the short run it buttressed the legitimacy of the new leadership as "progressive modernizers."

Planned industrialization involving a division of labor between the state and capital thus suited India's nationalist leaders and private entrepreneurs.[23] While interests and actions do not always correspond in the short term, there is a long-term tendency in all societies towards the privileged of that society discovering — either through conscious actions or through trial and error — politico-economic arrangements suitable for enhancing their position. In the case of India, the mixed economy was such an arrangement. It lent itself to the strengthening of the new rulers on the one hand, and to the profitability of private enterprise on the other.

Land Reforms

If the issue of planned industrialization highlights the mutually beneficial alliance between a loosely organized nationalist elite and weak capitalism, land reforms further highlight the incapacity of the Indian state to confront propertied interests. It is well documented that India's land reforms, especially the implementation of "land ceilings" and the consequent redistribution, have not been very successful.[24] What, therefore, needs further attention is not the extent of success or failure, but rather the causes of this failure.

The existing explanations of the failure of India's land reforms tend to follow one of two lines. On the one hand, some scholars tend to view it primarily as a "political failure." This is seen as stemming either from the

22. See Nordlinger, *Democratic state,* esp. chs. 3-5. Nordlinger's delineation of the types of state autonomy is also discussed above in chapter 1.
23. I have chosen not to discuss the economic (growth and distributional) consequences of planned industrialization in India in any detail. These have been discussed in many standard works. For example see Myrdal, *Asian drama,* chs. 23 and 24. While there is debate in the literature on the appropriateness of a focus on heavy industry for long-term economic growth, there is a fair amount of consensus regarding the fact that the contribution of this pattern to the creation of employment, and therefore to the alleviation of poverty, has been minimal. Given this, the primary concern of this study is not to reiterate this conclusion, but rather to analyze the political and social forces responsible for the adoption of this mode of development.
24. See Government of India, *Report of the National Commission on agriculture* (15 vols., Ministry of Agriculture and Irrigation: New Delhi, 1976) Part xv, entitled 'Agrarian Reforms', esp. ch. 66.

incapacity of the Indian bureaucracy to implement policies (the type of argument stressing centralization versus decentralization) or, more broadly, from the absence of a well-institutionalized polity capable of authoritatively translating leadership goals into a concrete outcome (the "soft state" argument).[25] On the other hand, other scholars conceptualize the failure as a social issue or a class issue, resulting from the relative power of the landed classes in the face of an unmobilized peasantry (the "organize the poor" argument).[26] Both the arguments are valuable but they need to be synthesized.

The strictly political argument fails to recognize that the process of institutionalization often involves a prior acceptance of given political arrangements by dominant social classes. It is seldom possible to transform mere organizations into cherished social institutions in the face of strong opposition from the socially powerful. Dominant classes bestow their support on institutions that are likely to pursue goals supportive, or at least not detrimental, to their interests. Established political institutions in class societies are therefore not simply neutral tools capable of translating all leadership goals into effective outcomes. Effective institutions are, rather, goal-specific. In other words, the social process of selecting legitimate political goals, and the development of capacities to pursue these goals authoritatively, go hand in hand. Because the process of political institutionalization occurs within the framework of social constraints, goals serving the interests of the privileged and the powerful tend to be "selected in," while those of the lower classes are "selected out" for political action and public policies.[27] Institution-building in class societies therefore tends to involve the creation not only of effective political tools, but also of tools that will preserve the interests of the dominant classes.

Viewed from this theoretical perspective, the argument that a better-institutionalized state apparatus would have facilitated the implementation of land reforms in India is not convincing. The problem is not only one of a degree of institutional development but also of the class biases of

25. That decentralized administration contributes to successful implementation of land reforms is an argument popular in some International Developmental Agencies. For an academic version of this argument, see John D. Montgomery, "The allocation of authority in land reform programs: a comparative study of administrative progress and output", *Administrative Science Quarterly*, 17, 1 (March 1972), 62-75. The "soft state" argument is, of course, that of Myrdal, *Asian drama*, p. 66. The more general argument regarding the significance of institutionalization as a prerequisite for efficacious political action is credited to Samuel Huntington, *Political order*, esp. ch. 6.

26. Many Marxist scholars as well as some "left–liberal" scholars have of late been attracted to this perspective. For a summary and a critique of this perspective, see chapter 1 above.

27. For a theoretical argument along these lines, but with reference to advanced capitalist societies, see Claus Offe, *Strukturprobleme des kapitalistischen Staates: aufsatze zur politischen Soziologie* (Suhrkamp: Frankfurt, 1972), ch. 3.

the institutions. It can be argued that the incapacity of the Indian state to implement land redistribution is part of the explanation of why the political authorities could maintain a vocal commitment to land redistribution without seriously jeopardizing their support from the landed classes. Further development of political capacities to implement redistribution would, therefore, either have to be accompanied by a decreasing commitment to redistribution, or face considerable opposition from land-holding groups. Opposition from powerful groups would in turn require some rearrangement of the political institutions aimed at either co-opting or confronting this opposition.

The alternative focus on class constraints on deliberate redistribution provides a useful antidote to the political argument, and yet it is also inadequate on its own. One cannot argue against this proposition, to the extent that it merely states that an increase in the political power of the lower classes would tilt the policy process in their favor. Land reforms in India would have indeed been more successful if somehow India's rural poor had been more powerful. But how does this power shift occur? In other words, what is far from clear are the conditions in which the class basis of political power alters without a total destruction of given social and political arrangements. To understand this variability in the class content of political power, one needs to complement a focus on social classes with a focus on the significance of ideology and political institutions in deliberately reinforcing or altering the balance of class forces. Only when we focus simultaneously on class and institutional variables — on the relationship of the state to society — can we understand how the relative power of the lower classes can increase within the framework of a democratic–capitalist model of development.

The failure of Indian land reforms, then, resulted from a failure to institutionalize elements of lower-class interests within the state. This in turn was primarily a failure of the dominant political force, i.e., the Congress regime under Nehru. The Congress party penetrated the Indian countryside, but not without being captured by the rural elite. As a consequence, the Congress leaders were able neither to utilize the party as a tool of direct politicization and social transformation, nor to use it to goad governmental and bureaucratic levels below the center to follow through with central policy directives. In the absence of an organizational tool designed to further lower-class interests, there was no force to counter the class power of landowners. Therefore, irrespective of the numerous legislation and policy statements, the landed classes were able to manipulate the workings of political power to their own advantage, making a sham of the Indian land reforms.

The Indian National Congress had emerged as the new rulers of India committed to rural reconstruction. This commitment not only reflected the socialistic orientation of the leadership, but also a desire to inflict some retribution on the *zamindars*, the landlords, who had been an important pillar of colonial rule. The early attempts at tenancy reform were moderately successful at breaking the back of the *zamindari* system, though not at improving the conditions of the majority of the tenants.[28] These twin consequences are explained if we remind ourselves that the *zamindars* were not only landlords but also revenue-collectors and "overlords" of a sort. They were political intermediaries between the government and the cultivator. They not only had access to considerable economic surplus but also possessed political power. Had this system been left intact, over time organized *zamindars* could have potentially posed a serious political challenge to the Congress party. To eliminate this threat, as well as to buttress their image as "progressive" leaders, the new rulers of India sought to abolish this "reactionary" system.

The leadership was not very successful in appropriating *zamindari* lands.[29]. The leadership nevertheless successfully withdrew the legal and political supports that had hitherto supported the local rights and powers of the *zamindars*. Some *zamindars* exchanged part of their lands for healthy compensation, and others sought to convert their lands into supervised production units. While the *zamindari* abolition thus did not significantly undermine the position of the *zamindars* as economic elites, it did eliminate crucial aspects of their role as local overlords. Having been left with considerable economic power, these "new" landowners would, of course, after a time, re-emerge as politically significant. This new pattern would, however, involve considerable political realignment. If *zamindari* abolition is, therefore, also understood as an aspect of political consolidation by a new set of rulers, rather than primarily as a redistributive measure, the limited success in eliminating *zamindars* as intermediaries as well as the failure to redistribute their lands are both comprehensible.

Land-reform measures in India since *zamindari* abolition have aimed at tenancy reform and the expropriation and redistribution of land over a "ceiling" — a specified upper limit on ownership. While the details of how these have been implemented in three specific states since the middle seventies will be discussed in the following chapters, these measures have generally not been very effective. The government's own reports document this failure.[30] The failure is readily understood if we travel the length

---

28. Thus Daniel and Alice Thorner concluded after their study of *zamindari* abolition: "In essence the bigger people have held on to a lot of land and are getting others to cultivate it." See, *Land and Labor in India* (Asia Publishing House: Bombay–New York, 1962), p.5.
29. See Government of India, *Report on agriculture*, ch. 66.   30. *Ibid.* ch. 66.

of the Indian political institutions from the center to the periphery and notice how, at every lower level, the bite of the reform laws was progressively weakened by powerful interests.

The Congress-dominated central government of India always left it to the state governments to specify the content of the national land-reform guidelines. While the center repeatedly reiterated the need to pursue land reforms vigorously, it was left to the lower levels of government to turn this into reality. This division of labor served important political needs. On the one hand, it buttressed the image of the central leadership as progressive and, on the other, it spared the leadership the wrath of opposition that the real implementation of these policies would have invoked from landowners. While the center was thus perceived, at least in the short run, as the champion of the downtrodden, the state governments were held to be responsible for the shortcomings.

A somewhat decentralized approach was of course necessitated by both constitutional jurisdictions and regional variations. This nevertheless gave landed interests an influential role in redefining the central policy guidelines in their own favor. Had the Congress been a more effective political party, able to translate leadership goals into compliance at lower levels, the scope for diluting the land-reform legislation at state level would have been minimal. After all, most of the state governments in this period were also Congress governments. If the party had had internal control mechanisms to translate party goals into supportive actions by "Congressmen," the entire story of land reforms would have been different. State governments could have then been goaded by party discipline into translating central goals into effective legislation and actions. As it was, Congressmen were often representatives of sectional social interests first and loyal party followers a poor second.

While the approach of the state governments varied, they consistently left many loopholes in both the tenancy and the "ceiling" legislation. Whatever bite was left proved difficult to implement. The actual task of implementation was left to lower levels of bureaucracy, mainly at block level.[31] The numerous ways in which local bureaucrats and landowners colluded to make a mockery of Indian land reforms is a tragicomedy. This has been told many times and does not need to be related here. What needs to be stressed is the analytical point that this experience highlights: local bureaucracy alone was singularly unsuited for the difficult political task of reordering the rural social structure by redistribution of property.

For example, if land records were not available, politicized individuals with local knowledge were needed to identify "surplus" land and local

31. Indian states are administratively divided into districts and districts into blocks. Blocks are a collection of villages, the latter being the lowest unit of administration.

tenancy arrangements. If there was fear of landlords, politicization of the potential beneficiaries was necessary. If the forces of law and order sided with the landlords, these forces had to be neutralized by political orders from above. If, following expropriation, land redistribution was to benefit the lower classes, politicized members of the lower classes would have had to be involved in the decision-making of who the recipients of land were to be. All of these were political and not bureaucratic tasks. All of them could have been performed only by the dominant political force in society, the Congress party. The Congress, however, as we have already noticed, was by then no longer an efficacious tool of social reform. Its internal control structure was weak and its recruitment far from selective, and it was building its rural electoral support through local notables, who were often closely tied to landed interests. In other words, Congress had failed to institutionalize elements of lower-class interests into the Indian political process. As a consequence, the story of Indian land reforms is one of continuous political failure.

To summarize this section, the Nehru years in India represent the years of political consolidation and the beginnings of industrialization. The INC emerged from colonialism as a legitimate but a heterogeneous political force. The leadership consolidated its position by compromising with the socially powerful, and this facilitated stability. In the long run, however, this strategy further weakened the capacities of the new Indian state for redistributive intervention. Being politically weak and yet desirous of economic development to buttress their image as modernizers, the Congress leadership had only one alternative. This was to eschew developmental tasks requiring the use of state compulsion or confrontation with dominant interests. Within the industrial sector this led to a tacit alliance between the nationalist rulers and a not-so-powerful capitalist class. State support for basic industries was the immediate consequence. While this pattern of industrial development contributed little to the welfare of the majority of the population, it did facilitate the profitability and growth of private manfuacturing. In the rural sector political weakness was manifest in the failure to implement a cherished Congress goal, the goal of land reforms. As the consciousness of this political weakness took hold, the state altered its half-hearted confrontational attitude toward the landowners and, in the later 1960s, moved toward an explicit support for agrarian capitalism.

The Political Origins of Agrarian Capitalism: The "Green Revolution"

Nehru died in 1964. Potential succession crises were avoided by finding compromise or weak candidates for leadership. Or at least this is how

Table 2.2 *Sectoral Allocations as a Percentage of the Total Public Outlay, 1955-1974*

	2nd plan (1955-61)	3rd plan (1961-6)	Annual plans (1966-7)–(1968-9)	4th plan (1969-74)
Agriculture	11	14	17	17
	20	23	23	24
Irrigation	9	9	6	6-8
Organized industry and minerals	20	20	23	21

Source: Government of India, Planning Commission, *Five year plans* [Second plan (New Delhi, 1954), Third and Annual (1966-7 and 1968-9) plans and Fourth plan (New Delhi, 1969) respectively].

both Shastri and Indira Gandhi were initially perceived by the competing factions within Congress, each hoping to manipulate a weak leader for its own benefit. From the perspective of this study, however, the significant aspect of Shastri and early Indira Gandhi rule was the "new approach" adopted toward the agrarian sector. While the basic industrial policy initiated under Nehru continued, the role of the state in agriculture underwent a considerable shift. These new agrarian policies, aimed at stimulating agricultural production, would later be hailed or decried as the "green revolution." In my discussion of these policy shifts, I shall pay less attention to the distributional consequences of the "green revolution" (already an under-documented but over-discussed area of enquiry),[32] and more to an analysis of the forces that gave rise to the emerging alliance between the state and agrarian capitalism. It will be argued that the "green revolution" represented a continuity in the unfolding of the basic political economy of India: a growth-oriented alliance between a heterogeneous political elite and private enterprise.

The "new approach" to agriculture represented more of a clarification of priorities within the agrarian sector and less of a shift in intersectoral patterns of public investment. As is clear from Table 2.2, the overall sectoral distribution of public expenditure did not undergo any marked change in 1966-7, when the new agrarian policies were officially adopted. What did undergo change was the mode of utilizing the share of public expenditure already assigned to the agrarian sector (see Table 2.3). Prior to the adoption of the "new approach," it would be fair to argue that Indian political authorities simply did not have a consistent agrarian policy. Their goals for agriculture were the same as for the rest of the

32. For a review of the evidence on the "green revolution" in India as well as for a bibliography of the relevant literature, see Terry J. Byres, "The dialectic of India's green revolution," *South Asian Review*, 5, 2 (January 1972); and Terry J. Byres and Ben Crow, *The Green Revolution in India* (The Open University Press, 1983).

Table 2.3   *Breakdown of Percentage Share of Total Agricultural Outlay, Third and*
Fourth Plans

	3rd plan	Draft 4th plan
Crop production	11.5	21.3
Major irrigation	37.3	28.6
Minor irrigation	15.3	15.4
Community development	16.5	7.7
Miscellaneous	19.4	27.0

Source: Government of India, Planning Commission, *Five year plans* [Third, and draft
Fourth plan (New Delhi, 1969) respectively].

economy: to improve production and facilitate some redistribution. The
means for accomplishing these goals were, at best, haphazard. Community development, agriculture extension, land reforms, improved irrigation, and even co-operative farming, were all tried. None of these
policies, however, facilitated any marked success in improving production or distribution. The "new approach" therefore reflected a clarification on the part of the government that agricultural production is a priority goal, and then the subsequent adoption of a seemingly consistent set
of policies to achieve this goal.

As is well known, the new policies were designed to subsidize the profitability of those landowners who were in a position to facilitate rapid
growth in output.[33] Regionally, these were farmers in areas with secure
access to irrigation and, in terms of class distinction, they were the better-off middle and rich peasants, well positioned to secure loans against land,
invest in chemical fertilizers and pesticides, and take risks by experimenting with high-yielding seeds. Political authorities argued that public support for these groups in the form of subsidized inputs, as well as price support for the output, offered the best hope for rapid growth in agricultural
production. It is now clear, however, that the impact of these policies on
total agricultural production has at best been moderate.[34] What is also
clear is that these policies did not contribute to the alleviation of rural
poverty. I will return to this last point in the next section.

There are questions that need to be addressed here: what political and
social forces were responsible for this pattern of agrarian transformation
in India? Did the "green revolution" represent, as Frankel has recently
argued, a "reversal" and a "retreat from the social goals of planning"?[35]

33. See Griffin, *The political economy of agrarian change.*
34. See the World Bank, *Economic situation and prospect of India,* (The World Bank,
Washington, D.C., 1979).
35. See Frankel, *India's political economy,* ch. 7.

If so, what forces contributed to this reversal? Or, as some Marxists have argued, did the adoption of "green revolution" policies only confirm what had been thought to be the case for some while, namely, that the landed classes play a significant role within the ruling Congress party?[36] When scrutinized in the light of the evidence, both of these arguments are found to be wanting. The "green revolution" was lot less of a "reversal" in the overall policy orientation than Frankel considers it to be. And the policies reflected not only economic interests, but also the interests and hopes of the political authorities in securing their power by facilitating rapid gains in food production.

While Frankel's emphasis on the role of external forces (especially USAID, the World Bank, and the Rockefeller Foundation) in influencing India's policy choices in this period is well taken,[37] her sense that these policies constituted a reversal is not accurate. To bear out Frankel's case, one would have to establish convincingly that Nehru's policy initiatives manifested a more serious concern with issues of redistribution than those of his successors. This case would not only be difficult to make, it would also represent a considerable misunderstanding of Nehru's policies. As argued in the last section, Nehru's main contributions were in facilitating political stability and in initiating the development of heavy industries. His agricultural policies, not to mention his land-reform programs, were, however, downright failures.[38] None of these results reveal a serious concern with economic redistribution. What exactly, then, were the "green revolution" policies reversing or retreating from? The question itself is inappropriate.

The adoption of the "green revolution" policies is better understood if one concentrates on the fact that the bulk of Nehru's economic initiatives were aimed at facilitating growth through industrialization. The developmental pattern adopted here revealed, as well as contributed to, the emerging foundations of the Indian political economy: a growth-oriented alliance between the dominant political elite and the less than self-sufficient private sector. The "green revolution" policies were then not a reversal but rather a continuity of this basic approach, resting on an alliance of the state with private enterprise. In industry this approach was adopted from the beginning. In agriculture it was only after some trial and error that the constraints of the "Indian conditions" were recognized. After this recognition it was clear that the only way to improve the "food situation" was to support private profitability by public actions.

36. For example, see Hari Sharma, "The green revolution in India: prelude to a red one," in Kathleen Gough and Hari Sharma (eds.), *Imperialism and revolution in South Asia* (Monthly Review Press: New York, 1973), pp. 77-102.
37. Frankel, *India's political economy,* ch. 7. 38. See Moore, *Social origins,* pp. 385-410.

The thrust of the Marxist argument is also misplaced. There is little evidence to support the contention that the interests of the landed classes were an important and direct consideration in the decisions leading up to a systematic state support for agrarian capitalism. One assumes that such a linkage between class and politics would be evident in the policy preferences of the majority of the Congress representatives. When presented with the "new approach" as a policy option for debate, however, the Congress representatives of the Lok Sabha (the lower house of parliament) as well as in the National Development Council (a consultative body that included the chief ministers of all the states) argued against it. Their preference was for higher investment in broad-based irrigation schemes, rather than for narrow subsidization of strategic inputs.

The members of the Lok Sabha, for example, when presented with the Draft Fourth Five-Year Plan, reacted by passing a resolution that the rural sector was being neglected and that the government "should give top priority to irrigation, electrification and water supply in the rural sector.[39] Furthermore, the Chairman of the Parliamentary Committee on the Draft Fourth Five-Year Plan, summarizing "the important observations" on which "there was full or near unanimity" noted that, "the provision for irrigation and rural electrification should be substantially stepped up. The strategy should be to concentrate on irrigation schemes."[40] Among the members of the NDC also, "There was a marked preference — for the allocation of more funds for rural water supply and minor irrigation works."[41]

In the light of the need to widen electoral support, and given that irrigation is a visible and essential input for a large proportion of their rural constituencies, these policy preferences of political representatives make sense. The immediate and electoral interests of the majority of the Congress representatives were thus not in a narrow pursuit of landlord interests. Their interests rather lay in a broad-based policy that, while benefiting the landed disproportionately to be sure, would nevertheless have positive consequences for larger numbers. In spite of these political preferences, the Congress leadership decided upon the "new approach," which would end up enhancing the profitability of a narrow group. The adoption of these new policies is, therefore, not readily explicable by an economic-interest hypothesis.

The leadership decision to adopt policies aimed at rapid production

---

39. See *Hindustan Times,* English daily (September 3, 1966).
40. See Government of India, *Report of the Lok Sabha Committee on the draft fourth five year plan (agriculture and rural economy)* (New Delhi, 1966), p. 40. Also see *Times of India* (August 21, 1966).
41. See *Times of India* (August 21, 1966).

growth resulted from three sets of conditions: the failure of past agrarian policies; the diminishing popularity of the Congress regime; and, in the face of food shortages, the increasing dependence of the leadership on foreign aid. These conditions reflected and contributed to the specific pattern of state intervention in India's deliberate development.

It had become clear by the early 1960s that the major planks of Congress's agrarian program, land reform and community development, were not producing the desired results. The critics as well as the government's own report tended to see the failure of land reforms as a political failure.[42] The absence of "political will" was held to be responsible for minimal land redistribution. This made the top decision-makers appear to be part of the problem, rather than a means to a solution. By that time it must have been evident to the leaders that radical restructuring of the countryside would require coercive political actions aimed at landed interests. Unwilling and unable to wield state power in this manner, the leadership was thus increasingly looking for a "new approach" to rural transformation. The failure of community development pointed in the same direction. Democratization of village communities without property redistribution was not likely to be successful. Similarly, the transmission of scientific know-how and modern agricultural practices had not released unbounded productive energies. The sluggish growth of agriculture provided the irrefutable evidence. Because the state was incapable of utilizing compulsion for social–structural transformation and because the manipulation of cultural variables had not altered the nature of production, something different was needed.

This search gained urgency because of the faltering popularity of the Congress regime, and because of failed monsoons that caused drastic food shortages in the mid-1960s. Multiple trends contributed to the declining popularity of the Congress. Central among these was simply a generational change in leadership. The legitimacy that Nehru and his contemporaries had enjoyed as champions of nationalism and anti-colonialism was increasingly falling into the background. The new leaders could not live off past accomplishments; they had to perform. And an important arena of political performance was the economy, especially agriculture. Continuing poor performance in agriculture had led not only to food shortages, but also to the slowing of overall economic growth. This in turn contributed to a more than occasional non-availability of goods and, more importantly, to rising prices of essential goods. Whether these economic conditions actually contributed to political dissatisfaction and to the declining popularity of Congress is not important. What is

42. See Government of India, *Progress of land reform* (Planning Commission: New Delhi, 1963), Parts I and IV.

important instead is that this is how Congress leaders perceived the relationship of economic conditions to their political popularity.[43] Accordingly, a leadership concerned with its political prospects in the approaching elections (1967) sought a "quick-fix" as well as a long-range policy as alternatives to the existing unsuccessful ones. The "green revolution" policies offered hope for both short-term and long-term problems.

The food situation in the mid-1960s was exacerbated by consecutive drought years. India was already dependent on food and monetary aid from external sources, and the resulting shortages led Indian leaders to request increased food aid from abroad, especially from the U.S. The U.S. government, as well as some U.S.-based private foundations used this opportunity to exchange food aid for "sensible" policies aimed at long-range "self-sufficiency" in food for India.[44] The aid donors demanded in unison what the Ford Foundation had already argued in the late 1950s: less attention to institutional reform and more attention to enhancing the profitability of those who were in a position to stimulate agricultural production.[45] The Indian leadership, faced by past failures in agricultural policies and a declining popularity, succumbed to external pressures. Aid was thus accepted with a commitment to treat production and growth as priority goals within the agrarian policy. The specific agrarian strategy adopted was not only consistent with the needs and the limited capabilities of the political leadership, but also with the views of aid donors.

These conditions leading up to the adoption of the "new approach" highlight the incapacity of the Indian state to translate the developmental vision of its leadership into a concrete outcome. In spite of a commitment to reconcile "growth with distribution," the political authorities finally adopted a policy that aimed primarily at facilitating economic growth. With the advantage of hindsight, it could be argued that such an outcome was predictable. A posture of state support for private enterprise in

43. Thus Mr C. Subramanium, the Minister of Food and Agriculture during the period the "green revolution" policies were adopted, when questioned about why the policies were adopted when they were, commented, "Our political survival was dependent on food production" (Interview, C. Subramanium, Madras, March 11, 1979). Similarly, Indira Gandhi later commenting on how the new approach was adopted, noted, "When it [the "green revolution" strategy] had been evolved, it was a question of sheer survival. It was hardly time to think of anything except increasing production" [*Hindustan Times,* English daily (April 19, 1968)].

44. See Frankel, *India's political economy,* ch. 7.

45. In 1959, a team of agro-experts, sponsored by the Ford Foundation, recommended a major shift away from land reforms and community development towards a technological solution to the problem of low agricultural growth. See Ford Foundation, *Report on the agricultural situation in India* (New York, 1959).

industry having been adopted, it was not likely that concerted attempts would be made to create "socialism" in rural India. Some redistribution may have been and still remains possible. However, the leadership would eventually have had to recognize that, given the nature of the state over which they presided, a pattern of development involving the authoritative use of state power on behalf of the lower classes was not probable. A recognition that radical rural transformation involving force was not on India's historical agenda — certainly not as long as the Congress presided — was thus inevitable. As the evidence regarding this political incapacity emerged, the need to maintain political support as well as external pressure combined to realign India's agrarian policies with its political–economic "realities."

From the very beginning the political "reality" had consisted of a state incapable and unwilling to utilize compulsion as a tool of social–structural change, and the economic "reality" of property owners, who were neither dynamic enough nor strong enough to impose their vision of the desirable upon the Indian society. This reality was recognized early in urban India and had led to state support for capitalist industrialization. In rural India, where the antagonism of Congress leaders towards the "reactionary" landed classes was part of the nationalist history, an explicit realignment was some time in coming. Once realigned, however, politically supported agrarian capitalism became the driving force of far-reaching changes in the rural social structure of India.

The Predicament of Distribution and Authority

The closer one comes to the present, the more difficult it is to discern the emerging patterns of social change. Looking back at the 1950s and the 1960s, it is evident that the Indian state has been incapable of directing socio-structural transformation in a manner capable of reconciling growth with distribution. As a consequence of this political incapacity, the political authorities have entered into a tacit growth-oriented alliance with the forces of private enterprise. While this arrangement has buttressed the dominant political and economic interests in the short run, it has also failed to solve some old problems and has created some new ones. In the emerging political economy, some trends are clearer than others.

Of the trends that are clear, the first is that the economy is increasingly on a firm capitalist footing. While there remain pockets of pre-capitalist agriculture, even significant ones, and some leader or another will occasionally make rumblings about "socialism," India's economy for the most part now operates on the principle of private property, wage labor, and commodity production. The capacity of this economy to generate self-sustained growth is by no means assured. India's mode of production has nevertheless undergone a decisive transformation from which there is no going back.[46] A second trend is that the adopted pattern of development has failed to alleviate the conditions of poverty for the majority of the population. Whatever the debates in the "poverty literature" — and these are mentioned below — so far there has been little or no significant alteration in the living conditions of the bottom half of the population.

If these economic patterns are relatively clear, what hangs in balance is the shape of the political arrangements to come. First, it is not clear whether the regime in control of state power will evolve towards a more or less democratic form. Second, whatever the degree of openness of the regime, the level of institutionalization it is likely to achieve remains in doubt. Similarly, while the links between the state and private enterprise are clear, the position the state is likely to adopt on any potential conflict between commercial peasants and urban-bourgeois interests is still an open question. And lastly, the degree to which future regimes are likely to be committed to distributional issues remains quite uncertain.

The Indian political economy is thus increasingly characterized by a state-supported capitalist economy, substantial rural poverty, and a more or less open regime, the future of which remains uncertain. Within this framework of a state and capitalist alliance, a question of considerable significance emerges: what type of regime, if any, can alleviate the conditions of rural poverty by planned state intervention? I will return to this below.

Trends in Distribution

What have been the distributional consequences of the pattern of development adopted so far? Prior to my taking a position on this issue, three caveats should be noted. First, my remarks here will be limited to the rural sector. Second, the quality of the available data, as well as their interpretation, marks a controversial scholarly terrain.[47] And third, given the macro-political-economy perspective adopted in this study, my interest in the distributional data is of a rough nature, as opposed to an interest in minute distinctions.

46. Ignoring much of the debate on the mode of production in India, the concept of "decisive transformation" is qualitatively akin to Barrington Moore's concept of "bourgeois revolution." It simply implies that major impediments to capitalist development in agriculture and industry have now been removed. For Moore, this had already happened with independence. See Moore, *Social origins*, section VI. 5 and VI. 6. I have asserted that this qualitative shift has come about with the spread of the "green revolution." After all, even for Moore, it is agrarian commercialization which marks the watershed between "tradition" and the capitalist route to "modernity."
47. For a sampling of the literature, see footnote 2 in the Introduction above.

Table 2.4   *Distribution of Operational Holdings in India by Size Group, 1953-1972*

Size of holding (acres)	1953-4[1] (%)		1960-1[2] (%)		1970-2[3] (%)	
	Number of households	Area operated	Number of households	Area operated	Number of households	Area operated
Less than 2.5	54.80	5.93	39.07	6.86	60.3	9.2
2.5–5	15.91	10.86	22.62	12.32	16.4	14.9
5–10	14.87	19.63	19.80	20.70	12.9	22.6
10–25	10.51	30.30	13.99	31.17	8.1	30.4
25 and above	3.01	33.28	4.52	28.95	2.2	22.8

[1] Government of India, *National sample survey*, eighth round.
[2] *Ibid*. Seventeenth round.
[3] *Ibid*. Twenty-sixth round.

Given these disclaimers, the distributional trends in rural India are not that difficult to document. Land-holding and consumption data both bear testimony to the conclusion that, while inequalities may not have widened, lower rural classes have gained little from planned economic development. In other words, the standard of living of as many as 220 million people in rural India — and these consist primarily of landless agricultural laborers, tenants, and marginal-to-small landholders — have not undergone any significant improvement over the last few decades.

Table 2.4 presents data on land distribution. It gives some indication of the overall patterns of distribution over time as well as data concerning access to land near the bottom of the ownership scale. As the accompanying Lorenz curve (Figure 2.1) reveals, there may have been a slight decrease in overall inequalities (among the land-holding population, but not including the landless) between the early 1950s and the early 1970s. While the shift is not all that significant, it does indicate that at least the direction of change in landholding is not toward increasing inequalities. There may also have been some increase in the average size of the holding of the marginal peasantry (under 2½ acres). What is not clear, however, is if this was at the expense of the larger landowners (25 acres and above) or, as is more likely, by a consolidation of the smallest of the marginal landholdings. The latter possibility is supported by the decline in the proportion of the number of marginal holdings over the two decades. The data further reveal that the notion that middle peasants (10 to 25 acres) have gained over both the larger and the smaller peasants is inaccurate. Whether this is true for incomes due to variation in land use is not clear from these data; what is clear is that the picture of a "broadening middle" does not hold for access to land. In general then, while the data highlight some fluctuations, they do not really indicate any significant shifts away

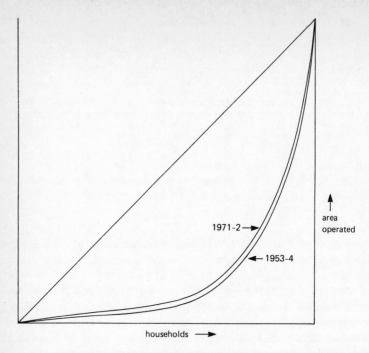

Figure 2.1 *Lorenz Curves: Operational Holdings in India, 1953-1954 and 1971-1972 (based on data provided in Table 2.4)*

from the existing pattern of landholding.

Given all the qualifications noted above, the safest conclusion from these data is that over the years the degree of inequality in rural India, as manifest in control over land, has not undergone any significant change. It should be noted that these data do not compare inequalities before and after the *zamindari* abolition, and so the conclusion refers to the situation since the *zamindaris* were broken up. This, of course, bears testimony to the shortcomings of land reforms and therefore to the limited political capacities of the Indian state for imposing a reformist pattern of development. Furthermore, to the extent that control over land has a bearing on the incomes of rural households, the data would support the conclusion that the incomes of the marginal and small peasants have not undergone any marked improvement. This issue of the incomes of the lower rural classes is, however, discussed better with reference to the rural consumption data.

Ahluwalia's computations of the National Sample Survey (NSS) data to chart out a profile of rural poverty in India are presented in Table 2.5.[48]

48. Ahluwalia, "Rural poverty."

Table 2.5   *NSS-Based Estimates of Rural Poverty in India*

Year	Percentage of rural population in poverty
1956-7	54.1
1957-8	50.2
1958-9	46.5
1959-60	44.4
1960-1	38.9
1961-2	39.4
1963-4	44.5
1964-5	46.8
1965-6	53.9
1966-7	56.6
1967-8	56.5
1968-9	51
1970-1	47.5
1973-4	46.1

Source: Montek Ahluwalia, "Rural poverty and agricultural performance in India," *Journal of Development Studies*, 14, 3 (April 1978), 298-324.

These data are more useful than the land data, because they reveal poverty where it matters most — at the level of consumption. They also include the rural landless, who are not covered in the data on land-holdings. The distributional and poverty trends highlighted by these data are, however, similar to those revealed by the land data. While the percentage of the population living in conditions of poverty has fluctuated, it does not reflect any clear trend over time. In other words, the proportion of those living under conditions of absolute poverty has neither clearly increased, nor decreased.

The decreasing inequalities in Ahluwalia's consumption data (Table 2.6), however, hide more than they reveal. First, one would not expect the increasing incomes of the rich peasantry to show up proportionately in their consumption patterns. Second, we know that the consumption levels of the lowest groups have not undergone a steady improvement. This suggests that the smaller Gini coefficients and the apparent trend towards reduced inequalities is a function of some other underlying changes. The reducing size of the area of inequality in the Lorenz curve here is then due, not to a reducing gap between the top and the bottom, but probably to the increasing incomes and consumption of the middle peasants. In conjunction with the land data, this would suggest that middle peasants have improved their economic status primarily by altering the patterns of land use.

While these data do qualify the earlier conclusions reached by Bardhan and others regarding a trend toward increasing, absolute impoverish-

Table 2.6   *Relative Inequality of Consumption: Gini Coefficients*

Year	Gini coefficient
1956-7	0.33
1957-8	0.34
1959-60	0.32
1960-1	0.33
1961-2	0.32
1963-4	0.30
1964-5	0.30
1965-6	0.30
1966-7	0.30
1967-8	0.29
1968-9	0.31
1970-1	0.29
1973-4	0.28

Source: Montek Ahluwalia, "Rural poverty and agricultural performance in India," *Journal of Development Studies*, 14, 3 (April 1978).

ment,[49] it is an overstatement to argue that the inequalities may be decreasing or that there is a "trickle-down" effect at work. The problems with this argument, as they are not directly germane to my discussion here, are outlined in Appendix II.

The macro-distributional picture revealed by the available data, then, is as follows: the overall relative inequalities have at least not increased; they have probably remained about the same. Similarly, with regard to the absolute levels of living, the proportion of the population living in conditions defined as poverty has not decreased. This implies that the number of people living in conditions of rural poverty has increased steadily over time — from about 180 million in the mid-1950s to about 240 million in the mid-1980s.

Changing Patterns of Authority

If state-supported capitalist development has failed to alleviate rural poverty, the resulting social changes have tended to undermine the inherited authority structures. During the 1950s and most of the 1960s India was governed by a relatively stable dominant party. The power of the Congress had itself rested on elaborate patronage-type networks. These networks facilitated the political incorporation of a large segment of the Indian society by virtue of the dependency of the lower classes on the upper classes. Dependencies inherent in the social structure had thus

49. Bardhan in Bardhan and Srinivasan (eds.), *Poverty in India*.

been politicized by the needs of electoral competition into patron–client networks manifest in "vote banks" and other forms of "intermediate aggregation."[50] In the last decade or so, however, both of these characteristics of political rule in India have been undermined. Neither single-party dominance nor patronage networks provide ready solutions to political stability any longer. What has emerged instead is a fragmented and potentially unstable center. This is barely held together at present by a dominant leader. During Mrs Gandhi's reign, moreover, populism emerged as a tool of direct political mobilization. Party organization was considerably weakened. As a consequence, not only is India's democracy rather fragile today, but the central authorities are even less capable of reformist intervention than before.

What forces have brought about this pattern of political change? The discussion is best begun by noting two important sets of underlying changes: a slow but steady erosion in leadership consensus; and a weakening of the vertical dependencies rooted in the social structure. A focus on the causes and the consequences of these political and social changes helps explain the transformation that authority structures are undergoing.

Multiple trends have contributed to the erosion of elite consensus. As the earlier unity generated by nationalism and the anti-colonial legacy has fallen more and more into the background, natural antipathies among the elite have surfaced. These antipathies have been heightened by a competitive political structure. Competition for leadership positions has probably been the most serious strain on any attempts to forge a substantial consensus. Of course, competitiveness exists in many polities, but it does not always lead to divisiveness. Even in India, a strong leader can keep chaos in check, as was the case during Mrs Gandhi's rule. The serious, long-range trend at work here, however, is the weakening of all consensus-imposing mechanisms. Interest and/or ideological parties are often such political mechanisms. Institutional arrangements of this nature are increasingly disintegrating in India. The old nationalist party is barely kept intact by a single leader whose legitimacy rests mainly on inheritance. New national parties based on either a clear interest representation or a coherent ideology are not on the horizon. Parties that blur their interest and ideological orientations, or those that openly take sides, are presently not succeeding in facilitating a workable consensus of the elite. Mr Rajiv Gandhi is able to portray an image of unified rule. As manifest more clearly in the experience of the Janata party, however, just below the surface lies a fragmented and divided elite.

50. The term has been used by Kothari. See Kothari. *Politics in India*, pp. 85-92 specifically and chs. 3, 4, 5, and 8 in general.

This emphasis on political variables is not to suggest that underlying economic interests have not contributed to political divisiveness. The emergence of new social groups, especially the commercial farmers, has thrust new leaders upon the scene who champion the *kisan* ("peasant") interests. Thus the state has not only facilitated the emergence of agrarian capitalism but now has to systematically accommodate the demands of rising new groups. There is nothing intrinsically impossible in the state simultaneously responding to the interests of agrarian and industrial capitalism. These conflicting demands do not constitute a struggle for different social orders, nor do they match the intensity of any potential conflict between the upper and the lower classes. Moreover, political conflict to date has been mainly among the elite, who would not disagree on the basic definitions of the Indian political economy, namely, a mutually beneficial alliance between the state and private enterprise. In the present situation, therefore, conflicting economic interests do not provide a ready explanation for elite dissension at the center. Economic factors have contributed, just as the dwindling nationalist legacy has played its part. The major reasons are only in part sociological: unabashed political competition on the one hand, and the absence of a consensus-imposing mechanism on the other.

Changes in the social structure have also had a considerable impact on the authority structure. Aside from the rise of a commercialized, land-owning class, the class relations in the countryside have been undergoing change. Vertical dependencies in the village communities had hitherto provided an important social mechanism preventing the politicization of class issues. Because the local notables of various types often controlled the votes of their dependents, electoral competition in the past did not always necessitate direct political appeals to the lower classes. In the last decade or so this pattern has altered.[51] The penetration of commerce in the countryside has probably been the single most important agent of change. Declining tenancy, the emergence of wage labor, and cash as a nexus of exchange have all contributed to the weakening of traditional ties. While these changes allow new political ideas to penetrate the lower rural classes, politicization has itself been an independent force weakening traditional vertical ties between land-owning notables and the peasantry. The twin forces of commerce and politics have therefore contributed to the emergence of the lower rural classes as a new political factor. While this process is far from complete, the way the new political forces are eventually accommodated, co-opted, or repressed, will probably be the single most important factor influencing the future of Indian politics.

51. While I have observed this process at first hand, the evidence to document this claim remains impressionistic. More research is clearly needed to highlight the nature of the changing rural social structure.

Elites competing for political power have sought to exploit these changing social–structural conditions. Indira Gandhi, for example, sought to build her support in the early 1970s by going directly to the masses. The popular slogan *garibi hatao* was of course an integral aspect of this mobilization strategy. She bypassed all or most "intermediate aggregators," and made direct appeals to the population. Blessed with leadership qualities, she gained considerable popularity. This was done, however, at the cost of undermining the intermediate links of the Congress between the center and the periphery. This mobilizational strategy was also accompanied by the broadening of the arena of legitimate demands, which has raised the expectations of the population concerning the distributional performance of the state. This, in the face of weakening capacities for reform, is a certain invitation for long-term instability.

During the mid-1970s the forces of political opposition adopted a similar strategy of direct mobilization. Thus Jaya Prakash Narain (JP) sought to oust Indira Gandhi by promising a "total revolution" that did not involve any attack on the propertied. Reminiscent of the days gone by, this may well have been the last time that a Gandhian-style mobilization strategy would strike a favorable chord among the Indian masses. After all, there are only so many times one can promise "national rejuvenation" or "total revolution" without any significant change. The class appeal of JP's movement was quite similar to that of other successful Indian leaders, including Indira Gandhi: it did not threaten the propertied and yet it offered a ray of hope to all those who had hitherto been bypassed by planned development. JP's position was somewhat unusual among the Indian political elite in that he alone could still claim to be an heir of sorts to the Gandhian legacy of saintly politicians, and this contributed considerably to his mobilizational success. As his movement to oppose Indira Gandhi gained support, and as the seeds of the Janata party were sown, Mrs Gandhi's power position was seriously threatened. In retrospect, this political struggle appears to have been the major cause leading up to the imposition of the "emergency." This in turn, of course, marked the brief authoritarian interlude in the otherwise democratic evolution of Indian politics.

The failure of Indira Gandhi to translate her authoritarian hold on power into concrete reforms, such as land redistribution, has led some analysts to argue that authoritarianism does not offer a solution to India's developmental problems. [52] That may well be so. The evidence, however, points toward a more radical conclusion. It suggests that neither democratic nor authoritarian regimes, presiding over the current political–

---

52. See Francine Frankel, "Compulsion and social change," *World Politics*, 30, 2 (January 1978), 215–40.

economic equation of India, are likely to be in a position to reconcile growth with distribution. The real issue, in other words, is not between democratic and authoritarian rule. Authoritarian rule does not always facilitate the autonomous use of state compulsion as a tool of social change. The debate is also not between capitalism and communism. Rather, it is, or ought to be, between a "captured" and an autonomous developmental state.

A captured state, whether run by a democratic or an authoritarian regime, is incapable of imposing social reforms. As a consequence, the adopted pattern of development usually reflects a compromise between the interests of the state and those of the dominant social classes. Whatever the merits of this pattern of development, it is singularly unsuited to solve distributional problems. An autonomous developmental state, by contrast, can translate leadership goals into a concrete developmental outcome. While it is usually coexistent with revolutionary and authoritarian situations, there is no intrinsic reason why partial autonomy cannot exist within a democratic–capitalist model of development. If ideologically committed to reformism and organizationally disciplined, such a state can selectively utilize compulsion against powerful interests so as to reform the social order from above. This political capacity, which I have discussed earlier and will discuss further in the following chapters, is a function of the leadership, ideology, and organization of the power-holders.

New Policy Directions

The Janata party swept into power in March 1977. While in the beginning it enjoyed popularity born out of its anti-authoritarian stance, leadership dissension soon gave rise to dissatisfaction. Even if popular support was not totally undermined, the incapacity of the leadership to act in unison led to governmental collapse. The same dissension further disabled the shortlived rulers from making even a respectable showing in the next elections. The Janata interlude will thus be remembered primarily for its successful dismantling of the emerging authoritarian regime.[53] Nevertheless, the failure of the Janata leadership to provide cohesive rule has also cast doubt on the viability of alternatives to a leader-dominant, stable government in contemporary India.

53. Dasgupta thus argues that, "a rapid reversal of the emergency regime, the reinstitution of the rule of law, and the swift dismantling of the structures of authoritarian control established by the Congress party were probably the most impressive accomplishments of the Janata party and its allies." See Jyotindra Dasgupta, "The Janata phase: the reorganization and redirection in Indian politics," *Asian Survey,* 19, 4 (April 1979), 395.

Given the present focus, how does one assess the distributional performance of the Janata regime? While the short duration of the regime makes any concrete assessment somewhat superfluous, certain trends were already clear. While investigating these trends, one should bear in mind that the discussion here, as above, is limited to the central government. The real impact of rural distributional policies, however, needs to be investigated at the state level. The performance in three selected states run by three different political parties is discussed in the following chapters. The trends at the Janata-controlled center were evident in the plan document, the 1979-80 budget, and the efforts directed at party organization. They all reveal that, as far as the issues of redistribution were concerned, the gap between rhetoric and action during the Janata phase, as in earlier periods, continued to remain large.

At a first glance the Janata plan document appeared to make refreshing departures from the past. It repeatedly emphasized the need to improve the living conditions of the bottom half of the population, assigning it first priority, even more important than economic growth, and went on to argue for "organizing the poor" as a means for accomplishing it.[54] This seemingly radical posture, as it turned out, reflected the outlook of some planners rather than those in position to make effective policies. The planners, taking their cue from the emphasis on redistribution in leadership rhetoric, saw this as an opportunity for "new beginnings." As they converted rhetorical goals into concrete policy proposals, however, the gap between the leaders and the planners became evident.

Raj Krishna, a prominent member of the Planning Commission, whose influence on the plan was evident, noted this gap: "The central cabinet is not very keen on land reforms and redistribution. Neither Morarji (Desai) nor Charan Singh are interested."[55] Given this leadership reluctance, it was impossible for the planners to translate the leadership commitment to alleviate rural poverty in ten years into concrete policies. Raj Krishna further argued: "Poverty can be removed in ten years. This is technically possible. Less than one-fourth of the total public outlay can remove poverty. Policy packages, including some land redistribution, exist, but they will not be delivered."[56] While many will challenge these judgements, they nevertheless are a commentary on the gap between what may be feasible and what the likely outcomes are in the absence of the political capacity for and commitment to redistribution.

This minimal commitment to redistribution was further evident in

54. See Government of India, *Draft five year plan, 1978-83,* especially sections 1.25 and 1.67 – 1.102.
55. Interview, Raj Krishna, New Delhi, May 22, 1979.
56. *Ibid.*

Janata's 1979-80 budget. This budget, more than anything else in the recent past, highlighted the emerging alliance of agrarian and industrial capitalism within India. The agrarian sector received a big boost in Charan Singh's budget. Much of this took the form of reduction of fertilizer and diesel-oil prices, substantial financial allocations to rural electrification and irrigation, and guaranteed procurement prices for selected crops.[57] These measures were aimed at boosting agricultural production. With regard to their distributional consequences, however, it is clear that the benefits would accrue primarily to the landed, the benefits being proportional to the size of agricultural holding. This is not to deny that, if sustained, these investments could also have some beneficial impact on the rural poor. However, one would have to be a diehard believer in the "trickle-down" or "urban bias as the root of all poverty" hypothesis to conceive of Charan Singh's agrarian tilt as a redistributive measure. This is especially true if one keeps in mind that production subsidies and price supports probably hurt more then help the rural poor because they, on the average, are net consumers rather than producers of agricultural products.

While agriculture received a boost, this was not at the expense of industry. State support for private industry, especially big industry, was maintained, while support was increased for the smaller industries. That industrial capitalists were pleased with the budget was underscored by the buoyant stock market in the days following its announcement.[58] Both agricultural and industrial producers thus received considerable state support. The resulting budgetary gap was filled in part by a wide range of indirect taxes. While all urban dwellers were hit by these taxes — taxes that were often regressive in character — they fell heaviest on the less well-to-do segments of the population. In view of these various measures, it is hard not to conclude along with A. N. Khusro that the budget "underscored the lack of emphasis on equality" on the part of the Janata regime.[59]

To highlight the same point further, it should be noted that the Janata party made only a minimal effort to penetrate the countryside by building a party organization. Rhetoric of decentralization aside, this absence of organizational development provides a strong indication that Janata leaders had little interest in facilitating state intervention aimed at the alleviation of rural poverty. The Janata's political and economic advisers had stressed the need for strengthening the organizational base, not only as a

---

57. See *Times of India* (February 28, 1979).
58. See the lead article by A. N. Khusro, "New emphasis on agriculture," *Times of India* (March 8, 1979).
59. *Ibid.*

means of sustaining support, but also as a vehicle for translating party goals into outcomes.[60] Raj Krishna, for example, had repeatedly stressed the contingent nature of "redistributive justice" and the "organization of the poor."[61] The party leadership were, however, too busy bickering among themselves to pay attention to serious organizational issues.

Janata was composed primarily of an anti-Indira Gandhi coalition. The various factions within the Janata were suspicious of each other. None of the major partners — the old Jan Sangh (the present Bhartiya Janata Party), the Congress (O), or the Bhartiya Lok Dal (BLD) — was a poor people's party to begin with. The ideology, leadership, and social support of these factions were anything but pro-rural poor. As coalitional partners in power, they collectively sought to portray a progressive image. Their actions revealed a different set of priorities. Not only was there no coherent leadership or ideology to build an organization around, but each faction worried about the others gaining in any drive to deepen political power. As late as the end of 1978, then, the Janata had only minimal party organization at the district level, even in the states where it was in power, and almost nothing below that level.[62] As a consequence, irrespective of the "class nature" of the party, the Janata could not have facilitated rural redistribution by utilizing the party organization even if it had intended to do so; it would have had to rely either on the inefficacious bureaucracy or the old faithful, "trickle-down."

The public policy and the organizational trends suggest clearly that the Janata party made little effort to steer state intervention in the service of the rural poor. On the contrary, the evidence indicates that the policies were aimed primarily at satisfying the interests of agrarian and industrial capitalism. This emerging alliance was probably as much by political design as by default. The Janata had few real political designs, and it was incapable of implementing them. Survival was of the essence. Competition within the heterogeneous leadership took up most of the political energy. Without a coherent leadership, ideology, or organizational structure, the Janata party was in no position to make a net political contribution to the developmental process.

Center and the States

Prior to a shift of focus from the center to the states, it is important to

60. Interview, Surendra Mohan (member and adviser, Janata party), Lucknow, June 14, 1979.
61. See Raj Krishna, "The next phase."
62. Interview, Surendra Mohan (as in footnote 60).

summarize briefly the argument so far. In this chapter I have suggested that the failure of redistributive reforms in India has resulted from both social–structural constraints and regime characteristics. As the former can often be taken for granted, it is the significance of the latter that I am interested in highlighting. Ever since the nationalist movement, through the periods in which the Congress was dominated by Nehru and Mrs Gandhi, to the Janata party, India has consistently failed to construct disciplined political institutions. The Indian state has, therefore, been unable to generate a sufficient degree of state autonomy to implement social reforms. Whatever autonomy existed at the time of independence has, moreover, declined over the years. While the open and consensual nature of India's dominant political institutions may well be credited for facilitating democratic stability, the same trait is also responsible for the failure to translate the leadership's socialistic ideologies into a corresponding pattern of development. To those with a distaste for the concept of "discipline" in political life, it ought to be said that the failure to alleviate poverty may well in the future contribute to the withering of cherished democratic institutions.

The central idea of this chapter, and of the rest of the study, is that regime type is an important variable for understanding the success or failure of social reforms. This is not likely to be a convincing hypothesis if the evidence provided is primarily negative, i.e., only if failure of reforms is associated with weakness of regime institutions. A stronger case can only be made by linking variations in regime type to variations in reformist outcomes. The rest of this study attempts this task by a comparative analysis of regional Indian materials.

States within India possess considerable constitutionally sponsored powers over the agrarian sector. While the central government provides guidelines, the states must translate these into legislation and implementation. This is especially true for redistributive policies. The nature of the political arrangement at the state level is therefore crucial for understanding the effectiveness of attempted redistribution. This significance is heightened in the conditions of a weak center, which the Janata phase characterized, and when the states are run by parties other than the one in control of the center. Both of these follow from the fact that the center has only a few formal control mechanisms to influence the behavior of the state governments. Periodic letters, the chief ministers' conference, and presidential approval of state-level legislation are the main formal mechanisms of control. Significant influence is, therefore, often indirect and is exerted through the party. When the party organization is weak, and when the state government is controlled by another party, fragmented central leadership can become powerless. Short of "presidential rule," the center in these cases has difficulty molding the decisions of the states. Under these conditions the role of the state governments in the rural sector takes on considerable independent significance.

These conditions existed during the Janata phase. This time period, therefore, provided an ideal opportunity to conduct comparative analysis within India. States run by different parties could be compared for their efficacy and performance concerning the issue area of rural redistribution. I chose three states for this purpose: West Bengal, under the Communist Party of India, Marxist (CPM); Karnataka, then under Devraj Urs and the Congress (I); and Uttar Pradesh under the Janata party. Irrespective of the orientation of the center, these states enjoyed a significant degree of independence in translating governmental power into redistributive policies. Of course, this independence was also constrained by the eventual power of the center and by the larger political–economic conditions of democratic capitalism. A degree of independence within the framework of larger constraints, then, provided an opportune area for raising and analyzing the following question: given social–structural constraints, what difference does variation in political rule make for the living conditions of the poor? Can one type of regime pursue (legislate and implement) such anti-poverty programs as land reforms, small-farmer schemes, and wage- and employment-generation projects for the landless more effectively than other types of regimes? Efficacy of varying regime types for facilitating reformist development is, then, the central theme pursued in the following chapters.

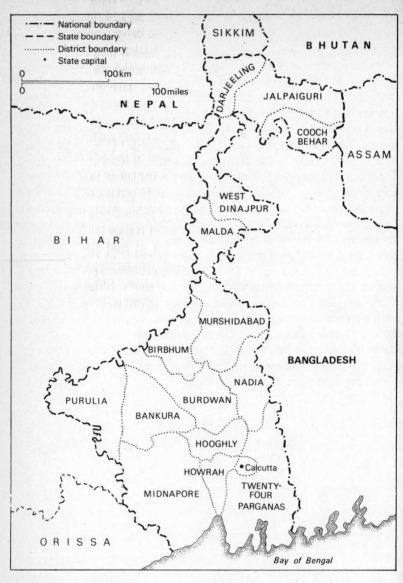

3.1 Map of West Bengal

3

West Bengal: Parliamentary Communism and Reform from Above

The Communist Party of India, Marxist (CPM) returned to power in West Bengal in 1977. This time, unlike the previous United Front Ministries,[1] the CPM had a clear majority. Alone it won 177 of the 293 assembly seats; along with its partners in the Left Front, the CPM now controlled a solid majority of 230 seats. The 1982 elections further confirmed the CPM's electoral popularity within West Bengal. These "parliamentary communists" have since 1977 sought to translate their power into developmental change. Central to their overall strategy is a concerted attack on the rural poverty of West Bengal. The creation of "red" *panchayats* (local governments), the registration of sharecroppers, the facilitation of credit for small landholders, and the mobilization of the landless for higher wages are all aimed at securing political position by improving the conditions of the lower classes. Whereas many others in India have paid lip-service to these redistributive goals, the CPM alone has made systematic and impressive beginnings towards accomplishing them. This is not to suggest that the CPM regime is without its share of failings, problems, and critics.[2] The CPM's redistributive programs are nevertheless impressive. If sustained, they promise to have a significant long-term impact on the living conditions of the rural poor.

What is it that distinguishes the CPM regime of West Bengal and its developmental efforts from other ruling parties in Indian states? To an-

1. For an analysis of the earlier experiences of the CPM and the United Front ministries, see Marcus Franda, *Radical politics in West Bengal*, Studies in communism, revisionism and revolution, 16 (MIT Press: Cambridge, Massachusetts, 1971); and Bhabani Sen Gupta, *Communism in Indian politics* (Columbia University Press: New York, 1972).
2. For a trenchant criticism of the CPM from the left, see Ashok Rudra, "One step forward, two steps backward," *Economic and Political Weekly* (Review of Agriculture), 16, 25–6 (1981), A61-A68. For other reviews of the CPM's programs, see the following articles in this same issue of *Economic and Political Weekly* as above: Nripen Bandyopadhyaya, "Operation Barga and land reforms perspective in West Bengal: a discursive review," A38-A42; Ratan Khasnabis, "Operation Barga: limits to social democratic regime," A43-A48; Ratan Ghosh, "Agrarian programme of left front government," A49-A55; Kalyan Dutt, "Operation Barga: gains and constraints," A58-A60; and Sunil Sengupta, "West Bengal land reforms and the agrarian scene," A69-A75. Another article which came to my attention only after this chapter was written is Biplab Dasgupta, "Share-cropping in West Bengal: from independence to Operation Barga," *Economic and Political Weekly* (Review of Agriculture), 19, 26 (1984), A85-A96.

swer this, I will analyze below the nature of the CPM as a ruling party and its distributional policies. It is argued that the capacity of the CPM to initiate a systematic attack on rural poverty stems from its political and class characteristics. The type of leadership, ideology, and organization the CPM regime brings to bear on the operation of political power enables it to perform two essential tasks: first, penetration of the countryside without being captured by the landed classes; and second, controlled mobilization and incorporation of the lower classes to buttress state power as a tool of social reform.

The CPM Regime

This discussion must begin with an important caveat. As a provincial government in a federal polity, the CPM in West Bengal operates under constraints. These not only involve the general constraints of India's political–economic arrangements, but also the more specific constraints of the constitution, and of the centrally controlled administration and finances, as well as those stemming from the prospect of presidential rule in case the governmental performance is deemed inadequate. Why then analyze a regional government as a "regime," implying that it has independent political significance?

While the constraints on independent actions are very real, as noted above, the CPM and other party-dominated regional governments have considerable control over the formulation and implementation of agrarian policies. This study is concerned with rural poverty. The large scope for rural intervention residing at the provincial level thus partly justifies treating constituent political units as analytically autonomous units. Second, as my purpose is to compare the efficacy of regional governments in anti-poverty policies, and as the regions share similar constraints, the analytical distortion caused by treating them as somewhat autonomous and therefore comparable units will be minimized. And third, political variation among the constituent units of a federal policy affords a unique opportunity to raise and analyze comparatively an important question: given the larger and similar social-structural constraints, what difference does the "regime" make for developmental outcomes?

To gain an understanding of the CPM regime in West Bengal, one must begin by analyzing the nature of its leadership, ideology, and organization. The important thing to note about the leadership is that it is neither concentrated in the hands of an individual nor, as one might expect, in the party alone. While the party wields great influence, leadership is shared by the three "wings" of the CPM, namely, the party organization proper, the Kisan Sabha (the peasant wing), and the parliamentary wing. Pramode Dasgupta, who was in charge of the party,[3] Binoy Chow-dhry, the head of the Kisan Sabha, and Jyoti Basu, the leader of the parliamentary majority, are three of the important leaders. As individuals, they represent varying leadership styles as well as somewhat different constituencies. And yet they, along with other CPM leaders, have managed to function in relative unison, avoiding major factional conflicts and open power struggles. As this characteristic of unity in shared power is rare in Indian politics, it requires some elaboration.

Pramode Dasgupta is the man most responsible for making the CPM into a well-organized, disciplined party. Of austere tastes, he used to live in a small room in the party headquarters located in the midst of the Calcutta slums. He eschewed luxuries and was known to do his own cooking and washing. Rare as this disposition is among the powerful of India, it is not surprising that Pramode Dasgupta was widely respected as a leader of integrity. He was the state secretary of the CPM, and thus its head in West Bengal. He not only wielded considerable political influence, but also remained the more radical of the prominent leaders.[4]

Jyoti Basu, by contrast, hails from a wealthy, upper-caste background. Educated in elite Calcutta schools and trained in law at the Middle Temple in London, he is closer to the social fiber of the Bengali *bhadralok* (the educated and cultured elite) than the other leaders. A competent parliamentarian and administrator, both in style and ideology, he evokes the "social democrat" rather than the "communist revolutionary."[5] As such he has been a natural candidate for heading the democratically elected, left-of-center government.

Binoy Chowdhry is the low-keyed, cerebral, peasant leader.[6] In contrast to the former Land-Revenue Minister, Hare Krishna Konar, Binoy Chowdhry eschews rhetorical fireworks and the use of leadership to provoke revolutionary sentiments among the peasantry. While of urban origins, he has spent most of his life organizing the peasantry. His power base is in the districts, specifically in Burdwan. Now the head of the Bengal as well as the All-India Kisan Sabha, his quiet strength within the CPM government is revealed by the fact that his favored programs for the sharecroppers top the policy-priority list.

In spite of this varied leadership, and in contrast to many other state governments in India, the CPM rule in West Bengal has not been marred

3. Pramode Dasgupta passed away after this chapter was written. The new party leader, Sarod Mukerjee, was a close associate of Mr Dasgupta.
4. For a biographical sketch of Pramode Dasgupta see, Bhabani Sen Gupta, "Pramode Das Gupta: party builder in eastern India," *Perspective* (Calcutta, April 1978).
5. Interview with Jyoti Basu, Calcutta, March 17, 1979.
6. Interviews with Binoy Chowdhry, Calcutta, March 12, 1979, November 2, 1981, and June 21, 1983.

by factional conflicts. This, of course, is not to suggest that factionalism is not a recurring theme in the evolution of the CPM. Born out of factional struggles, it still has conflicts among the more and the less radical, the older and the younger groups, and along the rural–urban cleavage. But this factionalism pales when compared to many other political organizations of India. Two important factors, one integral to the CPM and the other circumstantial, have tended to mitigate the fragmenting tendencies.

First and foremost of these factors is the party discipline. The CPM being organized along "democratic centralist" principles, its internal disagreements and power ambitions, while played out within the party, have not become impediments to a coherent policy. It is in the nature of "democratic centralism" as a principle of organization that a party position, once adopted, is binding on all the members. While in many cases this opens up the prospect of harsh, authoritarian tendencies, given the electoral framework of the CPM, the organizational leadership of the party has not been able simply to dictate its terms and preferences. Party positions have had to take account of various factors, including the Kisan Sabha, which provides the vital link with rural voters, and of parliamentary leaders, who run the government. The fact that the CPM is a "Leninist" party within a democratic polity has thus facilitated a degree of balance: some dissipation of power among the various wings of the leadership on the one hand, and on the other hand, a unifying umbrella that limits incapacitating power conflicts and disagreements at the top.

The second and circumstantial factor that has facilitated leadership unity is a shared perception of the common enemy — the central government of India in conjunction with the bourgeois–landlord forces. Whatever the accuracy of these perceptions — and some of this is discussed below — the consequence has been that the process of securing and maintaining power is conceived of as an ongoing struggle.[7] The costs of competition over the rewards of power are seen as high; there is a perceived vested interest — political survival — in unity. As a result of both objective (party organization) and subjective (perceived common enemy) factors, then, the CPM leadership in West Bengal has been characterized by shared but coherent leadership.

Over the years the CPM's ideology has shifted from a revolutionary to a reformist orientation. The doctrine of "class confrontation" as a means

7. A potential intervention from the center was a fear and a theme repeated by all senior ministers in interviews. For example, Ashok Mitra, Minister of Finance, argued eloquently: "What we have to constantly experiment with is how far we can push without invoking some intervention — or what is the feasibility frontier: we have the experience of Kerala in 1959 very much in our mind." Interview, Ashok Mitra, Calcutta, March 16, 1979.

of establishing the "dictatorship of the proletariat" is no longer central to the party line. Instead, the CPM has evolved a somewhat moderate stance. This is best characterized as a developmental and a democratic–socialist ideology. It emphasizes the preservation of democratic institutions on the one hand, and on the other hand emphasizes the use of state power for facilitating "development with redistribution." In practice, as I will argue below, this results in leaving capitalism intact as a mode of production, but directing efforts towards the consolidation of electoral power by channeling some public resources to the lower agrarian classes.

In the aftermath of the emergency, the renewed emphasis on democracy was clear at the CPM's Tenth Congress. The "immediate" as well as the "long-term objective," according to the resolution adopted, was "expanding democracy and introducing new clauses in the constitution putting the fundamental rights of the people beyond the mischief of any ruling party or government." To accomplish this, the program recommends the mobilization of "the broadest possible support" including "elements who do not support the economic program of the party."[8] The struggle for preserving and strengthening democratic institutions is, in other words, now treated by the CPM as a struggle prior to that involving class issues.

This moderation was evident even earlier in the agrarian program adopted in 1976. The party line that evolved stressed that "land redistribution," while a useful "propaganda slogan," should not be made into a "slogan of action." In contrast to past practices, land seizures (which were to be encouraged in a resolution adopted in 1969) were from then on not to be encouraged as a tool of mobilization and politicization. Instead, "the Kisan (peasant) movement led by our party . . . will have to channelize many other agrarian currents, like the question of wages for rural workers, the issue of rent reduction, the abolition or scaling-down of peasant indebtedness, fair prices for agricultural produce, the reduction of tax burdens . . . etc."[9] Pramode Dasgupta explained this reorientation as he argued that the only way to gain the support of all the peasantry, "rich and poor," was to pay attention not only to the "land question," but also to the issues of "irrigation, seeds, and fair prices for the produce."[10] The thrust of the agrarian program was, in other words, increasingly to shift its focus away from "class confrontation" to issues of "development with redistribution."

8. See, Communist Party of India (Marxist), *Political resolution*, adopted at the Tenth Congress (Jullundur, April 2-8, 1978), p. 18.
9. Communist Party of India (Marxist) (Resolution of the Central Committee), *On certain agrarian issues* (New Delhi, March 1976).
10. Pramode Dasgupta's speech to the Silver Jubilee Celebration of the Kisan Sabha, reported in *Ganashakti* (February 10, 1979).

The democratic–socialist tilt of the CPM is even clearer in its political analysis of who the "enemy" is and who is on "our side." In contrast to the Marxist emphasis on social classes, the CPM now mixes class with political and other criteria in deciphering potential allies. The only class of individuals to be isolated in the agrarian sector are the "big *jotedars*" — the class of large and often absentee landowners. They are enemies not only because they own more land than anyone else, but also because they do not participate in agricultural activities.[11] The support of all other agrarian groups, including the largest landowners who supervise production and therefore resemble capitalist farmers, is to be sought. The resolution on the *Tasks on the kisan front* makes this explicit: "The unity of the agricultural labourers, poor, middle and rich peasantry based on agricultural labourers and poor peasants, is sharply emphasized."[12] Accordingly, even "exploiting" individuals — rich peasants utilizing agricultural laborers and poor peasants — are not enemies as long as they are productive and willing to extend political support. A view of society and politics that only conceives of non-productive property owners as enemies is certainly a far cry from Marx's own analysis. Exploitation, in this view, is not a function of "surplus appropriation" but of parasitic life-styles. In and of itself this is neither praise nor an indictment; it highlights the non-communist, social–democratic nature of the CPM. Like the Italian Communists, the CPM in India can reconcile the prospect of a communist state in a capitalist society only by arguing that there are few real enemies in a capitalist society. Broad-based political unity aimed at reform is of the essence; revolutionary confrontation with the propertied classes is not really on the agenda.

Underlying this ideological shift are several factors: the dynamics of electoral–constitutional politics, the CPM's past experiences, and the need to maintain a healthy economy. As the CPM has sought electoral success, the need for broad-based political support has been deemed important. Knowing well that the rich and the middle peasants not only are numerically significant but, if alienated, can mobilize considerable opposition on behalf of other parties, the CPM has sought to soften its

11. "Big *jotedars*" (landowners) are differentiated from "rich peasants" by the CPM, not only on the basis of the size of the landholding, but also, and mainly, on the basis of whether they are absentee or supervisory landlords. It indeed makes for a funny type of communism which treats pre-commercial, "feudal" landlords as enemies but not those involved in the capitalist mode of production. CPM's class analysis was explained to the author in an interview with Maujam Hussain, Member of the Legislative Assembly, West Bengal, and Secretary, Local Committee, Debra Block, Midnapore, April 2, 1979.
12. Communist Party of India (Marxist) (Resolution of the Central Committee), *Tasks on the kisan front* (New Delhi, March 1976).

ideological position.[13] Moreover, having accepted constitutional limits, the leadership clearly realizes that the scope for radical property redistribution is minimal.[14] If these electoral and constitutional constraints were not evident in the early life of the CPM, active participation in political life for a few decades has clarified both the conditions for electoral success and the boundary conditions for the operation of political power. Crucial to this "organizational learning" have been two interrelated experiences. First, the slogan of "seizure of *benami* land" (land registered in false names), adopted in 1969, let loose forces that the CPM itself could not control. This not only led other political forces, especially the Naxalites, to gain support at the expense of the CPM, but also to widespread dissatisfaction with the CPM among the landed and the middle classes, culminating in center-sponsored repression. That a re-evaluation of the agrarian strategy followed is not surprising.[15] Related to this has been the experience of United Front ministries, both in West Bengal and in Kerala. Because these state governments collapsed under the duress of internal class problems and central governmental pressures, the CPM has now decided to go slow, while reassuring the propertied by specifying the limits of its socialist intent.

In addition to these constraints, the need to maintain economic growth has led the CPM to take a reconciliatory stance towards the propertied. In the recent past the economy of West Bengal has been characterized by moderate to low growth in agriculture and by a tendency for industrial capital to move out of the area. Both of these characteristics could be easily accentuated for the worse by a radical regime. Had the CPM decided to withdraw its support from agrarian productive activities (such support does benefit the larger landowners disproportionately), agricultural growth would have suffered; had the leadership adopted a more radical stance encouraging labor unions, and other forms of activism, there would have been a continued tendency to keep capital away from Bengal.[16]

13. No wonder that party platform and speeches have emphasized the "unity" of all peasantry, "rich and poor." For example, see the reference to Pramode Dasgupta's speech to the Kisan Sabha quoted in footnote 9 above.
14. Thus Jyoti Basu argued that, "we recognize that within the larger constraints we are operating under, we cannot bring about fundamental change." Interview, March 17, 1979.
15. As a party cadre active in block-level organizational tasks explained to the author, "The slogan 'seize *benami* land' was first raised in 1969. The resulting movement was quite irregular and confused. It was not clear as to whose land was to be seized — whether *khas* or *benami* or both. Illegal and irregular seizures occurred. When we went out of power, massive repression followed. Only in 1976 did we clarify this whole issue." Interview, Johar Santra, Secretary, Local Committee, Ghatal Block, Midnapore, March 24, 1979. (*Khas* land = land which is "above ceiling" by law.)
16. For example, see "Wooing business to West Bengal," *Indian Finance* (September 10, 1977).

As the legitimacy of the regime remains a function of its capacity as an economic manager, no democratic regime, if it values survival, can afford to take actions that discourage economic growth and lead to shortages, unemployment, and general dissatisfaction. In other words, a democratically elected, left-of-center regime within the framework of an economy with private ownership is constrained by the very nature of the arrangement: measures perceived as radical will discourage privately controlled economic activity. In order to avoid this outcome, the CPM regime has from the outset sought to appease those in a position to facilitate economic growth—landowners and urban capitalists alike. The CPM has learned that for the sake of survival, it cannot afford to be revolutionary; the most it can achieve is to facilitate development with distribution.

At the core of the CPM as an organizational force is a tightly knit and relatively small party. In an area with a population of close to 50 million, the CPM in the recent past used to boast no more than 40,000 party members in West Bengal.[17] Over the last several years in power, this membership has reportedly grown to about 100,000.[18] In order to understand how the CPM has generated a popular and efficacious political presence with less than 2 percent of the population as members, one has to understand the nature of the party as well as the linkages between the party and various support groups such as the Kisan Sabha.

The core membership of the party is a highly disciplined and select group. Each member actually gains that status after several years of party work. This work is typically in the trade-union movement, or in the Kisan Sabha, or in the student movement. Those sympathetic and dedicated to the party's mission are observed closely by those who are already members. Meeting periodically in small groups for political discussions, party members are able to observe at close quarters a prospective member's political development and dedication to the party. The prospective member in turn absorbs the party line as well as the belief that discipline and loyalty to the party line constitute the highest virtues, enabling one to become a member.[19]

The pre-recruitment period ends only when a potential member has proven to existing members that he or she understands the party line well and is willing to be a loyal follower of party directives. Those who become members have, therefore, already agreed to give party considerations

17. Interview, Abdullah Rasool, former leader, Bengal and All-India Kisan Sabha, at the party headquarters (State Committee of West Bengal), Calcutta, March 14, 1979.
18. Interview, Biplab Dasgupta, party member, Calcutta, June 22, 1983.
19. This account of the workings of the party is based on information gathered from many interviews with party cadres as well as the CPM leaders.

considerable weight. Once one is a member, the tendency towards loyalty and discipline is accentuated by the democratic–centralist principles on which the party is organized. Aside from loyalty or imposed discipline, as the ascent in the party hierarchy is a partial function of dedication to the party, some of those seeking success find it advantageous to go along with the party line. Loyalty, discipline, and opportunism thus combine in a tightly knit organization. While these characteristics do not totally eliminate internal dissent or factionalism, they do create a cohesive political force consisting of individuals representing primarily the views and interests of the CPM.

Until recently, the majority of the membership has consisted of urban professionals, middle peasants, and such urban–rural linkage groups as city-educated but rural-based school-teachers. While this clearly indicates that the CPM membership is not recruited from landless agricultural laborers, sharecroppers, and the working classes, the significance of this fact needs to be clarified.

The relationship between the social origins of members and the political practices of a party is anything but straightforward. This is especially true for the CPM. The party line here is decided upon at the highest levels. In arriving at the party line, the leadership takes into account a complex series of calculations involving electoral success, political feasibility, long-term versus short-term strategies, etc. The party program, in turn, is binding on the membership on the one hand, and becomes a guide for governmental policy on the other. While the leadership must account for the social backgrounds of its members, especially if this will lead the members to oppose a program strongly, this is only one among many considerations that result in the adoption of a specific program. No hasty conclusions should therefore be drawn about the nature of a party from the social origins of its members. It would especially be erroneous to conclude that the CPM's reformism results primarily from its middle-class membership and that a lower-class membership would necessarily be more revolutionary.

Within West Bengal, the CPM has deep roots in some areas but lacks them in others. For example, the Burdwan District and large tracts of Twenty-Four Parganas have long been CPM strongholds, while Midnapore, except for small pockets, has relatively little CPM strength. Such variation is only in small part explained by social-structural conditions. Burdwan has a higher concentration of disaffected tribal population than most other districts and it is further down the road of commercial penetration. This, however, is not sufficient to explain the political differences. Midnapore itself has a large tribal population and other areas such as Murshidabad have made rapid strides towards commercialization without parallel political changes. In addition to social conditions, therefore, one has to account for the leadership variable. Important leaders like Hare Krishna Konar and Binoy Chowdhry hail from Burdwan. On the one hand they have benefited from conflict-ridden social conditions; on the other, however, they have also contributed to the politicization of these conditions and thus to the deepening of the party base in their respective areas.

It is important to note in passing that caste does not play as important a role in West Bengal politics as it does in other parts of India. This is a well-known fact about Bengali politics. The causes of this are rooted deep in Bengal's history and do not concern us here.[20] As a consequence, however, all political parties, including the CPM, seldom use caste appeals as a mobilizing tool in this part of India. This is not to suggest that local loyalties are somehow unimportant political considerations. On the contrary, the CPM is sensitive to the fact that eastern districts have concentrations of Biharis and Jharkhandis, that Darjeeling is dominated by Gurkhas, that interior areas have tribal concentrations, and that districts such as Burdwan are dominated by land-holding agricultural castes. These variations become important considerations in selecting local candidates for elections; candidates not only have to be politically "correct" but should also attract support on the basis of "primordial loyalties." None of this in West Bengal, however, adds up to the "backward castes" movement of a Bihar type, or the concern with the "dominant castes" in Karnataka.

The other characteristic of the CPM that needs to be mentioned is the shifting nature of its rural–urban base. In the recent past the CPM was primarily urban-based. The peasantry was only "discovered" in the late 1960s. Various conditions facilitated this discovery.[21] The loosening control of landlords over their dependents was rightly perceived as an opportunity to gain the electoral support of this newly released political resource—the peasantry. The more radical elements within or outside of the party, following Mao's teaching, were already beginning to prove that the peasantry could be politically mobilized. Peasant leaders such as Konar had also gained prominence within the party. He argued for a "worker–peasant" alliance along Leninist lines. It was furthermore clear, even to the moderate leadership, that electoral success would require successful penetration of the countryside. To facilitate this rural tilt, the CPM undertook the recruitment of those university-level students in dis-

20. I have explored this issue elsewhere. See Atul Kohli, "From elite radicalism to democratic consolidation: the rise of reform communism in West Bengal," in Frankel and Rao (eds.), *Class, caste and dominance in India* (forthcoming).
21. For a detailed analysis see Bhabani Sen Gupta, *CPI-M: promises, prospects, problems* (Young Asia Publications: New Delhi, 1979), chs. 3 and 5.

trict towns and in Calcutta who had active rural roots.[22] It was hoped that these students, often turned primary- or secondary-school-teachers, would go back to their areas as party members or near-members, continuing the task of "propaganda and organization."

In addition to the role of the Kisan Sabha, this strategy has facilitated a degree of penetration of the countryside. However, while the students turned teachers and party workers are often quite politicized, many of them belong to land-owning families.[23] As a consequence, the CPM's rural base has continued to develop with the help of groups other than the poorest of the poor. This has certain important consequences. It is true that the social origins of the membership, as argued above, are not always important in influencing the party line. Nevertheless, I will argue below, membership interests become a constraint on what the governmental party can hope to implement through the party.

As a party in West Bengal, then, the CPM consists of a relatively small group of disciplined and organized cadres. These cadres generally originate from the middle strata in both the cities and the countryside. Their concentration varies from district to district, and the hitherto urban focus has been undergoing a considerable shift. This party structure has been supported by various "interest group" auxiliary organizations. These include the student movement, the women's movement, the trade-union movement, and the peasant movement organized under the Kisan Sabha. These groups provide important linkages between the party and society. While the relationship between the party and the auxiliary groups tends to be party-dominant, there are some built-in elements of reciprocity. A discussion of the Kisan Sabha will help elucidate not only this relationship but also the pattern of the CPM's rural penetration.

Kisan Sabha is recognized as the peasant wing of the CPM. Organizationally, however, though the two are linked, they are also distinct — while the CPM is a political party, the Kisan Sabha is not. As an autonomous organization, the Kisan Sabha has its own internal elections (in West Bengal, as well as on an all-India basis) and makes its own programmatic decisions. The aim of the organization is to represent the interests of the peasantry. Until recently, in terms of both membership and program, the interests represented were primarily of the middle peasantry. The slogans, therefore, while paying some attention to the "land question" and the "rights of the *bargardars*" (sharecroppers), emphasized issues of land

22. Interview, Sukumar Sen Gupta, Party Secretary, District Committee, Midnapore, March 22, 1979.
23. Only land-owning families of rural areas are generally in a position to finance the education of their children in district towns, not to mention in Calcutta.

taxation and fair prices for agricultural produce.[24] In the 1960s, however, paralleling the shift in the CPM, Kisan Sabha sought to increase its strength among the lower peasantry, as well as among the landless laborers. The agricultural labor union (Krishi Mazdoor Sangh) is now affiliated with the Kisan Sabha. The current slogans also pay attention to the needs of the rural poor. In spite of these shifts, the Kisan Sabha continues to be dominated by the middle peasantry. By one knowledgeable estimate, from someone who had an interest in emphasizing the "lower-rural class" nature of the Kisan Sabha, the internal strength is about 60-65 percent middle peasantry and 30-35 percent landless peasants and share-croppers.[25]

The linkages of the CPM and the Kisan Sabha are varied and multiple. In terms of personnel, sixty of the seventy-one members of the Kisan Provincial Committee are members of the CPM; 6 of the 28 members of the Executive Council of the Kisan Sabha are members of the CPM State Committee.[26] Moreover, individuals like Binoy Chowdhry, not only lead the Bengal and the all-India Kisan Sabha, but are also leading members of the CPM government. With regard to the program, Kisan Sabha accepts the CPM's "people's democracy" line. At the same time, however, the party is not able simply to dictate the peasant program to the Kisan Sabha. On the contrary, the Sabha makes an important, autonomous contribution.[27] This among other things is evidenced by Binoy Chowdhry's favored programs as priority items in the CPM's rural policies.

The elements of reciprocity stem from the vital functions of the Kisan Sabha. First, grassroots propaganda-and-organization work not only has a significant bearing on CPM's electoral support, but also provides a base from which future party recruits are selected. And second, the CPM needs the help of the Kisan Sabha in the implementation of rural programs. Conversely, however, the Kisan Sabha's attempts to represent peasant interests would be of little consequence if they were not part of a larger political program. The relationship between the CPM and the Kisan Sabha (or other auxiliary organizations) is thus marked by the

---

24. Interview, Mehbub Zahidi, party member, CPM and Sabhapati, *zila parishad*, Burdwan, March 27, 1979.
25. Interview, Mehbub Zahidi, as above. Similar estimates were given by Abdullah Rasool (footnote 17).
26. Interview, Abdullah Rasool (footnote 17).
27. Abdullah Rasool summarized the relationship as follows: "The CPM provides the political leadership. It defines the nature of the overall struggle. The Kisan Sabha helps with this. On the peasant organizational questions, however, the Kisan Sabha leads. CPM does not dictate." *Ibid.*

Table 3.1 *Results of 1977 and 1982 West Bengal Assembly Elections*

Parties	Assembly seats won		% of total valid votes	
	1977	1982	1977	1982
CPM	177	174	35.8	38.5
Other left-front parties	53	47	10.5	9.9
Janata	29	—	20.5	0.8
Congress (I)	20	49	23.4	35.7
CPI	2	7[1]	2.7	1.8
Others	12	17	7.1	13.3
Total	293	294	100	100

[1] The CPI joined the left front in the 1982 elections.
Source: compiled from official reports of the Election Commission of India.

former providing overall political leadership, while the latter facilitates electoral support and programmatic inputs.

The CPM swept into power in 1977. The number of assembly seats captured by the left front — composed mainly of the CPM, but also including the Forward Bloc and the Revolutionary Socialist Party — was impressive. The percentage of votes secured, nevertheless, was ·less decisive (Table 3.1). Had Janata and Congress not split up the votes between them, the CPM's overall majority could have been substantially reduced. The significant increase in the share of the vote received by Congress (I) in 1982 highlights how real this threat to the CPM continues to be. Even minor rearrangements in electoral alliances could hurt the CPM considerably in the future. Any potential future alliance between "bourgeois" parties is thus very much a part of the CPM's overall calculations regarding how to consolidate its power. The large number of ministries offered to other parties of the left front indicate this electoral vulnerability. In spite of these reservations, however, the repeated victories have been a heady experience. For the first time in its history, the CPM has won clear majorities enabling it to form and sustain a government free of united-front entanglements.

The factors underlying the CPM's success in part reflect its own widening political base and in part the failure of other parties. In the aftermath of the emergency, the Janata party cut deeply into the Congress' support. As these two split the votes, the CPM was the beneficiary. Furthermore, having aligned itself with the Congress during the emergency, the CPI lost its credibility and electoral support. As the opposition lay in tatters, the CPM emerged as the major political force in West Bengal. The CPM's own political work contributed further to this success. As is known, throughout the early 1970s the left in West Bengal had suffered

Table 3.2	*Changing Strengths of the Major Parties in West Bengal*

Parties	Seats won				
	1967	1969	1971	1977	1982
CPM	43	80	113	177	174
Congress	127	55	105	20	49
CPI	16	30	13	2	7
Janata	—	—	—	29	—
Forward Bloc	13	21	3	25	28
Revolutionary Socialist Party	6	12	3	20	19

Source: compiled from official reports of the Election Commission of India.

harsh political repression.[28] Moreover, because the United-Front government was dismissed, the landlords used this opportunity to reverse many of the fragile social gains of the tenants. Mass evictions of *bargardars*, involving the use of police force, followed.[29] Instead of breaking the CPM's back, political and social repression seems to have strengthened it. According to a party member, "While this repression was let loose, many of us continued, in a quiet way, to spread our propaganda and organize the peasantry. The electoral results bear out that our efforts have borne fruit."[30] While this member may exaggerate the class basis of the CPM's success, the steadily increasing strength of the party (see Table 3.2) is a testimony to the fact that not only has the CPM consolidated its old political base, but it has continued to broaden and deepen it.

Institutional Innovation: The Politicized *Panchayats*

Since coming to power, the CPM has sought to consolidate its rural power base further. In order to incorporate the lower rural classes institutionally, the leadership has undertaken a comprehensive penetration of the countryside. Central to this task are the new politicized *panchayats*. The CPM's decision to allow political-party competition for local government elections constituted a sharp break from past Indian practices. Given that the CPM was in control of the government and that its popularity within West Bengal was widespread, the leadership probably calculated that its own candidates were likely to do well in party-based *panchayat* elections.

28. According to Amnesty International, over 25,000 cadres, mostly of the CPM and the CPML, were in jail in the first half of the seventies. See Marcus Franda, "Rural development, Bengali marxist style," *American Universities Field Staff Reports*, Asia, 15 (1978), 4.
29. Interview, S. Sarkar, Director, Land Revenue and Surveys, West Bengal, Calcutta, March 19, 1979.
30. Interview, Johar Santra (footnote 15).

The calculations were right. Candidates running on CPM tickets won a massive majority in 1978: 87 percent of the seats at the district level (*zila parishad*); 74 percent at the block level (*panchayat samitis*); and 67 percent at the village level (*gram panchayats*).[31]

The results of the 1983 *panchayat* elections were not as impressive for the left as those of 1978. The proportion of seats captured by the left front in the 1983 elections was 73 percent at the district level, 65 percent at the block level, and around 60 percent at the village level.[32] There was therefore a minor but across-the-board decline in support. Two important factors caused this relatively minor decline in the CPM's position. First, there is the natural antipathy toward a ruling party whose performance is continuously under scrutiny. Charges of local corruption have especially hurt the CPM. And second, with the total decline of the Janata party, the Congress' position has been strengthened within West Bengal. The Congress is now the major opposition party. Because opposition votes were not divided up in the last election, the Congress was successful in cutting into the CPM's electoral successes. In spite of the small decline, however, the CPM is still very clearly the dominant political force in West Bengal's local government.

These "red *panchayats*"[33] are important in the CPM's overall political and developmental strategy. Finance Minister Ashok Mitra went as far as to argue that, "if *panchayats* fail, the CPM experiment fails."[34] It is therefore important to analyze this institutional innovation in some detail.

First, what has led the CPM to focus on transforming the local governmental institutions? To answer this, we need to remind ourselves of the CPM's overall goals. Like any political party, the CPM seeks to win and consolidate power. In contrast to most other Indian parties, the CPM intends to accomplish this political goal by building its power base primarily on the lower and lower-middle classes. This necessitates involving these groups in the political process, as well as transferring some of the benefits of power to them. Old institutional arrangements, however, did not facilitate the pursuit of this left-of-center type of politics. Local government in the past had been dominated by propertied elites, and the bureaucracy had repeatedly proven ineffective in implementing reforms. If reformism was the new goal, new institutional mechanisms were needed.

31. Information from the Secretary, Ministry of Panchayat Raj, West Bengal.
32. Information from the same as above. For a discussion of these elections, see Ajit Roy, "West Bengal panchayat elections," *Economic and Political Weekly* (June 25, 1983), 114.
33. The term was coined by Bhabani Sengupta, *CPI-M*, ch. 6. While Sengupta's assessment of the *panchayats* is far too optimistic for the minimal evidence he cites, he nevertheless deserves to be credited with being one of the first to recognize the novelty of the CPM's experiment in West Bengal.
34. Interview, Ashok Mitra (footnote 7).

The CPM had two options: rapid expansion of the party or restructuring of the local government. Communists generally understand better than most the complexities of building and sustaining reliable institutions. The "communist" leaders of Bengal, therefore, probably knew well that rapid expansion would destroy the party as a cohesive and disciplined political force. Instead of attracting loyal and committed cadres, the party would draw opportunists seeking the rewards of power. The party might then grow, but the leadership would not be able to utilize it to translate its goals into effective rural reform. Thus the CPM must have decided to restructure local government. The strategy has been to control the *panchayats* through "CPM sympathizers," while leaving the disciplined party cadres to play the crucial supervisory role over the local governmental institutions.

Who are these "sympathizers" now manning the *panchayats*? The results of my interviews with sixty members of *gram panchayats* are summarized in Table 3.3. Because these interviews were always carried out in group situations, which included members of the local community, it was difficult for the respondents to hide the length of their party involvement, as well as their ownership of land and the mode of land use. Considering, however, that there are about 28,000 members who won *gram panchayat* seats on a CPM ticket, a sample of sixty is by no means representative. The accuracy of the sample is nevertheless somewhat greater than its size would suggest, as a degree of control was built into its selection by choosing areas of CPM strength (Burdwan) and weakness (Midnapore). The emerging profile reveals that the majority elected on a CPM ticket are party sympathizers rather than full members, small landowners rather than landless or sharecroppers, and utilize hired labor to cultivate their lands.

Table 3.3   *Political and Class Profile of the Members of Gram Panchayats*
Table: 3.3 A   *Political Profile*

Relationship with the CPM	Distribution in %
Opportunists[1] (less than two years of party involvement)	13.3
Sympathizers (over two years of party involvement)	58.3
Part-time members (over five years of party work)	21.7
Full-time members (card-carrying members)	6.7

[1] The assumption here is that those who started getting involved with the CPM only after it came to power had opportunistic motivations.

Table 3.3 B   *Vocation*

Type of work	Distribution in %
Agriculturalist	60.1
Landless agricultural laborers	8.3
Non-agriculturalists (mainly teachers and social workers)	31.6

Table 3.3 C   *Land-Ownership*

Size of holding in acres	Distribution in %
0–2	8.3
2–5	69
6–10	19.4
10 and above	2.8

Table 3.3 D   *Mode of Land Use*[1]

Land use	Distribution in %
Only family labor	0
Use hired labor	83.3
Use sharecroppers	16.7

[1] Breakdown is for agriculturalists only (see Table 3.3 B).

A considerable minority are not agriculturalists at all, but rather teachers and social workers. The significance of this minority is greater than the numbers reveal, as the non-agriculturalists were generally more politicized and in positions of leadership within the *panchayats*. Thus, in Midnapore, for example, a survey of 515 *pradhans* (heads of the *gram panchayats*) by the district administration revealed that 217 of them were teachers. Of these, 207 had an educational level of at least a B.A. degree.[35] Being more educated and politicized, rural-based teachers were in positions of *gram panchayat* leadership out of all proportion to their numbers.

This overall profile is consistent with several other pieces of evidence. The District Panchayat Officer in Midnapore estimated the social backgrounds of *gram panchayat* members in his district as follows: 20 percent well-off landowners; 30 percent small farmers; 20 percent landless and *bargardars*; and 30 percent teachers.[36] Considering that his sample

35. Information from District Panchayat Officer, Midnapore, West Bengal.
36. Information from the same as above.

included both CPM and non-CPM *panchayat* members, the higher percentage of well-off landowners here does not really contradict the results of my survey. Confidence in the survey results was also enhanced because the results meshed well with the CPM's criteria for who would be given electoral tickets. As a local committee secretary explained, "Those who were with the movement were given tickets. The candidates were generally from lower peasantry or non-cultivating groups, such as teachers."[37] The predominance of party sympathizers, small landowners and teachers in my sample accords well with these criteria for selection.

At other levels of *panchayats*, the socio-political profile of the members is somewhat different. The *panchayat samiti* (block-level) membership closely parallels the nature of party organization in the block. In well-organized blocks, the *sabhapati* (head of the block *panchayat*) is usually a party member. Midnapore and Burdwan provided contrasting cases. In Midnapore, only eight of the fifty-two *sabhapatis* were party members, while in Burdwan, as many as 70 percent of the blocks were headed by members. These variations, of course, reflect the varying party strength in the two districts. In terms of social composition, however, the membership in both areas was similar: more or less equally divided between small peasantry, middle peasantry, and teachers.[38]

Because the party tends to be deeply entrenched at the district level, the *zila parishad* (district *panchayat*) is very much controlled by prominent party members. From the perspective of this study, however, the district *panchayats* are of lesser interest. Tasks of rural reform have been assigned to lower-level *panchayats*. The block-level *panchayats* are thus in charge of all activities related to land reform. The village-level *panchayats* are in turn responsible for administering the Food-For-Work Program, credit and agricultural inputs for small landholders, and many rural development projects in their respective areas.

Given the social and political composition of the lower-level *panchayats*, what deductions can we make about the functioning of these reconstructed local governmental institutions in the context of reformist rural development? First, the new *panchayats* of Bengal represent a sharp break from the past political patterns in rural India. There may be some similarities between the Bengal pattern and those of other states where middle castes are becoming politically prominent. But these similarities are more superficial than real. The political contribution of middle castes in such states as Uttar Pradesh is to tilt the policy process in favor of commercial agriculture. By contrast, politicized lower-middle classes of

37. Interview, Maujam Hussain (footnote 11).
38. Based on information provided by the offices of the party secretaries of Midnapore and Burdwan respectively.

West Bengal, committed to party goals, represent a qualitatively different pattern. The *panchayat* membership in West Bengal, and in most parts of India (except for, possibly, Kerala), has never been so free of landlord and rich-peasant domination as in contemporary West Bengal. The CPM has thus achieved what no other Indian political force has been able to achieve as yet, namely, comprehensive penetration of the countryside without depending on large landowners. From this perspective, it may not be an exaggeration to argue that the politics of West Bengal are undergoing a fundamental structural change. While the class structure remains intact, not only has institutional penetration been achieved but also institutional power has been transferred from the hands of the dominant propertied groups to a politicized lower-middle strata.

The role of the party in this transition has of course been central. Through its core as well as its auxiliary members, the CPM has combined class with political criteria in selecting its supporters. These supporters, riding the wave of the CPM's popularity, now man the local governments across the province. The resulting penetration is not as deep and as permanent as would follow if all the sympathizers were actually hardened members. The results are nevertheless impressive. First, the new institutional arrangements bypass the traditional pattern of the political elite building their support through the landed notables. And second, the degree of organizational and ideological linkage between the CPM leadership and their supporters in the rural areas is considerably more than often achieved in Indian politics. In other words, the new *panchayats* represent two interlinked patterns of political change: an organizational penetration of the center into the periphery, and a simultaneous shift in the class basis of institutional power.

While structural change may be emphasized in enthusiastic terms, three important qualifications should be noted. First, the change is in the organization of regime power and in the underlying class alliances rather than in the class structure. To what extent a shift in the former can influence the latter is, from the theoretical stance of this study, an empirical question, further examined below. Second, the structural political change is not from the upper to the lower classes, but rather from the former to an in-between group. Nowhere, for example, are the landless or the sharecroppers in prominent political positions. The new office-holders are either from lower-middle peasant backgrounds or from such "petty-bourgeois" backgrounds as teaching. And lastly, the majority of the new office-holders are party supporters rather than party activists. The question for analysis now is this: given that political change is both significant and yet somewhat limited, what is the likely impact of this change on the CPM's capacity to implement policies for the rural poor?

Wherever the party is well-organized, the social origins of *panchayat* members are not likely to be a major impediment to the government's redistribution programs for the rural poor. Several conditions facilitate such an outcome. First, the social backgrounds of political representatives are important, as they sensitize us to the types of interests these actors may bring to bear on their political roles. A communist party seeks to define the roles of its followers in the image of the party. The more disciplined a party, therefore, and the more incorporated political actors are into the party, the less significant are their social backgrounds as guides to their political behavior. As the CPM is a reasonably well-disciplined party, in the areas where party organization is strong, party followers as governmental representatives are likely to comply with leadership directives.

Even where party representatives do not control governmental institutions, and in the lower levels of *panchayats* this is in the majority of cases, the patterned linkages between the party and government are also likely to facilitate compliance. Party members are actively involved in the supervision of the *panchayats*. During my visits to the *panchayats*, it became clear that the major local governmental decisions were made in continuous informal and formal consultation with the local party representatives. If in a given area there were no party members, the block representative attempted to provide the supervisory role. Here, however, the oversight was weaker. Aside from supervision, there are built-in incentives in the current arrangement for the new representatives to comply with the party program. As the new political elite, who have displaced traditional local notables, these *panchayat* members owe their political power to the party. As long as they wish to share the benefits of power, compliance with central directives is likely to be maintained.

All this is not to suggest that the social background of the representatives is inconsequential. If the members were from large land-owning backgrounds, the prospects of implementing redistributive programs through them would not be very good. The lower-middle-class origins of the majority of the representatives are of consequence, as these members are not likely to oppose redistributive programs. Many of these programs will not directly affect the socio-economic interests of the *panchayat* members. Thus, given that the political interests of the new members will be enhanced by pursuing redistribution policies, compliance with the party program is likely. The major exceptions to this will be twofold: less than enthusiastic compliance wherever the party organization is weak; and reluctance to implement those programs that benefit the landless or the sharecroppers at the expense of *all* land-owning groups, including the small and medium landowners.

Party supervision of local governmental activities also minimizes the corrupt and non-developmental waste of scarce public resources. As is well known, local public and bureaucratic officials, in conjunction with local notables, have often in the past frittered away developmental resources. While I am not suggesting that those belonging to the CPM are somehow above these practices, the institutional arrangements of the CPM are aimed at minimizing these problems. These arrangements include close party supervision of *panchayats*, an open accounting system for *panchayats* (all accounts have to be periodically written on blackboards for verification by the community and the party), a shift of developmental resources from the entrenched bureaucracy to the new *panchayats*, and the designation of the local bureaucracy as an executive arm serving the locally elected governments. While the effectiveness of this arrangement is further investigated below, the last point about *panchayat*–bureaucracy relations requires further comment.

Aside from the penetration of the countryside, a related goal of the *panchayats* is to "tame" the local bureaucracy. According to a new law passed in 1977 the bureaucrats at each level — district, block, and village — are from now on to be the executive arm of the parallel, elected governments. The hitherto powerful district commissioners are, in other words, from now on to take their orders from the elected *zila parishad*. Similarly, the activities of such "local czars" as the block development officers and of others such as the junior land-reform officers and the *kanun gos* (local-level administrators) are now to be carried out in close co-operation with the *panchayat samitis* and the *gram panchayats*.

How effective are these attempts to "tame" the bureaucracy likely to be? Given that the power of local bureaucracy has long been considerable, and that it has come to be accepted by the respective communities as such, the transition will have to be sustained for quite some time before significant change is manifest. The key to a long-term shift in authority will be the extent to which the elected officials become full-time office workers, combining the "red" with the "expert." The elected officials already have legal authority over the bureaucrats. Moreover, as the elected officials carry the support of the party in government, the threat of "transfers" is an important power resource in the hands of the political elite. The legal and the informal power resources should therefore allow some compliance from the bureaucrats.

Conversely, however, the well-established bureaucrats possess all the skills for administering a district, or a block, or a village. Political control over the activities of the bureaucrats will necessitate the newly elected representatives gaining considerable familiarity with such bureaucratic tasks as how land records are maintained, how accounts are kept, what the system of files is, and how development projects are designed and co-ordinated. While none of these skills is intrinsically difficult to acquire — especially considering that over 50 percent of the heads of *gram pan-chayats* and 70 percent of the heads of *panchayat samitis* have an education at least to the level of a B.A. degree [39] — they will require full-time work. Full-time work requires that the remuneration is sufficient to sustain it. At present, the remuneration for being a *panchayat* officer is minimal; only party members who receive a regular salary from the party and who double-up as local government officials are likely to be full-time office workers. In the absence of full-time work by elected officials, the bureaucrats are likely to maintain considerable *de facto* power. The "taming" of the bureaucracy, in other words, like the success of many other aspects of the CPM experiment, will remain a function of the further development of the party itself.

In the short run, certain changes are already evident in the political–bureaucratic relationships. At the district level, the web of political control over the district commissioner is growing. While the district commissioners are in part always beholden to local political leaders, especially the Legislative Assembly members, in West Bengal they also now have to pay attention to the district party leaders and the elected *zila parishad* officials. A significant consequence of this increased control has been the changing use of police to quell "civil disturbances." By influencing the district commissioner's rulings on when the police may or may not be used to settle civil disputes, the CPM has sought to neutralize the police as a tool of landlord interest. This has been especially important in tilting the power balance in many of the conflicts between landlords and share-croppers over the share of crop at harvesting time. [40]

At lower levels of bureaucracy also, established bureaucrats were disgruntled with "political interference" in their work. [41] This was a good indicator of the curtailment of their powers. The *panchayat samitis* are already working closely with the land-reform bureaucracy in deciding issues of possession and distribution of surplus land. In conjunction with the party members and the Kisan Sabha, the block-level members are also working with the *kanun gos* in the registration of *bargardars*. At the village level, the power of the bureaucracy is being curtailed by transfer-

---

39. Based on information from District Panchayat Officers of Midnapore and Burdwan, West Bengal.
40. This is necessarily based on the impressions I gained during my village-level research in both Burdwan and Midnapore. The conclusion should therefore be qualified by (1) emphasizing its impressionistic nature; and (2) noting the limits of my sample. This issue of the role of police is further discussed under the section on the "operation *barga*" below.
41. Based on interviews with block-level and lower-level bureaucrats.

ring programs formerly administered by it to the new *panchayats*. Though the consequences of these changes are discussed below, it is necessary here to repeat a qualification on the nature of the change itself: the changes are more significant in areas with a strong party organization and less so where it is weak.

To summarize the discussion on *panchayats*, the politicization of *panchayats* in West Bengal is aimed at a purposive penetration of the countryside. The purpose is to bring lower and lower-middle rural classes within the influence of the party. It is hoped that by increasing the role of these classes in the governing institutions, as well as by transferring some benefits of development to them, the party position will be strengthened. The past patterns of rural power have involved the political leaders, bureaucrats, and landowners in a tacit pact of domination. The new ruling alliance seeks to diversify this pattern by isolating the significance of the landed to the social sphere, by taming the bureaucracy, and by recasting local government to enhance the political role of hitherto excluded social groups. *Panchayats* are an integral part of this new pattern of rule. As institutions, however, not only are they new and fragile, but they are also manned by small landowning groups instead of the poorest of the poor. A similar social basis of power has been noted for the party and the Kisan Sabha. Given that the CPM regime wishes to pursue anti-poverty policies, the question follows as to the capacity of the given political arrangements to facilitate a redistributive orientation. I now turn my attention to an analysis of this issue.

The Attack on Rural Poverty

The CPM regime has utilized its political organization to improve the living conditions of the rural poor. The attack on poverty is multi-pronged. Some programs have been accorded priority; some are also more successful than others. While the short-term results are less than spectacular, some concrete achievements have been made, and the foundations for systematic reforms are being laid. If sustained over time, these efforts promise to mitigate rural poverty by planned political intervention. In what follows, I analyze the CPM's attempts to implement three major programs: land reforms, especially tenancy reform; programs for small farmers, mainly credit for sharecroppers; and employment and wage schemes for the landless laborers. The analysis focuses on the links between political organization and these redistribution programs.

In order to appreciate and understand the attempted solutions, it is first important to get some sense of the nature of the poverty problem in West Bengal. In general the problem is both massive and complex. The per-

Table 3.4 *Distribution of Land in West Bengal by Size Class of Operational Holdings, 1953-1972*

Size class of household operational holding (in acres)	1953-1954		1961-1962		1971-1972	
	Percentage of households	Percentage of area operated	Percentage of households	Percentage of area operated	Percentage of households	Percentage of area operated
"Landless"[1]	0.89⎤	—	33.9⎤	—	30.94⎤	—
	⎰48.55		⎰48.6		⎰50.74	
0.005–1	47.66⎦	3.90	14.7⎦	2.3	19.80⎦	4.34
1–2.5	16.61	10.49	16.90	11.50	22.42	20.45
2.5–5	17.52	23.27	19.70	27.90	15.77	28.94
5–10	12.15	31.38	12.40	32.20	8.95	31.05
10–20	4.14	20.78	3.80	19.10	1.87	12.32
20 and above	1.031	11.18	0.70	6.60	0.25	2.90

[1] The drastic change in the numbers of the "landless" between 1953-4 and 1961-2 reflects a change in survey procedure.

Source: Government of India, *National Sample Survey*, Eighth Round for 1953-4, Seventeenth Round for 1961-2 and Twenty-Sixth Round for 1971-2.

centage of the rural population living in conditions of poverty has for decades hovered around the 65 percent mark.[42] This contrasts with the all-India average of about 45-50 percent (Table 2.5). The overall inequalities as measured by the Gini coefficient of consumption patterns also reflect little change in the pattern over the last two decades.[43]

Data on access to land (Table 3.4) reveal that, over the years, larger landholdings have been breaking down. This reflects several trends at work. Under the pressure of land laws, large holdings have often been divided among family members or broken up and sold in parcels. Inheritance laws further tend to divide up landholdings. While these trends contribute to the breakup of large holdings, they do not necessarily mean gains for the lower rural classes, nor do these trends mean that the family incomes of large landholders necessarily decrease (as supported by the unchanging patterns of inequality of consumption). The breakup of the old *zamindaris* has probably also contributed to the above trend. That the breakup of the largest estates did not reach the rural poor is, in turn, made clear by the fact that, at the bottom end of the scale, the percentage of the landless and the marginal peasants (taken together) has, if anything, continued to increase. At over 50 percent of the rural population, this combined group comprises the bulk of the rural poor.

In terms of land use, while the overall tenancy has declined over the years, sharecropping has increased in comparison to fixed-rent tenancy

42. See Ahluwalia, "Rural poverty."   43. *Ibid*.

Table 3.5   *Changes in Tenancy in West Bengal, 1953-1971*

Year	% of cultivated area under tenancy	Area under sharecropping as a % of area under all forms of tenancy[1]
1953–4	25.43	89.57
1960–1	17.65	92.53
1970–1	18.73	96.44

[1.] Includes sharecropping and fixed-rent tenancy.
Source: adapted from Pranab Bardhan, "Variations in extent and forms of agricultural tenancy," *Economic and Political Weekly*, 18, (September 11, 1976).

Table 3.6   *Structure of Leasing in West Bengal, 1953-1972*

Size of operational holding (in acres)	1953-1954		1971-1972	
	% of households operating leased land	% of area "leased in"	% of households operating leased land	% of area "leased in"
0–1	46.6	4.6	18.9	5
1–2.5	15.8	11.4	38.6	29.2
2.5–5	19.7	29.8	29.7	37.1
5–10	14.4	39.1	11.3	24.1
10–20	2.9	11.9	1.2	3.1
20 and above	0.5	3.1	0.2	1.5

Source: Government of India, *National Sample Survey*, Eighth Round for 1953-4 and Twenty-Sixth Round for 1971-2.

(Table 3.5). Sharecropping now constitutes nearly 96 percent of overall tenancy and is virtually the only form of tenancy in West Bengal. While the majority of the sharecroppers operate holdings of less than 2.5 acres, a considerable amount of leased land is operated by sharecroppers with access to larger landholdings (Table 3.6). This suggests that though the majority of the sharecroppers have low incomes from the small areas they cultivate, a significant minority may be better off than the poorest of the poor. As sharecropping arrangements have tended to be informal and variable, the lack of security of tenure is the other social problematic aspect of their existence.

What these data reveal is that as much as 65 percent of the rural population continues to live in conditions of abject poverty in West Bengal. Most of these poor are the landless agricultural laborers, marginal peasants, and sharecroppers. Moreover, there have been no dramatic changes in these conditions over time. In the face of this poverty profile, it would take a callous ideologue to argue that higher rates of economic growth will somehow solve the poverty problem in and of itself. Con-

Table 3.7   *Food and Rice Production in West Bengal, 1961-1981*

Period	Average food production (million tons)	Average rice production (million tons)
1961–6	54.4	49.6
1966–71	63.5	55.1
1971–6	74.7	61.9
1976–81	78.3	65.8

Source: Government of West Bengal, Directorate of Agriculture, *Estimates of area and production of principal crops in West Bengal* (Calcutta, 1982).

Table 3.8   *Annual Rates of Growth in West Bengal, 1961-1981*

Growth rates in:	Annual rate (%)
Food production	2.9
Rice production	2.2
Rice acreage	0.8
Rice productivity	1.4

Source: Government of West Bengal, Directorate of Agriculture, *Estimates of area and production of principal crops in West Bengal.*

versely, it would take a romantic ideologue to suggest that redistribution of assets would largely eliminate rural poverty.

Prior to the analysis of reforms, it should also be noted that there is no obvious evidence within West Bengal to suggest a decline in food production. The agricultural growth rates have continued to hover around 3 percent. This was the case prior to the CPM coming to power, and has remained so since. As Table 3.7 documents, food production in general, and rice production in particular, have steadily increased. And as Table 3.8 suggests, the bulk of this increase stems from improvements in productivity. There is therefore no reason as yet to fear that the CPM's reform programs have been detrimental to the growth process.[44]

Land Reforms

Once in power, the CPM faced the option of focusing its efforts either on the redistribution of "above ceiling" surplus lands or on tenancy reform. During its first term the leadership chose to concentrate on "operation *barga* [sharecropping]," a form of tenancy reform aimed at improving the conditions of the *bargardars*. In order to analyze why this choice was

44. For further evidence generally supportive of this conclusion, see James K. Boyce, "Agricultural growth in West Bengal, 1949-50 to 1980-81: a review of the evidence," *Economic and Political Weekly* (Review of Agriculture), 19, 13 (1984), A9-A16.

made, one has to first understand the reluctance of the leadership to tackle the issue of surplus land.

As is known, the legislation prescribing limits on land ownership has not been successfully implemented in West Bengal (or in any part of India for that matter). According to Binoy Chowdhry, the Minister of Land Revenue, the lowering of ceilings in 1972 should have resulted in as much as 3 million acres of surplus land available for redistribution in West Bengal.[45] In actuality, however, less than 40,000 acres have been successfully redistributed.[46] Even this has not always reached the needy. An understanding of why this has happened, and with what consequences, is essential for comprehending the difficulties of dealing with the land redistribution problem in the current context.

Land-ceiling laws have occasionally led landowners to sell their lands, or, more often, to transfer them legally to various real or imagined individuals and organizations, while maintaining *de facto* control over their property. In addition, the land records in West Bengal, due to the historical conditions of the *zamindari* system, are of very poor quality. As a consequence, under the current conditions, it is impossible to locate the surplus land by legal and bureaucratic means. This is especially problematic because local bureaucrats are often easily bribed to falsify land records. From a legal perspective one might therefore conclude that there is little or no surplus land available for the West Bengal government to acquire. From a more political standpoint, however, there is as much as 2-2.5 million acres of "above ceiling" land currently held as *benami* land. The complexity of *benami* land can best be exemplified by some of the actual cases I encountered during my research:[47]

Case 1, Balichak Area, Midnapore.
The big landlord family is an old *zamindari* family. Fifteen to twenty years back they used to own 500 acres. Now they own 270 acres. The rest they have sold. Of the land they have kept 150 acres is between the four sons and held *benami*; 120 acres is kept as religious land. All four sons are in business. One is a well-known cinema producer in Calcutta. He was also the *anchal pradhan* (head of local government) in the ex-Congress government. The second son had a rice mill in Balichak, but was killed in 1970 by the Naxalites. Two other sons own a cinema and live in Balichak. Two managers live in the old mansion. Seventy to eighty *bargardars* work the land. They also live on the family property.

45. Interview, Binoy Chowdhry (footnote 6).
46. The figures refer to land distributed under the Land Reforms Act. See, Government of West Bengal, *Land reforms in West Bengal, a statistical report* (Land Revenue Department: Calcutta, 1981).
47. The cases are based on information gathered from local party cadres and *panchayat* members in the respective areas. The information was often checked for accuracy in conversations with other members of the local community.

Case 2, Daspur Area, Midnapore.
A money-lending family. They own 44 acres. Father is dead. Two sons own 22 acres between them. The mother and the third son also own 22 acres. Two of the sons work in the city. Most of the land is on *barga*. Some land is under the personal supervision of the third son. He uses hired labor.

Case 3, Kaksha Area, Burdwan.
Nine *jotedars* (landlords) are in possession of 3000 acres. Five of these use *bargardars* and hired labor. Some of them have additional urban incomes. One of them has many contracts in bus routes. His brother-in-law was an M.L.A. in the Congress government. Four landlords use hired labor. Most of the land is *benami*.

All of these cases are fairly typical and represent varying situations within which land that was formerly surplus (land over 15 acres for a family of 5) is now held on to as *benami* land. If the CPM government ever hopes to acquire this land, several implications for action are clear from the nature of the land situation itself. First of all, new legislation will be needed to make *benami* land illegal. This will require making many past transactions retroactively illegal and redefining the "family" in a much stricter sense. Such legislation, now passed by the CPM government, awaits approval from the Indian Central Government.[48]

In addition to new legislation, the implementation of these laws will not be possible through the established bureaucracy. It would have to involve the active participation of the local population. Aside from the issue of mobilized political support, community participation will be necessary for identifying *benami* land and the prospective beneficiaries. Because attempts to establish local land-reform committees are bound to resemble a revolutionary situation that might bring about central intervention, the CPM was reluctant in its first term to move in this direction. At the time of writing this, however, the CPM was seriously considering this policy option.

Finally, the active involvement of the citizenry in property redistribution is an inherently volatile task. It is likely to release considerable pent-up frustrations, including "excesses." If constitutional limits of "property and order" are to be observed, any mobilization effort will also have to be controlled. Controlled mobilization is, however, fraught with difficulties. It requires a large number of loyal and disciplined cadres, who combine the functions of information-supply and mobilization, and who are also close followers of party directives. Because the CPM does not possess a party structure of this nature, it is probably wise of the leadership to have avoided tackling the issue of redistribution of surplus land so far.

Whether the CPM will in the future make a concerted effort to acquire

48. Interview, Binoy Chowdhry (footnote 6).

benami land remains unclear. While the party development remains uneven, the new *panchayats* enhance the CPM's capacity to combine centralization and decentralization aimed at reform. In order to strengthen this new political arrangement, however, the CPM is moving slowly. The *panchayat samitis* already have land-reform committees working closely with the junior land-reform officers in the block offices. However, this work is aimed, not at acquiring new land, but at identifying beneficiaries of the land already in the possession of the state. Both Binoy Chowdhry and Ashok Mitra argued that this will be a "learning experience" for the *panchayats*.[49] The new legislation is now in the works, presumably to be implemented once the center approves. The slow movement towards the issue of land redistribution has, of course, invoked criticism from both the left (not fast enough!) and the right (moving toward a dangerous law-and-order situation!).[50] A more objective perspective regarding the CPM, however, must note its political maturity in slowly testing the "feasibility frontier,"[51] rather than running headlong into adventurous schemes.

While the CPM regime has only cautiously proceeded on the issue of *benami* land, it has undertaken a concerted effort to register the sharecroppers. A registered sharecropper can enjoy legal protection already on the books for sharecroppers, including security of tenure and modified "rents." In the past these protections have not been very effective, owing to the informal nature of much tenancy. The burden of proof that a tenant was indeed a legal tenant, and thus protected by tenancy laws, has hitherto been on the tenant himself. Sharecropping laws have therefore been inherently biased against the sharecroppers. This legal bias has also been reinforced by socio-economic inequalities. Because the sharecroppers often depend on the goodwill of the landowner for their livelihood, it is understandable that they are reluctant to invoke the wrath of these landowners by pursuing legalistic demands. In the past the landlord–sharecropper relationship has therefore been marked by an insecurity of tenure and levels of rent that many would consider exploitative.

To alter these conditions, the CPM has thrown the weight of the party and the state behind the sharecroppers. Once in power, the CPM government moved quickly to amend the land-reform laws in order to transfer the burden of proof regarding who is a sharecropper to the landowners. Under this new amendment one who claims to be a sharecropper has the legal rights of a sharecropper until a landlord can prove to the contrary in

---

49. Same interviews as in footnotes 6 and 7 above.
50. For a "left" critique, see Ashok Rudra, "Two steps backward;" the "right" critique can often be seen in such newspapers as *The Statesman*.
51. The useful metaphor was suggested by Ashok Mitra, see footnote 7 above.

the courts.[52] Such laws are generally within the jurisdiction of the provincial governments. In this case, however, the Governor of West Bengal, an authority more closely associated with the center than with the CPM, decided that this amendment needed presidential approval. The bias of the Central Government of India towards the propertied and against both the CPM and the lower classes was clearest in the reluctance of the President to sign this amendment. It took the center six months to give the presidential approval, a time period long enough to allow the eviction of quite a few tenants by landowners.[53]

In the wake of this new law, the CPM has undertaken an intensive drive to register sharecroppers across the state. Termed "operation *barga*," the program has sought (1) to identify areas with a concentration of sharecroppers; (2) to send in teams of bureaucrats and members of the party and Kisan Sabha to meet, inform, and politicize the sharecroppers; and (3) eventually, after field verification and other actions, to register sharecroppers as legal sharecroppers. Once they are registered, it is hoped that the vulnerability of the *bargardars* to eviction will be reduced. It is further hoped that over a longer period of time an improved incentive structure will contribute both to rising incomes and agrarian productivity.

How well has "operation *barga*" worked? As all measures of success are relative, the CPM's accomplishments have to be put in perspective. Less than 60,000 sharecroppers were registered over the last three decades in West Bengal. In about five years, however, the CPM regime has succeeded in registering over 1.2 million *bargardars*.[54] Compared to the past performance of the Congress and other governments in the area, therefore, the CPM's current success is spectacular. Had this type of program been undertaken in a concerted manner by past regimes, the living conditions of Bengal's *bargardars* might well have already undergone some important improvements. In the light of this evidence, I have come to the view that, if sustained, the CPM's programs promise to have a long-term impact on the living conditions of the rural poor. However, when the record is compared to the size of the problem — there may be 1.5 to 2 million tenant families in West Bengal[55] — one's enthusiasm has to be restrained. More important here than the assessment of success, how-

---

52. The new act was passed in September 1977. As the presidential assent, however, took six months, it was officially announced in *The Calcutta Gazette*, West Bengal Act XXXIV, only on February 3, 1978.
53. Interview, D. Bandopadhyay, Land Reforms Commissioner, West Bengal, November 2, 1981.
54. See Government of West Bengal, *Land reforms in West Bengal, statistical report VII* (Board of Revenue: Calcutta, 1982).
55. Interview, Binoy Chowdhry (footnote 6).

ever, is the analysis of conditions that have facilitated or hindered "operation *barga.*"

A seemingly simple task of registering sharecroppers strikes at some of the fundamentals of the traditional rural social structure. The act of registration involves state intervention in and modification of long-established social relations. This intervention is, moreover, aimed at modifying the inegalitarian relationship between the landowners and the sharecroppers. The new laws aim to reduce the landowners' control of and income from their property, while increasing the rights and income of those who work the land — the sharecroppers. Such a change from above is resisted by the landowners and is only hesitatingly embraced by the sharecroppers. While the resistance of the landowners is understandable, that of the sharecroppers requires comment.

The sharecroppers depend on landlords' goodwill for their livelihood. While an opportunity to improve one's socio-economic status is a powerful motivating force, an uncertainty about whether or not the change will lead to improvement remains an obstacle. Because what is offered is mere registration, without any convincing guarantees that access to land will continue uninterrupted, "rational" calculations lead the *bargardar* to approach the offers of political outsiders with hesitation. The rational is, moreover, buttressed by the traditional. Pre-capitalist social relations are built around bonds of reciprocity. The resulting value system does not easily legitimize a straightforward calculated pursuit of gain, especially if it is at the expense of those with whom there are some ties. The reluctance of the *bargardars* to embrace the CPM's programs enthusiastically are thus rooted in both rational and traditional considerations.

The emphasis on a reluctance built into the social structure is not to suggest that under the right conditions, the reluctance does not dissolve, leading to a wholehearted embrace of change. These right conditions in West Bengal, however, have to be created politically. Here we do not have a case of widespread class conflict, upon the backs of which the communists can ride. Rather, reformist change is being politically generated. The interaction of social–structural conditions with the party, the government, and the bureaucracy therefore deserves further analysis.

The CPM regime has utilized both the bureaucracy and the party (including the Kisan Sabha) to implement "operation *barga.*" The bureaucratic half of the program is under the jurisdiction of a senior civil servant with impeccable credentials in implementing land reforms.[56] Because the

---

56. The individual in question is D. Bandopadhyay. He made his reputation as an effective land reformer under Hare Krishna Konar. Then he moved to New Delhi for a while. Once the CPM ministry was formed in West Bengal, Mr Bandopadhyay was especially asked back to help implement the new government's programs.

senior civil servant was appointed especially for the implementation of land reforms, continuous momentum for "operation *barga*" is generated from the top. The next rung of relevant civil servants are the Assistant District Magistrates (ADMs) in charge of land reforms and land settlement at the district level. Most of these are young officers of the Indian Administrative Services (IAS). They think of their positions as temporary and so their primary consideration is task completion as a means of upward mobility. There was no evidence of obstruction of or enthusiasm for "operation *barga*" at this level. The primary job of the ADMs was to instruct the lower-level bureaucrats how to conduct the program and then to continue supervising it. From the available evidence, this work seemed to be effectively in progress.[57]

The point here is that the upper echelons of the bureaucracy do not create hurdles in the implementation of "operation *barga*." The same, however, cannot be claimed for the lower-level bureaucrats. The lower-level members of the land bureaucracy — the *kanun gos*, and *amins*, and the Junior Land Reform Officers (JLROs) — generally make up the field staff. The field staff is in charge of camping in selected village areas, clarifying the new laws in public forums, urging the sharecroppers to come forward to register, explaining the benefits, verifying from the local sources the validity of claims and counter-claims, and, finally, registering the sharecroppers of the area.

It is during this phase of the operation that there is considerable opportunity for both corruption and class bias. The local bureaucrats often have strong local connections, including well-entrenched relationships with the landowners. Many field officers I interviewed expressed their personal dissent regarding the new laws, arguing that the rights of the landowners should be taken into consideration. Moreover, as a group, these are the same officers who have in the past repeatedly colluded with landowners to foil attempted land redistribution. It would be naive to believe that they have all turned over a new leaf under the CPM regime, and are now enthusiastically implementing reformist change. Party cadres repeatedly complained about corruption and the class bias of the administration. While some of these complaints were self-serving — and there was little evidence to support this at the upper levels of bureaucracy — at lower levels the party perspective indeed had a ring of truth.

This is not to suggest that in the absence of bureaucratic hurdles "operation *barga*" would have been considerably more successful. It would have made some difference, but the primary variable in the success of

57. This conclusion is based on long interviews with the ADMs in Burdwan and Midnapore. This information was further confirmed by the potential "adversaries" of the ADMs, namely, the members of the respective *zila parishads*.

implementation is not the bureaucracy, but rather the party. In my visits to the "operation *barga*" sites, it became clear that wherever the party or the Kisan Sabha had carried out prolonged propaganda and organization work, the *bargardars* were more willing to come forward to register. The prior politicization increases the sense of efficacy, while reducing the fear of dependence in the *bargardars*. Moreover, visible party presence, now perceived as the presence of state power, created a sense of sustained external support. In a local struggle involving inherently unequal social actors, sustained external support on the side of the underdog was essential to modify the power balance. Active party involvement further minimized bureaucratic corruption while short-circuiting the bureaucrat–landlord alliance. In other words, the role of the party was central in overcoming socio-structural and bureaucratic obstacles, enabling the government's reformist intervention to achieve a modicum of success.

Because the party organization and presence is uneven within West Bengal, so was the success of "operation *barga*." Where the party is strong, the program was doing well; where the party is weak, the success was more limited. For example, during my visits, the registration drive was considerably more successful in the districts of Burdwan and Twenty-Four Parganas, areas with strong party presence, than in a weak party area, namely, Murshidabad. The ratio of registered *bargardars* to the agrarian population was 0.133 for Burdwan, 0.115 for Twenty-Four Parganas, and only 0.084 for Murshidabad.[58]

Members of the land bureaucracy in West Bengal often attributed the problems of "operation *barga*" to the "middle peasant" nature of the CPM's rural support.[59] The argument was that members of both the Kisan Sabha and the new *panchayats* owned land and used sharecroppers to have it cultivated. As such, the argument continued, the party's own supporters were not backing a program that would undermine their interests. I did not find evidence in support of this argument. While many members of the Kisan Sabha and the new *panchayats* own land, they are mostly smallholders. In the majority of the cases, the mode of land use was not sharecropping but personal supervision with hired labor. (see Table 3.3). The more prominent members of the *panchayats* are often not even agriculturalists, but rural-based teachers and social workers. To the

---

58. Based on "operation *barga*" statistics provided by the Government of West Bengal, *Land reforms in West Bengal* (1982), and agricultural working population figures (cultivators and agricultural laborers) from Government of West Bengal, *Economic review, 1978-9, statistical appendix* (Calcutta, 1979), Table 2.4.
59. This almost appeared to be the bureaucratic line on "operation *barga*." Senior civil servants like D. Bandopadhyay (footnote 53) and S. Sarkar, Director of Land Surveys, West Bengal, both stressed it during interviews. It was also repeated at lower levels of bureaucracy.

extent, then, that the social origins of the CPM's rural support add a class bias to the party, one has to conclude that the bias is more likely to be against the landless laborers (against higher wages) and not against share-croppers or the issue of land redistribution. Even this conclusion would rest on a too-simplistic view of political behavior resulting primarily from class interests; it would ignore issues of political interests and ideological commitment.

The members of the party and the bureaucracy blamed each other for the shortcomings, while claiming the successes. The evidence suggests a more complex pattern at work. The obstacles are rooted in the social structure, the lower level of bureaucracy, and the uneven development of the party. Conversely, the forces pushing toward success are the result of momentum generated by the top government leaders and bureaucrats, as well as by the action of the party and the Kisan Sabha. The role of the party itself was central. Because party development is uneven, so is the success of "operation *barga*."

Knowing the problems of the lower-level bureaucracy and the uneven development of the party, the CPM leadership has undertaken the recon-struction of the *panchayats*. The role of the *panchayats* in the "operation *barga*," however, has not been significant. This is mainly due to the new-ness of the *panchayats*. "Operation *barga*" got under way about the same time as the elections for the *panchayats* were being held (summer 1978). "Operation *barga*" has involved both political and administrative compo-nents. The political and mobilization tasks have so far been the responsi-bility of the party, while the legal and administrative tasks have been handled by the bureaucracy. In other words, the implementation of "op-eration *barga*" has involved both the "red" and the "expert" roles. In their early life, the *panchayat* members are neither all that "red," nor to any degree "expert." As the institutional development of the *panchayats* proceeds, they are likely to become active in various land-reform activities. In this early intensive drive to register sharecroppers, however, their role has not been all that significant.

The partial success in registering West Bengal's sharecroppers has thus resulted from the manner in which the CPM authorities have used regime power. Once in control, the leadership has utilized both the party and the governmental resources to implement "operation *barga*." The party's capacity (1) to penetrate the countryside without being co-opted by the landed classes and (2) to facilitate controlled mobilization of the share-croppers to buttress state power for reform has been the decisive variable in success. Social reform has been, in other words, a function of the nature of the regime controlling state power.

The next issue that needs to be investigated is the impact of registration on the actual living conditions of the sharecroppers. The issue is complex, in part because improvements in living conditions manifest themselves over a long time, and in part because improvements involve tangible and intangible changes. Psychological gains from increased security of tenure, a sense of efficacy in the local community, absence of fear and dependence on local notables, and substitution of independent social action for the ethos of servitude are all significant but difficult to measure and therefore difficult to assess in a concrete manner. The suggestion is not that all these changes are occurring and that the only problem is their measurement and documentation. Rather the point is that, if politicization is sustained and if the state support for the underprivileged is maintained, both material and non-material improvements in the living conditions of the *bargardars* are likely to result.

In order to assess the changes in economic conditions, I surveyed 300 registered sharecropper households. These households were spread over three districts: Twenty-Four Parganas, Burdwan, and Midnapore. Once again, this is by no means a statistically representative sample of West Bengal. It nevertheless provides a good indication of how the reform measures have or have not been working at the ground level. The results are reported in Table 3.9. They broadly tend to support the conclusion that CPM's "operation *barga*" has had a considerable positive impact on living conditions of the poor sharecroppers.

Questions 1, 2 and 3 of the survey help chart out a profile of who has been affected most by the reform measures. The majority among those who have lost control of their lands — nearly 80 percent — were absentee landlords (see question 3, Table 3.9). Those gaining control in turn are largely small and marginal peasants — 85 percent own less than 1 acre of their own land (question 2, Table 3.9). The amount of land these marginal peasants have secured access to is also relatively small — less than 1 acre for 66 percent and between 1 and 2 acres for an additional 25 percent (question 1, Table 3.9). It is thus fair to conclude that the CPM's reforms have hurt absentee landowners while benefiting the insecure sharecroppers. The reason to highlight such a simple conclusion with data is the rarity of such an outcome within India.

Questions 4, 6 and 7 refer to the problem of debt and are discussed below. What is most important for the immediate discussion are the results to question 5. This question was aimed at finding out what had happened to the share of the crop since registration. As the result indicates, the crop share has increased since registration in nearly 70 percent of the cases. For the majority of these cases, this increase has been from an even sharing of the crop between the sharecropper and the landowner to the sharecropper now keeping the legal share of 75 percent. This shift

Table 3.9   *The Impact of "Operation Barga": Household Survey of Registered Sharecroppers*

Question	Tabulated answers		
1. How much sharecropping land did you register?	*Below 1 acre*	*1-2 acres*	*2-5 acres*
	66%	25%	9%
2. Do you own any land other than the land held under a sharecropping agreement?	*No*	*Yes*	
		Under 1 acre	*More than 1 acre*
	37%	49%	14%
3. Where does the landowner live?		*In or around the village*	*Elsewhere*
		19%	81%
	Before registration		*After registration*
4. Did the landowner provide any inputs?	*Yes*	*No*	*Yes*	*No*
	14%	86%	3%	97%
5. How is the output shared?	*Before registration[1]*		*After registration[1]*
	50-50	*60-40*	*50-50*	*60-40*	*75-25*
	87%	13%	32%	2%	66%
6. Have you taken out a loan?	*Yes*		*No*
	36%		64%
7. If yes to no. 6, how did you use the loan?	*Family maintenance*		*Investment*
	28%		72%

[1.] The first share figure refers to the share of the sharecropper. For example, "60-40" refers to 60 percent of the share belonging to the sharecropper and 40 percent to the landowner. *Source:* based on a survey of 300 households in the districts of Twenty-Four Parganas, Burdwan, and Midnapore. The surveys were carried out in July–Sept 1983. I would like to acknowledge the valuable help of Dr. Sajal Basu in supervising the surveys in Burdwan and Midnapore. I did the survey in Twenty-Four Parganas.

constitutes a remarkable improvement in the incomes of sharecroppers.

For those who can prove their *bargardar* status, the new laws stipulate the ratio of crop sharing. Most sharecroppers used to pay higher than the legal shares, and their registration has now freed them from the old arrangements. What has caused the old arrangements to snap is, of course, not the mere shift in legal status. It is rather the process of politicization whereby the sharecroppers came to understand the law, got closer to the party, and took the final and important step of coming forward to register. An act of defiance against the traditional patron, this act itself did more to help implement the sharecropping laws than the refined qualities of the laws.

In some areas of West Bengal, the party and the government did not have to intervene significantly to facilitate implementation. The southern tracts of Twenty-Four Parganas, for example, have had a long history of sharecropper activism. Starting from the days of the Tebhaga movement,[60] the sharecroppers have long held a view that they are paying an unfair proportion to the landowner. This local sense of justice, born out of memory of historical peasant movements, itself facilitated rapid implementation of the new laws. Once the laws were proclaimed and registration completed, most sharecroppers — who are CPM activists in any case — tended to hold on to their larger shares.

Sustained party and governmental actions have further contributed to the implementation of crop-sharing laws in other parts of West Bengal.[61] In case of any dispute between the sharecropper and the landlord, the sharecropper can now deposit the landlord's legal share with the local bureaucracy, get a receipt, and be free of any legal obligations. The landlord can then collect his share from the bureaucracy. The local police have moreover been instructed by the government at minimum to refrain from taking sides with the landlords and, at maximum, to provide the *bargardars* with protection in conflicts over crop-sharing and disputes over evictions.[62] Wherever the landlords have hired their own "thugs" to settle conflicts by force, the party has attempted to counter by militant mobilization. In an area of Burdwan, for example, where a landlord shot and injured a sharecropper, the party mobilized 5000 supporters within twenty-four hours. These supporters supervised and shouted slogans as the crop was cut, the share divided, and each party — the injured sharecropper and the landlord — given his legal portion. The landlord also

60. For a discussion, see Hamza Alavi, "Peasants and revolution," in Gough and Sharma (eds.), *Revolution in South Asia*, esp. pp. 321-5.
61. I did, however, find one piece of evidence which would contradict the thrust of this argument. Of the 300 sharecroppers I interviewed, 100 were in Burdwan. The share these registered sharecroppers were keeping was often no more than half. As the party organization is quite strong in Burdwan, one wonders why the government's stipulated laws are not being implemented there. As the sample in each district was quite random, I have chosen to put greater thrust in the overall results than in a part of the sample.
62. Thus from a memorandum forwarded by the Office of the Board of Revenue to all land administrators, including the District Policy Officers, clauses 4 and 12 are worth quoting in full. Clause 4: "Where the dispute is between the landowner and the recorded *bargardar*, the latter should receive full protection from the administration in harvesting the crop and getting proper share of the produce." Clause 12: "Government expects that the functionaries at all levels in the district administration should act impartially. They should always bear in mind that the weaker sections of the community who have so far been deprived of and denied their legitimate rights and privileges are given full benefits and protection that they are entitled to under various laws." See Government of West Bengal, *Guidelines for the settlement of harvesting disputes — protection of bargardars and assignees of vested land* (Office of the Board of Revenue: Calcutta, 1978).

backed off from his insistence on evicting the specific sharecropper.[63]

The political message for all concerned is increasingly clear. The CPM intends to take both its legal and its distributive roles seriously. Mobilization power can be generated, but it is controlled mobilization. As in the incident above, mobilization led neither to vengeance, nor to a grabbing of land. As excesses were avoided and only laws implemented, the CPM remained very much within its constitutional limits. At the same time, however, it effectively neutralized elements of the old alliance of domination between landlords, police, and the local thugs. It was therefore not surprising to notice that the majority of the registered sharecroppers had increased their share of the yearly crop. So effective has been the CPM's strategy of controlled mobilization, that the last few years of harvesting (1977-81) have been the most peaceful ones in a long time. Even some landlords I interviewed were appreciative of the CPM for bringing harvesting violence, a major problem in the past, under control.

For *the bargardars*, increased incomes, security, and political efficacy have been the important positive consequences of registration. Some critics have suggested that such gains must be weighed against the disruptive consequences.[64] One common criticism focuses on the consequences of the breakdown of the old nexus of goodwill between the *bargardars* and the landowners. *Bargardars*, it has been argued, used to depend on the landowners for timely credit and crucial agrarian inputs (implements, seeds, bullocks, fertilizer, etc.). While the *bargardars* often paid exploitative rates for these goods and services, the critical argument continues, they were at least in the past assured of their timely availability. State intervention in this relationship has undermined the past elements of reciprocity. What has come into place instead is a somewhat hostile — some may say contractual — relationship. The registered sharecroppers must therefore increasingly fend for themselves. This transition from a somewhat protected, pre-commercial environment to struggling in a market-like environment is, in the short-run at least, a difficult one. The psychological costs involved are compounded by the concrete problems of how to secure timely credit and inputs.

---

63. The incident occurred in a village in Kalna I block of Burdwan. The various events were related to me by the local party members in the presence of members of the local community and the injured sharecropper. The story was later confirmed by the landlord himself, with the difference that he labelled party representatives as "hoodlums."

64. For a criticism of the "operation *barga*," which arrives at conclusions quite different from mine, see Ashok Rudra, "Two steps backward." Disruption in the countryside was also emphasized by bureaucrats who wanted to highlight the CPM's failings and maintained that "operation *barga*" was actually creating more problems for *bargardars* rather than alleviating their poverty. Interview, Mr. S.C. Kol, Land Settlement Officer, Burdwan, April 3, 1979.

I also made such an argument in print at an earlier date.[65] A closer look at the grassroots reality, however, suggests that this criticism is misplaced. As the answers to question 4 (Table 3.9) make clear, input dependency of the sharecropper did not alter significantly after registration. What is of considerable importance is the fact that the majority of the sharecroppers were not receiving any inputs from the landowner even prior to registration. The common conception that sharecropping involved considerable elements of reciprocity — with the landlord providing timely inputs and necessary loans in exchange for a large proportion of the crop — may very well be incorrect. This conclusion is buttressed by the fact that as many as 80 percent of the landowners in the sample were absentee (question 3, Table 3.9). The most common sharecropping arrangement, therefore, was probably one in which the landowner only leased land to the sharecropper, lived away from the village, and returned to the village periodically to collect the share of the crop. If this view is correct, it is not likely that the breakdown in the old nexus of goodwill will have disruptive consequences for either the personal welfare of the sharecropper or agricultural production in general.

This is not to suggest that the credit constraint is unimportant for the registered sharecroppers. Unavailability of cash loans, or exploitative rates for loans, is a perennial problem for the village poor. It affects welfare in lean periods and reduces the prospect of improving production on smallholdings. As the village environment has become more politicized along class lines, loan availability from interpersonal connections has probably declined in the recent years. The CPM government has thus undertaken new programs to support the registered sharecroppers and smallholders.

Support programs for Sharecroppers and Smallholders

Organized credit markets in rural India have in the past been notoriously ineffective. The ineffectiveness is manifest not only in the relative scarcity of credit (relative to urban markets) but even more in defaults on payments and, as a rule, in their skewed distribution favoring the larger landowners.[66] In the face of these past patterns, the CPM in West Bengal has undertaken the difficult task of facilitating low-interest loans to smallholders as a whole but especially to the newly registered sharecroppers. Governmental authorities have entered into a series of negotiations with the

65. See Atul Kohli, "Parliamentary communism and agrarian reform," *Asian Survey*, 23, 7 (July 1983), 783-809, esp. p. 801.
66. See Marcus Franda, *Organizational alternatives in India's rural development* (Wiley Eastern Limited: New Delhi, 1979), ch. 2.

nationalised banks aimed at channeling "subsidized" credit for the lower agrarian groups. While the program is in its beginning stage, the novelty of the experiment deserves some analytical attention.

The CPM would like the commercial banks to enter the rural credit markets on a large scale. While the enthusiasm of a "communist" government for the spread of commercial capitalism may seem ironic, it fits into the CPM's overall redistributive emphasis. It is hoped that the penetration of organized credit markets will ease the hold of the "feudal" moneylenders on the smaller peasantry. This will not only contribute to material improvements for these groups, but will also help the CPM consolidate its political position. The commercial banks are, however, reluctant to enter the rural markets on a major scale.

Several factors underlie this reluctance.[67] First, rural lending with a focus on smallholders will result in a great number of small loans that, even when considered as a whole, do not amount to large sums. The process is therefore likely to be costly from a management standpoint. Second, rural lending will require considerable diversification in banking patterns. Bankers will have to adopt to rural living conditions, agrarian experts such as agronomists and veterinarians will have to be added to the staff, and thousands of new bank branches will have to be opened. Buttressing both of these issues is the third and the central factor: the banking pay structure. Unionized bank employees are remunerated considerably above their equivalents in other services. Any suggestions to diversify and expand are therefore considered to be cost-heavy proposals and are met with reluctance.

From the point of view of the banks, any new activity must fit favorably into their cost-benefit calculations. In the simple words of a senior bank employee: "We work with other people's money. We have to make sure that we use this money sensibly." Credit markets, in other words, have to be both lucrative and reliable, and for banks the lucrativeness and the reliability of rural credit markets remain in doubt. Even though research has indicated that smallholders are more reliable in their debt repayments than the larger ones,[68] the labor and therefore the cost-heavy aspect of rural banking remains an important obstacle to diversification. Understanding the reluctance of banks to enter rural markets, the CPM has entered into negotiations with the banks aimed at subsidizing the process of loaning to smallholders.

Concerned especially with the consequences of its favored "operation *barga*," the CPM would like to institute a credit program for the share-

---

67. The discussion is based on interviews conducted with both government and bank officials. Especially useful were the insights of D. Bandopadhyay (footnote 53).
68. See Franda, *Organizational alternatives*.

croppers. This would not only support those who have already registered but also encourage others to break older patterns of dependence. Because the sharecroppers do not own any land, the problem of "collateral" is the first obstacle to any credit program for them. The CPM has argued and the banks have "in principle" agreed that loans ought to be given out against crops as well as against land.[69] In practice, however, the principle of loans against crops creates the messy problem for the bankers of identifying the *bonafide* sharecroppers and their shares in village communities. Because this task is labor intensive and potentially controversial, the bankers definitely do not want to be involved in this part of the process. As a result, the CPM has offered the services of the newly created *panchayats* in undertaking the labor-intensive groundwork requiring community knowledge.

The local *panchayats*, according to the agreements reached, now prepare a list of the registered sharecroppers in their areas as well as identifying their anticipated share of the yearly crop. This information is passed on to the banks. Using this information, the banks decide who is eligible for loans and for what amount. Only a part of the loan is cash. As much as 50 percent of the total is in the form of vouchers for fertilizers and other inputs. The interest rates for the sharecroppers are only 4 percent, the balance being paid to the banks by the government. Moreover, if the sharecroppers pay back their entire loan by March 31 of the next year, the loans are interest-free, the total interest being paid by the state.[70]

This program of subsidized credit (indirect subsidies to the bank in the form of labor cost and direct subsidies to the sharecroppers to cover interest rates) is presently in its early stages. In 1981 and 1982 approximately 130,000 and 300,000 registered sharecroppers and other smallholders received institutional credit respectively.[71] These numbers, while small, are not unimpressive. As questions 6 and 7 of my household survey further revealed (see Table 3.9), a sizeable minority of registered sharecroppers have used institutional credit for investment purposes. What is the likely future direction of such a credit scheme?

The banks are not likely to make major rural investments until they have some clear sense of the longevity of the CPM regime in West Bengal. What if the CPM were to lose in a future election or, more likely, were to be ousted by yet another round of presidential rule? Could banks count on the new regime's willingness to provide the support necessary

69. Interview, Binoy Chowdhry (footnote 6).
70. Based on interviews with Binoy Chowdhry (footnote 6) and D. Bandopadhyay (footnote 53).
71. Government of West Bengal, *Guidelines for bank financing to sharecroppers and patta holders* (Calcutta, 1983), p. 11.

for rural diversificiation? In other words, the CPM regime will have to be sustained for quite some time before the banks enter rural banking on a major scale. Even if banks were to come forward, the role of the *panchayats* would remain crucial. If corruption was to jeopardize the process of identifying sharecroppers and their portion of the crops, the entire program of credit for sharecroppers would be undermined. As discussed above, the smooth working of the *panchayats*, in line with CPM's electoral goals, is likely to remain a function of the party–*panchayat* linkages and of the development of the party itself.

The prospects for credit for smallholders are thus likely to depend on the continued viability of the CPM as a political force. The CPM's attempts to facilitate loans for the registered *bargardars* highlight dramatically the difficulty of a state's redistribution intervention within the framework of a democratic–capitalist model of development. The democratic element makes regime longevity doubtful. While this is desirable for various well-known reasons, it also causes difficulty for long-term changes requiring sustained state intervention on behalf of the underprivileged. Commercialism as an obstacle is also clear in the obvious fact that banks are in the business of making profits and not of providing welfare. If the state wishes to work through the private sector to buttress the position of the lower classes, then it is for the state to make such activities attractive for those operating on the principle of profitability. This is not to suggest that the obstacles to planned redistribution cannot be overcome. Rather, it is to point out that the task is a formidable one and not likely to succeed in the absence of imaginative and sustained intervention by left-of-center regimes.

Wages and Employment Schemes for the Landless

So far I have concentrated on the actions of the CPM that are aimed at improving the lot of the sharecroppers. Sharecroppers are, however, only one target group of the below-the-poverty-line population. The other major group consists of the landless agricultural laborers. As much as one third of all the rural families in West Bengal — about 2.2 million families or about 4 million adults — belong to this category of the landless. The primary source of income for these families is agricultural employment. Less than 30 percent of the land is irrigated in West Bengal and, as a consequence, much of the agricultural activity revolves around the *kharif* crop (that is, the crop that depends on the monsoons). On the average, this generates three to four months employment per year for the landless. The poverty problem of the landless is therefore rooted both in limited employment opportunities and in low wages. In this section I analyze the

CPM's attempts to create additional employment opportunities and to improve the wage conditions of the landless.

Prior to investigating the CPM's actions, two caveats should be noted. First, changes in the employment and wage conditions of the landless are influenced by a whole set of social, political, and economic conditions. It is therefore not always easy to isolate the impact of political actions. The following discussion nevertheless traces the consequences of political actions in two areas: the creation of non-agricultural, rural jobs; and the unionization of the landless, aimed at improving their agricultural wages. My discussion will not analyze the consequences of changing economic conditions or even the consequences of politically stimulated economic changes, such as public investments in irrigation. The second caveat has to do with the fact that the costs of programs for additional employment are often shared by the central and the state governments. The central support is, however, common to all states. Since I am pursuing a comparative analysis of three states, my analytical interest is not on the role of the center; I am primarily concerned with the differential performance of the three state governments utilizing central funds.

One of the major programs for creating additional employment for the landless is the Food for Work Program (FWP) or, as it is now called, The National Rural Employment Program (NREP). Sponsored in part by the center, the CPM government has implemented the program with considerable effectiveness. The evaluation of FWP by India's Planning Commission singled out West Bengal for its "better coordination in the planning and implementation of the program."[72] Research conducted in the seven blocks (three in Burdwan and four in Midnapore) revealed a fairly consistent pattern of policy outcomes.[73] On the average, twenty-eight days of employment per year were generated by the FWP projects for the landless laborers. The standard wage was 6½ lbs. of wheat plus 2 rupees cash per day, a wage that was higher than the average wage in the area. Because the total employment available from agriculture each year is approximately three to four months, and because the FWP projects were contributing about 1 month of employment, it is fair to conclude that the FWP contributed about 25 percent over and above the yearly income derived by the landless from agrarian employment.

The FWP employment was, of course, not available to all the landless. Approximately one third of all the landless households have had yearly

72. Quoted in Government of West Bengal, *National rural employment programme in West Bengal* (Development and Planning Department, Calcutta, 1983), section 2.1.
73. The results are based on interviews which by no means constitute a representative sample. Figures cited should therefore be treated as broadly indicative, rather than as precise data. The possibility of data being different from other parts should also be borne in mind.

access to this employment.[74] In recent years the program was supposed to have spread further, but the problems with the Central Government have slowed the progress. While neither the yearly increment in incomes nor the extent of the program's coverage is sufficient to alleviate poverty, a 25 percent increment in yearly income for about one third of all the landless households is not an insignificant achievement. Because the FWP is sponsored by the center, neither the credit for initiating the program nor the credit for funding it goes to the CPM. What is attributed to the CPM, however, is its effective implementation. This deserves attention.

The FWP projects are now implemented by the village-level *panchayats* in West Bengal. In conjunction with local party cadres, the *panchayats* decide the projects to be undertaken, choose who will be employed, and administer the funds. While a series of socio-political implications flow from this powerful role in the rural communities, certain immediate consequences are also notable. Among these is the major accomplishment of maintaining a "clean administration." Many of those interviewed suggested that, as a result of the party–*panchayat* linkages and the party's need to sustain a clean reputation for political purposes, public funds under the new local leadership were not being appropriated for private benefits,[75] or certainly not to the same degree as under previous Congress governments. The projects chosen also fit better into the shared needs of the community than those selected in the past, which had been based on the narrow preferences of the village elite.

Compared to the past practices through which development projects ended up in the backyards of the local notables, the new projects often benefited a broader population. The projects included the building of roads connecting isolated villages to main roads, the cleaning and fixing of village tanks, and the drainage and cleaning-up of canals used by many members of the village community. The new CPM *panchayats* reduced corruption and class bias and were considerably more effective in facilitating mass-oriented rural development than were the past institutional arrangements.

Aside from the FWP, the village *panchayats* are now also in charge of several other employment-generating developmental schemes. The Rural Works Program (RWP) brings together some of the projects formerly carried out under the jurisdiction of the Public Works Department, the

74. In 1977-8, 100 million rupees were spent on the FWP in West Bengal. As the average person employed in 1977-8 received 28 × 5 Rs. (4½lbs. of wheat, at approximately 1 R. a pound, and 1 R. cash for each day of employment) = 140 Rs./year, approximately 100,000,000/140 = 714, 000 landless laborers were employed. This constitutes about a third of the 2.2 million landless households in rural West Bengal.
75. While this is based on interviews throughout West Bengal, for a confirmation of this by others, see Franda, "Rural development;" and Bhabani Sengupta, *CPI-M*.

Block Development Office and the old *panchayat* bureaucracy. In terms of reducing corruption and class bias, the new *panchayats* are proving more effective in facilitating the hitherto mythical development from below. For example, in a remote Santhal village (Bhatar Block, Burdwan) that I visited, the major RWP project was the construction of a road linking the Santhal community to the main road. For the first time in three decades of rural developmental activities, this road would allow the local Santhal population to leave their villages in the monsoon season without having to wade through knee-deep water. The settlement of "vested tanks" (that is, tanks over which specific individuals have rights) will also be administered now by the *panchayats*. Instead of being leased to the highest bidder, who in the past was generally a well-off notable, the tanks will now be assigned to groups of fishermen sponsored by the *panchayats*. This will provide not only incomes for some of the landless but also additional *panchayat* funds (to be matched by the state government) for sponsoring new projects. While none of these schemes, or the future ones to be assigned to the *panchayats*, is in itself radically new, there is significant change in the politicized administration.

Effective implementation of redistributive programs is integral to CPM's political design: the CPM favors its political sympathizers and gains electoral popularity by channeling resources to select groups. The CPM is, after all, a political party and not a charitable organization. Partisan political behavior nevertheless means that funds poured in for rural development are likely to help the lower classes, both by direct employment remunerations and by the projects themselves serving broader social needs.

It is too early to document substantial improvements in the standards of living of the poorest of the poor. The poverty problem in the area is a severe one and even under the best of political circumstances the solutions will come over a long period. However, important and impressive beginnings have been made, and it is the direction of change to which I wish to draw attention. For the first time in modern India, political institutions capable of facilitating rural development with redistribution are being developed at the behest of the CPM leadership. Increased bugetary resources are to flow into these institutions. The CPM is broadening its own budgetary base by a series of new taxation measures, including another first — the progressive agricultural taxation bill, which is now in the works.[76] If a developmental pattern of this nature had been pursued over the last three decades, the profile of rural poverty might well have been quite different; if it is sustained for the next three decades, the

76. For details see *People's Democracy*, "West Bengal budget breaks new ground" (March 11, 1979), 6.

impact on rural poverty in the area is likely to be significant.

Other than the developmental impact, the control of the CPM *panchayats* over local decision-making and public resources is beginning to have socio-political consequences that should be noted. First, increasingly there is a clear separation of social and political power in the countryside. Even though the landowners and other notables remain socially powerful, political power is being concentrated in the CPM and its representatives. Whether this situation of dual power will prove to be a stable one in West Bengal remains an open question. The workability of this somewhat unique situation will nevertheless depend on both sides being willing to leave each other with their core resources: the major portion of the land for the landowners, and control over political offices and policy for the CPM.

Another impact of the CPM's growing social control is that as public resources come to be controlled by a new local elite, new patterns of patronage are developing. Instead of the old landlord-dominated "vote banks," the *panchayat* leaders are becoming politically powerful. Many of the landless working on the FWP projects noted in interviews with me that they were grateful for the role of the *panchayat pradhan* as a benefactor. Over time, the *pradhans* will be able to convert this new-found influence into a tool for mobilizing electoral support. As long as the CPM remains in power, it will be able to buttress its position further through these patronage networks linking the party, local government leaders, and poor beneficiaries. If the CPM is weakened, however, the loyalty of many of the intermediate sympathizers may prove to be shortlived.

Presently the CPM's popularity is enhanced by its capacity to facilitate economic benefits for the rural poor. Some of this capacity is, however, buttressed by the center-supported projects, such as the FWP, administered by the CPM provincial government. The central leadership has come to resent this indirect political subsidy that it is providing for the CPM. The Congress leadership in Delhi has therefore terminated, temporarily at least, the wheat grants for the FWP, arguing that developmental resources are being used for "political" or "partisan" purposes. The argument has some validity, because those who gain employment from FWP projects tend to be CPM sympathizers, or as a result of the gained opportunities, become CPM supporters. The central charges are, nevertheless, mostly hollow, as all political parties in India utilize the benefits of power to strengthen their respective positions. In the case of the CPM, the developmental resources are at least not frittered away on corruption and on the privileged. The Congress resentment towards the CPM in West Bengal therefore masks a blatant power struggle couched in legal and constitutional euphemisms.

In addition to the employment-generating developmental projects, the CPM has made efforts to unionize the landless laborers. The unionization is aimed both at building organized political support (i.e., "consciousness-raising" by propaganda and organization) and at conducting "wage struggles." In this decisively political task, the role of the party and the Kisan Sabha is here more important than is the role of the state and local governments. The issue that I will address is the impact of CPM-initiated union activity concerning the wages earned by the landless laborers of West Bengal.

It is in general difficult to isolate the consequences of unionization on the wages received by the landless agricultural laborers. Reliable data over time are virtually non-existent, and what does exist is difficult to interpret. For example, even if increments in real wages over time could be established, the causal contribution of changing economic conditions, as distinct from that of unionization, would be difficult to isolate. Cross-sectional wage comparisons between more or less unionized areas are only somewhat less problematic. Again, for example, peak wages in the Burdwan district tended to be somewhat higher (around 6 rupees including rice and meals per day) than in Midnapore (around 5 rupees including rice and meals per day).[77] As party presence and unionization are stronger in Burdwan, can we make any conclusions about the impact of unionization on rural wages? Since the economic conditions in Burdwan are also more advanced, the chances are that any such conclusions could easily be spurious. It is difficult to know whether increments in commercialization, employment availability, unionization, and wages come as a package in Burdwan or if unions indeed make a net impact over and above the market conditions.

In order to avoid these problems, at least in part, I compared union activities and wage rates within Midnapore. Of the four blocks I studied, Ghatal and Debra are highly politicized, while Daspur I and II do not have a strong party presence. Moreover, Ghatal and Debra have strong agricultural labor unions, with a history of active wage struggles. Local labor and the entry of incoming migrant labor are controlled by the CPM and Kisan Sabha in these areas. In Debra, for example, the local leadership sought to implement the minimum-wage legislation. To dramatize the issue, a strike was organized on the lands of a prominent landowner who was also an ex-Congress legislator. So effective was the CPM's control, that the lands under consideration were kept uncultivated for a whole season. Only when the landlord decided to comply with the minimum-wage law, was labor released to cultivate the lands. While cases

77. The qualification noted above in footnote 73 should be borne in mind for these figures as well.

of this nature are a distinct minority, they highlight, for all concerned, the potential political capacity of the CPM's rural unions.

The wage levels in the unionized blocks tended to be somewhat higher than in the non-unionized ones. The peak wage in Debra and Ghatal was closer to 5.50 rupees per day, while in the Daspur area it hovered between 4.50 rupees and 5 rupees per day. Whether some economic conditions were responsible for this small differential was not immediately evident. One is thus tempted to conclude that unionization had made some impact on wage increments.[78]

The safest conclusion is probably that the CPM-led unions have made some, but by no means a dramatic, difference in the wages received by the landless laborers. The unionization is, however, quite uneven, generally paralleling the variations in party strength. Moreover, the CPM leadership finds it difficult to balance the needs of the middle peasantry, who often employ landless laborers, against the task of organizing the struggles of the landless laborers for wage increments. The needs of electoral politics make it difficult for the CPM to pursue a more aggressive strategy of class mobilization. Since it is now a party in power, agitational modes of political behavior are not preferred. There is concern within the party that as party cadres are used more and more in the process of governing (e.g., in *panchayats*), the politicization activities of the party may suffer at the expense of the more administrative activities.[79] Given these obstacles, unionized agitation for higher wages, though not unimportant, is not likely to remain a priority item on the CPM agenda.

The improvements in the living conditions of the landless in West Bengal are thus likely to remain primarily a function of additional employment opportunities. As the CPM is committed to increasing budgetary resources for this task and, more importantly, now has the institutional capacity to implement it, one can view the prospects with moderate optimism. This optimism is, of course, conditional on the CPM remaining in power in the near future. The unionization of rural labor is also likely to make some, albeit a small, positive contribution. As unionization facilitates organized political support, the CPM is likely to pursue it continually. Even if wage agitations are not on the agenda, this will, at minimum, allow the landless laborers to maintain their share in a growing economy and, at maximum, may even facilitate a somewhat greater share.

---

78. For further data supporting this conclusion, see Pranab Bardhan and Ashok Rudra, "Labor employment and wages in agriculture: results of a survey in West Bengal, 1979," *Economic and Political Weekly*, 15,45-6 (1980), esp. p. 1948.
79. For a discussion of this concern, see *People's Democracy* (March 11, 1979), 10-11.

Conclusion

To summarize and conclude this chapter, West Bengal is currently ruled by a communist party that is reconciled to operating within the constraints of a democratic-capitalist framework. This left-of-center ruling party has both reasons and the capacity to pursue incremental reforms. The reasons have to do with the nature of the support for the regime from the middle and lower classes. More important, however, are the political arrangements of the CPM, which enable it to generate a considerable capacity for reforming the social order by political fiat. While the results of attempted redistribution are less than spectacular, concrete achievements have been made. Programs for sharecroppers are especially noteworthy. If these efforts are sustained, they promise to make a significant dent in the rural poverty of West Bengal.

Four political characteristics are important for understanding the CPM's reformist capacities. First, the rule is coherent. A unified leadership allows not only clear policy thinking but also sustained political attention to developmental tasks. Second, the ideological goals as well as the disciplined organizational arrangements of the CPM do not allow direct access to the upper classes. This minimizes the prospects of the co-optation of reformist programs by those whose interests are threatened. Third, the CPM's organizational arrangement is both centralized and decentralized. While the decision-making power is concentrated, local initiative and knowledge can be combined within the framework of central directives. And fourth, the CPM's ideology is flexible enough to accommodate the continued existence of propertied classes as dominant in the social and economic sphere. This makes the prospect of reformism tolerable for the socially powerful.

The role of the CPM as a party is central in generating these political traits. An organized, left-of-center party allows a reformist orientation to be institutionalized within the regime. Even though the regime exists within the framework of a democratic–capitalist political economy, the pattern of regime and class interactions facilitates a degree of separation between social and political power. Propertied classes remain dominant in the sphere of production and civil society; they do not, however, control political power. Power-holders accommodate the interests of the propertied; but they also channel some of the public resources to the lower classes. The regime is controlled by a well-organized, ideological party. Because this party rests its power on classes other than the propertied, it generates a degree of political autonomy from the dominant classes. This enables regime authorities to push through some reforms of the agrarian social order from above.

4.1 Map of Karnataka

4

Karnataka : Populism, Patronage, and Piecemeal Reform

Devraj Urs ruled Karnataka for most of the 1970s. He came into power in 1972 and was ousted in 1980. His rise to power, while complex, was largely a byproduct of the earlier split in Congress and the later rout of the old Congress by the Indira-dominated Congress.[1] As the "Indira man" in Karnataka, Urs sought to create a new power base. The old ruling pattern had consisted of the nationalist generation of Congress leaders in alliance with the propertied of the "dominant castes."[2] With the goal of displacing this ruling alliance, Urs diversified Karnataka's political scene. He consolidated his own position by including propertied groups from castes other than the dominant ones, the hitherto excluded members of the dominant castes, and some members of the backward classes.

The mechanisms of inclusion in and exclusion from the ruling alliance were primarily the distribution of the spoils of political power. Additionally, however, the new ruling alliance, based on patronage like the old one but with a diversified social base, was cast in a populist idiom. Promising "welfare for the masses" and a commitment to the Congress slogan of *garibi hatao* ("eradicate poverty"), Urs sought to implement some visible redistributive programs. In this chapter I analyze both the nature of the Urs regime and the anti-poverty programs pursued in Karnataka. The general issue concerns the capacity of a patronage-based, populist political arrangement for redistributive reforms.

I will argue that the reformist capacities of the Urs regime were limited.

1. For an analysis of the earlier periods of politics in Karnataka (or Mysore), see James Manor, *Political change in an Indian state, Mysore 1915-55*, Australian National University Monographs on South Asia, 2 (South Asia Books: Columbia, 1978); James Manor, "Structural changes in Karnataka politics," *Economic and Political Weekly*, 12,44 (1977), 1865-9; B.B. Patil-Okaly, "Karnataka: politics of one party dominance," in Iqbal Narain (ed.), *State politics in India* (Meenakshi Prakashan: Meerut, 1976); and R.K. Hebsur, "Karnataka," *Seminar*, 278 (August 1978), 21-6. Another interesting article on Karnataka under Urs and Gundu Rao, which came out after this chapter was mostly written, is M.N. Srinivas and M.N. Panini, "Politics and society in Karnataka," *Economic and Political Weekly*, 19, 2 (1984), 69-75.
2. M. N. Srinivas has defined a caste as "dominant" when "it preponderates numerically over the other castes, and when it also wields preponderant economic and political power." See his "The social system of a Mysore village," in McKimm Marriott (ed.), *Village India, studies in the little community* (University of Chicago Press: Chicago, 1955), p. 18.

Strong leadership and patronage-based support facilitated the implementation of some redistributive programs. Conversely, however, exaggerated claims were made on behalf of these small successes. The tenancy reforms of Karnataka especially require scrutiny. The evidence indicates that while some achievements were made, several serious qualifications on the reformist performance are in order: (1) reform policies in Karnataka were not aimed at securing the redistribution of surplus lands; (2) given the size of the tenancy problem, the achievements are not all that significant; (3) those who lost their lands were not the well-entrenched landowners in close association with the ruling faction; and (4) the beneficiaries of reforms were not always, and not even predominantly, the rural poor.

In contrast to West Bengal, the Urs regime was neither based on a well-organized political party, nor able to prevent the landed elites from controlling the governing organizations. An attempt to institutionalize lower-class power within the state, in other words, was neither intended nor achieved. The resulting reforms therefore tended to be piecemeal and superficial rather than deep and systematic.

The Urs Regime

An understanding of the ruling arrangements in Karnataka, as in the case of West Bengal, begins with a focus on the leadership, ideology, and organization of the regime. While formally ruled by a Congress (I) government, Karnataka during the 1970s was very much dominated by the person of Devraj Urs. A heavy-handed ruler, Urs had the leadership style of a power-manipulator and a "machine operator." He used his control over political spoils to buy support. The following that he attracted was thus not based on caste or other primordial sentiments. Urs himself belonged to an elite but minority caste. Moreover, shared agreement on policy issues was also not the basis of the leader–follower relationship. Rather, the support that Urs generated was based in part on his leadership qualities and in part on his capacity as a person in control of patronage, especially control over the access to power positions within the region. The leader–follower relationship was thus largely one of mutual opportunism. This is evidenced by the fact that as soon as Urs' control over power resources (though not necessarily economic ones) dried up in the aftermath of his split with a resurgent Indira Gandhi in the late 1970s and early 1980s, his capacity to attract political support within Karnataka declined sharply.

The "leader as a patron" and the "follower as a client" is a widely recognized form of socio-political interaction in Karnataka and elsewhere.[3] At the core of this political arrangement is an individual, tacitly recognized as a leader, and his or her followers. The leader as a patron bestows patronage on the client followers in exchange for support. Because patronage usually involves the use of public resources for private aggrandizement, the whole arrangement is seen, both by the participants and by outsiders, as representing the sordid side of politics. The participants clearly recognize the rival factions and the respective leaders and followers. It is, however, difficult for an outsider to penetrate this arrangement; it is in the interest of the participants to preserve the secrecy of arrangements deemed to represent political corruption.

Politics in the Congress-dominated old Mysore, and now Karnataka, has always represented this genre of "clientalism." Urs' leadership was no different. While, as discussed below, he clearly diversified his clientele and pursued some innovative redistributive programs, he continued to buy his political support through patronage, rather than build it through a class- or issue-oriented party organization.

That Devraj Urs was a powerful leader was most clearly evidenced in his policy-making style. Decision-making during his reign was highly personalistic. As an important insider, who wished to remain anonymous, made clear:

Even the Cabinet did not matter in important decisions. He [Urs] would make it look as if he was taking everyone's advice, but then would go on to make his own decisions. He did, however, have close and good advisers. Some top bureaucrats and people like M.V. Ghortade [Finance Minister] were very close to him.

It would, therefore, not be unfair to conclude that Urs, like Indira Gandhi at the center, operated a highly centralized political machine.

As a leader favored by the central leadership, Urs controlled the crucial resource — the right of others to run for elections on a Congress (I) ticket. Urs utilized this resource repeatedly to pack the Legislative Assembly with his supporters. Party tickets were given by Urs, as by other leaders, to his own men. Irrespective of their public image, work in the party, commitment to the party principles, or ability, the primary criterion for candidate selection was "loyalty to the leader." And "loyalty invariably meant unconditional submission to the leader."[4] Aside from party tickets for assembly elections, Urs arranged for his supporters to have seats on district boards, *taluk* boards (administrative-unit boards),

3. With reference to Karnataka, see all the sources in footnote 1 above. For a more general statement on patron-client politics, see James Scott, "Patron–Client politics and political change in south-east Asia," *American Political Science Review*, 66, 1 (March 2, 1972), 91-113.
4. Patil-Okaly, "Karnataka," p. 145.

and co-operative societies. These seats, in addition to being positions of power, are coveted because they offer considerable opportunity to divert public funds for private benefits. Moreover, enough evidence was collected by an independently established enquiry, the Grover Commission, to substantiate accusations that illegal funds had been amassed by the Congress (I) under Urs and used for buying political support on an ongoing basis.[5]

As a leader, Devraj Urs thus presided over a machine that remained loyal to him as long as he had the capacity to grease it generously. This, however, was only one significant aspect of Urs' political strategy. The other was to cast his regime in a populist ideology. The ideology was not, as in West Bengal, so much a coherent set of ideas explaining the present and providing a vision of an alternative future, as it was a set of idioms aimed at creating a political mood. And the mood was one of "people's power." With the goal of undermining the legitimacy of the old ruling arrangements and, by the same token, enhancing his own, Urs sought to contrast the mass nature of his regime with the elitist character of past regimes. More specifically, Urs shifted the nature of political debate from caste issues, which to him obfuscated the "real issues," to "more important ones" concerning "redistributive justice" or class issues.[6]

In order to understand this shift from a caste to a class idiom, it is first important to have a clear understanding of how caste and class as aspects of social structure interact with political reality. Because the issue is often quite muddled in Indian political sociology,[7] a brief digression aimed at clarifying it in the context of Karnataka is in order. Scholars tend to agree that Mysore politics in periods prior to Urs' ascendance was dominated by the unified Congress in alliance with the "dominant castes," namely, the Vokkaligas (peasant castes) and the Lingayats (non-Brahmin priestly castes).[8] While this scholarly consensus is clearly useful, it fails to elucidate certain aspects of state–society interactions in Karnataka. Specifically, it fails to distinguish between who supports a ruling alliance and who benefits from it.

For example, as a dominant-caste group, the Vokkaligas include merchants, traders, landowners, tenants, laborers, and even servants.[9] Significant numbers of the Vokkaligas are therefore not propertied and rich, but rather poor. In the past, rich and poor Vokkaligas alike tended to sup-

5. See *Deccan Herald*, English daily (Bangalore, January 4, 1979).
6. Interview, Devraj Urs, Bangalore, April 25, 1979 and November 8, 1981.
7. One scholar who has done much to illuminate the interactions between caste and class in India is Andre Beteille. See his *Inequality and social change* (Oxford University Press: New Delhi, 1972); and *Inequality among men* (Basil Blackwell: Oxford, 1977).
8. See the references in Footnote 1.
9. See Srinivas, "The social system."

port specific Congress factions. The reasons for the rich of the dominant caste supporting a faction were not the same as those of the poor. Caste leaders, often of landed origins, made political choices based on the calculations of concrete rewards. The poor of the same caste, however, followed their leaders, in part because of primordial loyalties, in part because of the influential role of caste leaders within caste communities (the influence of "traditional leadership" *à la* Weber), and in part from their sheer material dependence, rooted in the pre-capitalist division of labor. The united, group-like political behaviour of the rich and the poor members of a dominant caste therefore resulted from different imperatives.

The rewards accruing to the rich and the poor of the dominant castes from state outputs also varied. The landed and other prominent members of the dominant castes benefited handsomely from their close association with the seats of power; the poor of the same castes did not. Scholars investigating this past pattern of Karnataka politics have noted that "the great skeleton in the closet of Vokkaliga and Lingayat raj in the state has always been the exclusion from political spoils of a great many members of these two groups... poorer Vokkaligas and Lingayats."[10] This suggests that it is important to trace the benefits of power along both caste and class lines.

The rewards of state power stem in part from the content of public policy and in part from direct access to political office. In the past politics of Karnataka, the rewards of public policy have tended to flow to the propertied classes, while the rewards of direct control over political offices have gone to the prominent members of the dominant castes. Both of these require elaboration.

The past patterns of public policy (taxation, pricing, subsidies, land reforms, etc.) have favored and protected the interests of the propertied in Karnataka. Irrespective of their caste origins, therefore, the landed in the countryside have continued to benefit disproportionately from state intervention in the economy.[11] This pattern highlights the importance of class domination in conditioning political outputs. Some scholars, however, noting that individuals sharing similar socio-economic positions do not associate as classes, have been led to argue that caste rather than class is the politically significant aspect of the social structure. This is an absurd claim. It confuses social–structural constraints with the more immediate determinants of political behavior — namely, caste loyalties (see Appendix I). If caste factors were indeed so important, how would one explain

10. Manor, "Structural changes," p. 1868.
11. For example, see Trude Scarlett Epstein, *South India: yesterday, today and tomorrow* (Macmillan: London, 1973).

the consistent pro-propertied bias of the public policies? An answer is not possible without analyzing class constraints; conversely, it is not difficult if one differentiates the political consequences of both class and caste factors.

Class domination in rural Karnataka has in the past been fairly complete. Patterns of material dependence have been reinforced by prolonged periods of state domination and ideological justification. The resulting patterns of political behavior, therefore, especially those of the lower classes, often appear to be devoid of class content. In stratified social settings, however, a focus on manifest political behavior is as important an indicator of the social forces at work as the absence of certain expected behavioral patterns. For example, if those at the bottom of the socio-economic hierarchy do not make any demands for improvements in their living conditions, this is more likely to reflect the severity of class domination than the absence of it. In the past this was generally the situation in rural Karnataka. Class problems here remained pre-political — they were solved within the framework of the traditional social structure. Distributional issues never got politicized and as a consequence, class cleavages were neither a basis for political association nor an aspect of policy debates. Public policies simply went on enhancing the interests of the landed classes. The propertied and other notables in the countryside, in turn, controlled the lower classes. Because the whole arrangement has had a semblance of stability, it has occasionally led to superficial claims regarding the irrelevance of social classes in Karnataka's politics.

If class-oriented political behavior has resulted from structural constraints, there is no denying that caste has provided a more active basis for political association. Caste groupings in Karnataka have become politicized for rewards above and beyond those of public policy, namely, for rewards stemming from access to political office. As the role of the state in society has increased, political offices have offered significant symbolic and material rewards. Access to office, moreover, provides an opportunity to build one's influence further as well as to divert public funds for private use. Electoral and bureaucratic offices are therefore coveted and are valued resources in the hands of the prominent political leaders. The dominant castes of Karnataka have in the past tended to monopolize these political spoils. Caste leaders have mobilized their caste following to help specific leaders or factions win elections. The political elite, in turn, have bestowed spoils on prominent caste leaders who are in a position to mobilize electoral support. Political conflict involved the winners and the losers in the struggle for spoils. Because these cleavages often represented rival caste groupings and factions within the Congress party, caste and factional conflict dominated the more visible aspects of Karnataka's politics.

Table 4.1 *Selected Castes and Communities of Karnataka*

Caste/community	Percentage of state's population
Brahmin	4.23
Vokkaliga	11.82
Lingayat	14.64
Kuruba	6.77
Beda	5.06
Arasu (Urs)	0.07
Scheduled castes	13.14
Scheduled tribes	0.79
Idiga	2.25
Muslim	10.63
Christian	2.09

Source: Government of Karnataka, *Report of the Karnataka backward classes commission* (1975), vol. II.

Caste and class as aspects of the social structure are therefore important for unraveling state–society interactions in Karnataka. Class domination in the past tended to be so thorough that class issues never even emerged as political variables. Public policies mirrored this pattern of social domination; they were consistently in favor of the propertied. Caste provided the basis for mobilizing electoral support. Dominant castes allied with specific factions of the Congress party to carve out the ruling arrangements in the state. Aspects of class were built into caste, as caste leaders were often the wealthy and the propertied. The rewards of power reflected this intermixing of class and caste variables. The landed classes of the area as a whole benefited from public policies. The upper-class members of the dominant castes benefited doubly — from public policies as well as from direct access to political offices. Conversely, the lower classes as a whole gained very little from this pattern of rule. The poor of the dominant castes may have gained a trifle more than the other poor due to some "trickle-down" from their flourishing patrons.

This was the general socio-political pattern within which Devraj Urs entered as a new political leader. Brief comments on the more specific aspects of coalitions and factions in the ruling circles will further set the scene for an understanding of the Urs regime.[12] Table 4.1 summarizes

12. The following is based on several interviews conducted in the cities of Bangalore and Mysore during the summer of 1983. The most important of these was a series of interviews with E. Raghavan, Special Correspondent, *Indian Express*, Bangalore. I am indebted to Mr Raghavan for generously sharing his immense knowledge of Karnataka politics. Others interviewed included the anthropologist M.N. Srinivas; G.V.K. Rao, former Chief Secretary, Government of Karnataka; M.A.S. Rajan, former Revenue Secretary, Government of Karnataka; and V. Balsubramanium, Personal Secretary to the Chief Minister of Karnataka.

the distribution of Karnataka's population according to caste. As data on landownership according to caste have further made clear, the largest amount of land within the state, especially in large landholdings, is owned by the two dominant castes — the Vokkaligas and the Lingayats.[13] The numerical (Table 4.1) and the land-owning significance of these two communities has given them considerable political power. As Table 4.2 makes clear, over 50 percent of the parliamentary seats have continuously been occupied by these castes since independence. All the Chief Ministers prior to Devraj Urs, moreover, were either Vokkaligas or Lingayats.

The influence of these communities is not aggregated through formal political organizations. The Lingayats' power, for example, is partially consolidated through the religious organization of Mutts. These are powerful bodies to which Lingayats are religiously attached. The heads of these organizations — the swamis — are in turn influential men. They not only control funds and can sway opinions, but they intervene politically and for the purposes of patronage distribution. It is reported, for example, that the swami at the powerful Mutt of Sringere controls from fifteen to twenty members of the Legislative Assembly at any one time. Favored candidates are decided upon by the swami in conjunction with influential men and then the faithful are asked to vote for them.

This dominant position of non-Brahmin groups, including the agricultural castes, provides an interesting contrast to such other Indian states as Uttar Pradesh. Agricultural castes in Karnataka have been powerful within the framework of the Congress party since independence. This is in part a function of the relative numerical insignificance of Brahmins in Karnataka and in part owing to the early successes of the non-Brahmin movement in Southern India. When opposition to the old Congress alliance arose in Karnataka, therefore, it did not take the form of the middle-caste movements of the Charan Singh style. The Vokkaligas — Karnataka's version of the Jats — were already in power in this part of the country. Opposition leaders have had to dig deeper into the social hierarchy so as to mobilize support against the ruling alliance. Devraj Urs, therefore, in addition to promising a better deal for the peasants, had to make populist promises to the poor. That, however, is moving far ahead in the story.

Throughout the 1960s Vokkaligas and Lingayats vied for power and patronage. That the Lingayats had the upper hand within the competitive ruling alliance is made clear by the fact that all the Chief Ministers

13. For example, see the land–caste data (Table 3) in G. Thimmaiah and Abdul Aziz, "The political economy of land reforms in Karnataka, a south Indian state," *Asian Survey*, 23, 7(July 1983), 810-29.

Table 4.2 *Composition of the Legislative Assembly by Caste, 1952-1972 Elections*

Caste/community	1952 no.	1952 %	1957 no.	1957 %	1962 no.	1962 %	1967 no.	1967 %	1972 no.	1972 %
Brahmin	14	11	9	6.75	8	6	8	6	11	6
Lingayat	45	35	47	33	45	34	49	36	43	24
Vokkaliga	33	26	35	25	35	27	36	26	52	29
Other Hindus	12	9	22	15	20	14	17	12	37	22
Scheduled castes	20	16	22	15	21	16	24	17	23	12.5
Scheduled tribes	—	—	2	1.50	1	1	—	—	2	1
Christian	—	—	1	0.75	—	—	1	0.75	5	3
Jain	2	2	3	2.25	1	1	1	0.75	1	0.5
Muslim	1	1	1	0.75	1	1	2	1.50	4	2
Total	127	100	142	100	132	100	138	100	178	100

Source: Government of Karnataka, *Report of the Karnataka backward classes commission* (1975), vol. IV.

between 1956 and 1972 belonged to this community. Devraj Urs stayed aloof from this dominant-caste conflict and positioned himself closer and closer to Nijalingappa, a powerful Lingayat and twice Chief Minister of Karnataka. Nijalingappa brought Urs into the Cabinet for the first time in the early 1960s. At the same time, however, Urs as a minority-caste member increasingly found himself squeezed out of the main factional struggles within the ruling coalition of Vokkaligas and the Lingayats. During the 1967 elections, Urs had a difficult time even getting a ticket for elections. He therefore slowly started cultivating Mrs Gandhi directly in Delhi. As Jatti left state politics, and Veerandra Patil became the Chief Minister, Urs became the head of the old Jatti faction. When the Congress party split nationally in 1969, Devraj Urs made the critical political decision of his career, namely, to oppose the dominant political figures within the state, including Nijalingappa, and to side with Mrs Gandhi.

Urs now had the mandate to build Mrs Gandhi's party within the state. Much of old Mysore and the Bombay and Hyderabad parts of Karnataka were, however, already controlled by Vokkaliga and Lingayat politicians. At this point it seems that Devraj Urs discovered the backward castes and the poor. Urs started putting together a coalition of third- and fourth-level disgruntled party members. He also built support in districts not fully controlled by the dominant castes, such as the coastal areas. While this coalition was a beginning, it was far from sufficient to displace the old guard successfully. For that Urs needed Mrs Gandhi's help.

When Mrs Gandhi won a sweeping victory in the 1971 national elections, numerous members of the Legislative Assembly switched sides, the Patil government collapsed, and the Urs faction emerged dominant within Karnataka. Urs therefore owed his initial rise to power more to being favored by Mrs Gandhi than to his personal political base. Once in power, however, Urs sought to undermine any possibility of revival of the older ruling pattern, consisting of the Congress old guard in alliance with the wealthy Vokkaligas and the Lingayats. In addition to broadening the social base of his regime, Urs altered the idiom of rulership. If the past political conflict had revolved around which caste groupings would obtain favors, or spoils, from the leadership, a new element was now added to the ideological debate — the rights of the lower classes. Taking his cue from Mrs Gandhi, and working within the constraints of state politics, Devraj Urs presented himself as a "man of the poor." This populist idiom was aimed at undermining the legitimacy of the elitist nature of past leadership. Because this populist posture has in recent years come to characterize not only politics in Karnataka, but much of Indian politics, it is important to unravel it in some detail.

The content of Urs' populism, like that of Mrs Gandhi, differed both from the lip-service paid to the "rights of the poor" in the Nehru era and from the clear pro-lower-class ideology of the CPM in West Bengal. In contrast to Nehru's "socialism," which seldom meant more than state participation in heavy industries, Urs' populism was a clear recognition of the failure of "trickle-down." In other words, the renewed commitment to the poor implied an ideological recognition of past shortcomings, including a recognition of the fact that the needs of the lower classes deserved special attention. Urs thus argued:

In the past, under planning, various programmes were launched for increasing production. It was believed that if total production increases, it will take care of poverty. This belief was belied... large cross-sections of the society... were unable to improve their productivity for several reasons. They have no ownership of the means of production like land although they toiled on it for decades... This necessitates a shift in policy emphasis. Production-promoting measures alone are inadequate. The removal of basic handicaps of the poor within an overall and consistent income redistributive development framework ought to be the guiding factor.[14]

While the idiom resembles the "growth with equity" emphasis of many international development organizations, Urs went further by recognizing how this can be implemented:

One of the most effective means of making the rural poor participate in the

14. Devraj Urs, *Socio-economic programme for the poor: some policy imperatives* (Office of the Chief Minister: Karnataka, April 1978), p. 1.

process of development is to break the rural power structure and make the rural poor get a proper share.[15]

Both in tone and content this ideological posture, which emphasizes the need to "break the rural power structure," indeed went beyond that of the Nehru years. Irrespective of the developmental outcomes, the idiom itself is important because it highlighted political change, and the gap between rhetoric and outcome is not without political consequences.

It is also important to recognize that Urs consciously sought to politicize state issues along class lines. For example, the Havanur Commission report sought to redefine the role of "backward" and "forward" communities within the state.[16] Urs added the class dimension to this debate. As a senior civil servant reminisced:

I wrote the implementing orders of the Havanur Commission report. I argued that visible jobs, such as district commissioners and senior police officers, should always include members of scheduled castes. Such positions become important symbols of group achievement. It was Urs, however, who added the economic criteria. That is to his credit. Irrespective of the caste origin, he argued that the poor should have access to important jobs.[17]

Urs knew well that it would be difficult for anyone in the state to argue against "affirmative action" for the poor. While caste privileges are old and highly controversial, class adds a new political possibility for mobilizing support. There is also no reason to doubt that Urs' populism had some elements of genuine sympathy for the poor.

While more radical than the Nehru era, this ideological posture is also distinct from that of the CPM. Specifically, it did not rest on the Marxist doctrine of class conflict. While the needs of the lower classes were emphasized, this was not at the cost of expropriating the propertied or even disrupting the class structure. While discussing the strategy of land reforms, Urs thus noted: "I believe that we have been entirely pragmatic in our whole approach to the challenge of restructuring the rural areas; the means employed are radical without being disruptive."[18] "Pragmatic" and "without disruption" were code words to appease the propertied and Urs repeatedly made it clear that he was not a Marxist in the guise of Congress. This was clearly seen in a personal interview in which I pressed Urs

15. *Ibid.* p. 11.
16. Reference is to Government of Karnataka, *Report of the Karnataka backward classes commission* (Bangalore, 1975), submitted to the Government of Karnataka by the Chairman of the Commission, Shri L.G. Havanur, November 1975.
17. Interview, G.V.K. Rao, former Chief Secretary, Government of Karnataka, Bangalore, June 11, 1983.
18. From a speech by Devraj Urs to a subregional workshop on agrarian reform organized by Asian Institute for Rural Development, Bangalore, November 10, 1978 (mimeo).

as to why the implementation of "land ceiling" laws had not been pushed through. He couched his answer in terms of the "just principles" of "private property":

Property is an inner urge. Just as I want property, so do others. Imagine a person who owns property. If he is always insecure about it, about when it will be snatched away, he is not happy. This hurts production and happiness. We do not believe in it.[19]

When not couched in the rhetoric of a social scientist turned speech-writer, Urs' ideological principles did not hold out any real threat to the propertied as a whole. And since it is this down-to-earth style that marked the personal interactions between Urs and the prominent economic elite of the area, the elite did not really find his rhetorical commitments to the poor very threatening.

Urs' populism was thus marked by an increased vocal commitment to the poor within the framework of the existing class structure. This populism, which resembled Mrs Gandhi's ideological posture, was similar to the Nehru years in its commitment to the poor, but went beyond the "socialism" of Nehru in terms of degree. When compared to the CPM, however, it varied in its basic approach to the poor. This difference is manifest in the all-important fact that Urs' commitment to the poor was not marked by a simultaneous commitment against the propertied classes.

This is clearly evidenced by the fact that even during Urs' rule, the Vokkaligas and the Lingayats continued to occupy up to 50 percent of the Assembly seats (see the results of the 1972 elections in Table 4.2). Moreover, a strong case can be made that Urs consciously sought to incorporate the Vokkaligas rather than exclude them from the ruling alliance. Several pieces of evidence can be cited to support this conclusion. First, Urs' own constituency (Hunsur) was a Vokkaliga-dominated one. Second, as the Basvalingappa incident highlighted, when confronted with the difficult choice of whether to favor the lower castes over the Vokkaligas, Urs fired Basvalingappa — a vocal scheduled-caste minister opposed by the dominant castes.[20] Third, Urs managed to have the Vokkaligas classified as a "backward caste" and thus eligible for favored treatments bestowed upon the underprivileged.[21] And lastly — and probably most importantly — the crucial reform measures of tenancy

19. Interview, Devraj Urs (footnote 6).
20. For details, see V.K. Nataraj and Lalitha Nataraj, "Limits of populism: Devraj Urs and Karnataka politics," *Economic and Political Weekly,* 17, 37 (1982), 1503-6, esp. p. 1506.
21. This classification was a result of Government of Karnataka, *Backward class report* (the Havanur Commission).

abolition did not hurt the Vokkaligas; they may even have benefited them. This is discussed in detail below.

Suffice it to note here that Urs' pro-poor populism was not anti-rich. In contrast to the CPM, therefore, for the most part, there was little effort made in Karnataka to isolate the propertied from the political sphere. The design of the political institutions did not reflect a conscious attempt to tilt the power balance in favor of the poor. This in turn narrowed the range of options available to state authorites for poverty reform.

It is also important to emphasize the political origins of this populist ideology. The ideological shift to the "poor" reflected primarily the needs of political competition and only secondarily did it indicate changes in the class structure. Devraj Urs, like Mrs Gandhi, discovered the poor when he needed an alternative power resource in his competition with the Congress old guard. To oust the older ruling alliance, Urs went directly to the "people." Of course, this was possible only because social-structural changes had released the "people" from their traditional loyalties and dependencies. At the same time, however, these social changes were not significant enough to be a driving force behind political change. There was little class conflict to speak of in the Karnataka of this period. Even in the latter part of his rule, Urs was still emphasizing the need to organize the rural poor.[22] In other words, it was not the emergence of the rural poor as an autonomous political force and the need to incorporate them politically that pushed Urs' ideological posture towards populism. Rather, it was the need to mobilize new political forces as a tool of electoral competition that was primarily behind the shifting ideology. James Manor's description of Karnataka as a "cohesive society" with minimal class conflict is essentially correct.[23]

That the ideological shifts were rooted in political needs is of considerable consequence. First, in the absence of politicized poor, the gap between rhetoric and actions can, in the short run at least, continue to be large without damaging consequences. Second, once the lower classes have become an object of political competition, no political party can resist the temptation to champion their cause. Especially since the rhetoric does not have to be matched by actions, all parties have been inclined to move towards populist commitments. By the same token, however — and this is the third point — a long-range consequence of such a drift is likely to be political instability. Continued commitments to the poor broaden the range of legitimate expectations from the regime. If the capacity to satisfy

---

22. Urs, *Socio-economic programme for the poor*.

23. See James Manor, "Karnataka: caste, stratum and politics in a cohesive society" (mimeo). This is a draft version of a future chapter to appear in Frankel and Rao (eds.). *Class, caste and dominance in India.*

these commitments does not expand proportionately, an increasing gap between promises and performance is a sure invitation to long-term instability.

In addition to the leadership and the ideological characteristics, the organizational arrangement of the Urs regime needs to be delineated. The organizational patterns were characterized as much by the absence of specific forms as by their presence. Especially notable here is the absence of a well-organized political party. Congress (I) in Karnataka, like Congress (I) elsewhere, of course, has a rudimentary organizational structure. However, this is activated primarily for electoral purposes and occasionally to influence intra-party factional disputes. The major functions of the party are to collect funds and to dole out tickets for elections. Those who control the use of party funds and/or the right of others to run on a Congress ticket are powerful individuals. Those who are attracted to the party often have their own opportunistic motivations. These motivations can vary from something as major as seeking a party ticket for election to something as minor as securing a job, a permit, or a favorable settlement of a dispute by virtue of association with party influentials. Leaders and followers alike hail from varying social backgrounds. They are in turn held together in an ideologically amorphous and a structurally loose organization, bound often by no more than a sense of mutual opportunism.

This organizational pattern contrasts sharply with that of the CPM in West Bengal. The CPM as a political party is characterized by a clear pro-lower-class ideology, by a membership largely exclusive of the propertied groups, and by a tight internal control structure. This organizational pattern allows the CPM to create a filter between itself and society at large. Party members belong to the CPM as much as or more than they do to society; the politically defined roles tend to dominate social roles. This allows the CPM to act as a cohesive nucleus, part of and yet distinct from society, and capable of generating politically directed social reform. The Congress in Karnataka, however, is penetrated by social forces and as a result the societal hierarchies are reproduced within the dominant political organization. The ideological commitments of the Congress party are multiple, its membership is open, and the internal control structure is weak. In such a loose and amorphous organization, social roles and interests influence political behavior more than the organizational imperatives do. As a consequence, class and caste structures are mirrored within the Congress party. The party itself tends to become primarily a vehicle for the pursuit of individual or sectional social interests. Organizational arrangements here, in other words, do not facilitate political autonomy from the social structure as a whole and from the dominant social classes in particular. These characteristics of Congress as a ruling party further narrow the options of state authorities pursuing politically directed social reform.

Congress as a party and the Congress government in Karnataka have not always worked in unison. Mrs Gandhi occasionally attempted to check the ever-growing power of Urs by assigning his rivals to the state party leadership position. Because Urs was a powerful political resource, Mrs Gandhi could not afford to alienate him beyond certain limits. For the most part, therefore — and this was especially true in the aftermath of the emergency — Urs managed to control both the party and the government. The party and governmental relationship was thus mutually reinforcing. The control of the party allowed Urs to pack the Legislative Assembly with his supporters and to use party funds to buy and sustain support. This facilitated control of the government. Governmental control in turn provided further opportunities to dole out patronage and thus to broaden and consolidate the base of political support.

Devraj Urs effectively presided over such a "machine" organization. In the early years Urs had to depend on Mrs Gandhi and central contributions to grease the political machine, but as time went on this situation reversed itself. The more powerful Devraj Urs became within the state, the greater was his capacity to attract contributions from the rich. Money came in through legal and semi-legal channels, but also through nefarious means. In addition to direct contributions to party funds, numerous "development boards" and other organizations were set up. These were reported to be controlled by Urs himself and acted as bodies for receiving and doling out funds — receiving funds from the rich wanting governmental favors and doling out funds to those whose support was crucial for the Urs regime.

The structure of corruption in Karnataka can be highlighted by an example described to me by a competent local journalist.[24] The state liquor industry is both regulated and heavily taxed. The powerful liquor-excise lobby paid large sums to relevant civil servants and politicians, especially Urs, to avoid these constraints. As a result, the liquor manufacturers diluted the alcohol content below regulation, produced more bottles than allowed, and paid less taxes than their due. The money thus made beyond legal earnings was "black money." Part of this black money was recirculated back to the politicians to facilitate the continuance of these arrangements.

Urs channeled the large sums of money he was accumulating both upwards and downwards. In moving upwards the money apparently went directly to Mrs Gandhi. This buttressed the crucial support Urs received

24. Interview, E. Raghavan (footnote 12).

from her. In channeling money downwards, Urs kept several potentially troublesome politicians in line. Lacking any formal party mechanisms for maintaining discipline and loyalty, Urs reportedly kept a number of Assembly members on the "pay-roll." While this is a fairly common organizational pattern in India, Urs' innovation lay in incorporating clients of diverse social backgrounds.

The recipients of patronage increasingly included members of varying social backgrounds. For example, fully 50 percent of the Congress tickets for the 1978 Assembly elections were given to members of scheduled castes and "backward classes." Lingayats and Vokkaligas, however, were by no means fully excluded. Close to one third of the total tickets were still given to the members of these dominant castes. While this was a substantial decline from earlier periods (see Table 4.2), the more troublesome opposition was at least partially co-opted. The remaining tickets were given to prominent individuals belonging to higher castes other than the dominant ones. Following the recommendations of the much-debated Havanur Commission report,[25] Urs also increased the share of reserved civil-service jobs for the backward classes. Moreover, many of the lesser but significant positions in the rural co-operatives and on the *taluk* boards were given to those groups previously excluded from political spoils by the Congress regimes.

Urs' political acumen lay in recognizing the need to buy off counter-elites. Once bought, his rivals had less motivation to mobilize opposition utilizing caste and other primordial appeals. By diversifying the recipients of spoils, Urs diversified his political base. The gains from this mode of accommodating opposition were not, however, shared by the majority, especially not by the rural poor. The elite of the backward classes gained, not the backward classes themselves. What was being offered to the counter-elites were offices or office-related spoils rather than concessions on public policy. Because it is only systematic shifts in public policies that have broad-based social consequences, it is to an investigation of the poverty-related policies that I now turn my attention.

To summarize this section, Urs' regime was characterized by strong leadership, a populist ideology, and a loose and amorphous organizational pattern revolving around the widespread use of patronage as a basis of political support. The presence of a strong leader gave the regime a semblance of coherence. At minimum, and unlike many other Congress-run states, Karnataka under Urs was not marred by debilitating factional conflicts. Populist ideology, while not threatening to the propertied in any fundamental way, created an aura of progressiveness around the

25. Government of Karnataka, *Backward class report*.

regime. The leadership evoked a sense of hope among those favoring the interests of the lower classes. Organization behavior, however, created a sense of *déjà vu*. Widespread use of patronage, as well as charges and counter-charges of corruption, reminded one that some important traits of the old Congress party remained intact. The party organization itself remained weak. The issue which I now want to investigate, therefore, concerns the capacity of this populist political arrangement — one that is leadership-dominant and patronage-based—for redistributive reform.

Poverty Reforms

In addition to diversifying the composition of those receiving patronage, Urs sought to channel the rewards of public policy to the hitherto excluded social groups. The pursuit of some highly visible redistributive programs was in keeping with his populist political strategy. Here I analyze three of the important programs aimed at alleviating rural poverty in Karnataka: land reforms, small-farmer programs, and the wage and employment schemes for the landless laborers. The focus of analysis, as in the discussion of West Bengal, is on the linkages between political organization and reformist outcomes. I argue that the piecemeal success of Karnataka's poverty programs highlights the limited reformist capacity of the Congress regime under Devraj Urs.

In order to understand Karnataka's poverty reforms, it is first important to delineate briefly the nature of rural poverty and inequalities in the area. The poverty problem here is serious, though not as serious as that of West Bengal. The percentage of the rural population living in conditions of poverty has for decades hovered around 50 percent.[26] This is close to the all-India average (Table 2.5) and contrasts with the 65 percent figure of West Bengal. The relative inequalities as measured by the Gini coefficient of consumption patterns generally reflect an unchanging pattern over the last two decades.[27]

This stubbornness of rural poverty and inequality ought to be viewed in the light of the economic performance of the area. Between 1950 and 1975, Karnataka experienced an average growth rate of 5 percent per annum. Karnataka has therefore been one of the fastest-growing states in India.[28] That this has had little consequence on poverty in the area ought to give pause to even the diehard believers in the "trickle-down" perspective on development. Micro-studies have also documented the failure of

26. See Ahluwalia, "Rural poverty."
27. *Ibid.*
28. See Government of Karnataka, *Draft five year plan, 1978-83* (Planning Department: Bangalore, 1983) pp. 9-10.

Table 4.3 *Correlation Coefficient for Rural Poverty and "Development"
in the Districts of Karnataka, 1974-1975*

District[1]	% of population below poverty level (V_1)[2]	Index of development (V_2)[3]
Belgaum	66.4	94.18
Bellary	56.7	86.42
Bidar	63.9	82.81
Bijapur	60.6	76.62
Chickmagalur	44	94.14
Chitradurga	63:06	99.93
Coorg	50.7	108.63
Dharwar	45.9	102.45
Gulbarga	67	67.04
Hassan	54.04	90.62
Kolar	63.5	100.79
Mandya	59.8	112.36
Mysore	44.5	116.81
North Kanara	39.6	100.09
Raichur	35.6	79.72
Shimoga	55.1	125.28
South Kanara	61.9	181.01
Tumkur	54.3	88.11
mean:	54.9	100.95
standard deviation:	9.6	25.02

Pearson's r (V_1, V_2) = 0.0443 (not significant)

[1] Bangalore, being a largely urban district, is not included.
[2] Based on NSS consumption data and taken from G. Thimmaiah, "Inequality of income and poverty in Karnataka," Paper presented at the sixtieth Indian Economic Conference, Madras, December 28, 1977 (mimeo). The definition of poverty levels is the same as that used by India's Planning Commission and by Montek Ahluwalia, "Rural poverty."
[3] The index is a composite index based on 12 variables including agriculture growth and the use of high-yielding seeds. The index is calculated by the Government of Karnataka and made available in the Planning Department document, *Draft five year plan, 1978-83* (1978), p. 20.

publicly subsidized agrarian transformation to benefit the rural poor.[29] The same point can be made by cross-sectional district-level data. When the index of development for the nineteen districts is correlated with the poverty levels in these districts, the results are insignificant (see Table 4.3). The Karnataka data therefore are consistent with the hypothesis that higher growth rates do not automatically relieve rural poverty.

Data on access to land are presented in Table 4.4. These data, like all the land data on India, ought to be interpreted as no more than broadly

29. For example, see Epstein, *South India.*

Table 4.4 Distribution of Land in Karnataka by Size Class of Operational Holdings, 1953-1972

Size class of household operational holding (in acres)	1953-4		1961-2		1971-2	
	% of households	% of area operated	% of households	% of area operated	% of households	% of area operated
0–1	29.5	0.4	34.2	0.2	34.4	0.4
1–2.5	13.4	3.9	9.8	2.4	15.6	4.7
2.5–5	18.1	10.6	13.2	6.7	16	10.7
5–10	21.5	25.1	21.3	21.3	17.9	23
10–20	11.5	26.3	12.6	24.3	9.9	24.8
20 and above	6	33.7	8.9	45	6.2	36.4

Source: Government of India, *National sample survey*, eighth round for 1953-4, seventeenth round for 1961-2, and twenty-sixth round for 1971-2. The data for 1953-4 are strictly not comparable to the later years, owing to the reorganization of the Mysore state.

Table 4.5 *Changes in Tenancy in Karnataka, 1953-1971*

Year	% of cultivated area under tenancy	Area under sharecropping as a % of area under all forms of tenancy
1953 - 4[1]	16.37[1]	24.72
1960 - 1	18.16	37.52
1970 - 1	15.9	43.98

[1] The data from 1953-4 are not strictly comparable to those of the later years owing to the reorganization of the Mysore state in 1956. Just after the reorganization of Mysore, a Land Committee estimated that about 23% of land in Mysore was under tenancy. See Government of Mysore, *Report of the Mysore tenancy agricultural land laws committee* (Government Press: Bangalore, 1958).

Source: adapted from Pranab Bardhan, "Variations in extent and forms of agricultural tenancy," *Economic and Political Weekly*, 18 (September 11, 1976).

indicative. What they indicate is a pattern similar to that seen in West Bengal. There has been a small decline in land concentration at the top of the scale. This reflects partly the legal (though not always operational) breakup of large landholdings in response to land-reform laws, and partly the breakup of these holdings due to inheritance laws. At the other end of the scale, families operating small-to-marginal holdings have continued to grow, both proportionately and in absolute numbers. If one adds to this the phenomenal growth of the landless laborers — from about 13 percent in 1961 to 26 percent in 1971 to around 30 percent at present[30] — the poverty picture is clear. The landless laborers and the marginal peasants form the bulk of the rural poor.

Tenancy patterns are indicated in Table 4.5. With increasing commercialization, the overall extent of tenancy has declined. Within this, the proportion of sharecropping has increased. The overall significance of sharecropping in Karnataka is, however, considerably less than in West Bengal. While nearly all tenancy in West Bengal is sharecropping, over half of it in Karnataka is carried out on the basis of cash arrangements. The socio-political consequences of this are explored below.

The data then reveal that about half of the rural population of Karnataka is living in conditions below the poverty line. In spite of the steady and impressive economic growth, this proportion of poor people has remained unchanged. Within the category of the rural poor, the proportion of landless laborers has grown consistently. The majority of the rural poor are now landless. The rest are cash tenants, sharecropers, and marginal landholders. With the aim of improving the living conditions of

30. The 1961 and 1971 figures are the census figures. The 1980 figures are the unofficial estimates of the Government of Karnataka.

these rural poor, the Urs regime had undertaken certain policy measures. What these measures are, and the extent of their success, is the subject of the following analysis.

Land Reforms

The most publicized redistributive program in Karnataka has been the renewed land reforms.[31] Until recently land reforms in Karnataka had been a sham. As part of the overall populist thrust, however, Urs' government in 1974 passed a series of amendments to the existing land-reform legislation. It was hoped that the new laws would inject enthusiasm into the seemingly hopeless and yet important distributional issue. In 1975, moreover, 183 special land tribunals were created, one or more for every *taluk*, to facilitate the implementation of the invigorated laws. With new laws, and new institutional arrangements, land reforms appeared to be on the move all over again. How successful have these renewed efforts been?

It is important at the outset to separate the issue of surplus land from that of tenancy reform. As in West Bengal, tenancy reforms have been pursued vigorously in Karnataka; but not the appropriation and redistribution of "above ceiling" lands. That the latter has been ignored is clear by the record. In spite of the high landownership ceilings in Karnataka (up to 54 acres depending on land quality), there should be close to half a million acres of surplus land in the state, according to the government's own conservative estimates. After four years of publicized land reforms, however, less than 45,000 acres, or less than 8 percent of the legal surplus

---

31. Karnataka's land reforms have attracted considerable scholarly attention. For two sympathetic assessments, see James Manor, "Pragmatic progressives in regional politics: the case of Devraj Urs," *Economic and Political Weekly*, annual number, 15, 5 - 6 (1980), 201 - 13; and Thimmaiah and Aziz, "Land reforms in Karnataka." For two contrasting interpretations, see Atul Kohli, "Karnataka's land reforms: a model for India?," *The Journal of Commonwealth and Comparative Politics*, 20, 3 (November 1982), 309-28; and Narendra Pani, "Reforms to pre-empt change: land legislation in Karnataka," Indian Institute of Management typescript (Bangalore, 1981). A number of papers on the subject were also presented during a symposium on land reforms, Bangalore, March 18, 1982. A mimeographed collection of papers from this symposium included the following relevant pieces: N. Parameshwara and P.H. Rayappa, "Collective and distributive land reforms in Karnataka;" M.A.S. Rajan, "Working of land tribunals of Karnataka;" V.S. Satypriya and S. Erappa, "Land reforms in Karnataka: some field evidence;" and A.J. Rajapurohit, "Land reforms and changing agrarian structure in Karnataka." Another article which does not assess Karnataka's land reforms but ably documents the failure of housing-schemes for the rural poor is Mira Bakhru, "Distribution of welfare: people's housing scheme in Karnataka," (in two parts), *Economic and Political Weekly*, 19, 10 (1984), 427 - 36, and 19, 11 (1984), 473-80.

and, had been redistributed.[32] This redistributed land constitutes less than 0.2 percent of the total cultivated land in the state. It would, therefore, be difficult to deny that redistribution of surplus land has been a low-priority item on the government's policy agenda.

Underlying the reluctance to tackle the issue of surplus land are factors not only of socio-political constraints, but also of leadership intentions. Surplus land in Karnataka, as in the rest of India, has over the years "vanished" as *benami* land (falsely registered land). It would take enormous political capacities to procure this land. The chances are that no government in India, short of a revolutionary one, is ever likely to tackle this issue seriously again. Even the communist government in West Bengal, with all its organizational capacities, has been hesitant. With landlord-dominated local governments and little or no party organization, the Urs regime was certainly in no position to pursue and appropriate surplus land for redistribution. The land tribunals, discussed below, also did not add significantly to this capacity. Even if the leadership had wished to get at the surplus land, the complexity of the problem, class opposition, and the absence of organizational capacities would have made it next to impossible.

The problem in Karnataka was, however, more fundamental. The leadership had no intention of appropriating surplus land for redistribution. A vigorous pursuit of "above ceiling" land implies nothing less than a frontal attack by the state authorities on the rural class structure. West Bengal communists are hesitant to undertake this as a matter of "pragmatic compromise." The Congress regime in Karnataka, by contrast, was not even committed to this as a goal. Urs' populist rule had some commitment to redistribution, but only within the framework of the existing class structure. The ideology and the organization of Urs' regime reflected this class commitment. In an interview discussed above, when pressed as to why surplus lands were not being appropriated more vigorously, Urs defended the government's actions in terms of the "rights of the private property." In other words, rhetoric for public consumption aside, preservation of the basic class structure is part of the regime commitment. India is, after all, a private-enterprise economy. And I do not mean to suggest or even imply that there is anything wrong with this. It is just that the gap between the political rhetoric of socialism and the reality of a privately-owned economy tends to be larger in India than in many other countries.

What has been pursued vigorously since 1975 are tenancy reforms. The new amendments to land-reform laws closed off many loopholes that had

32. Figures from Government of Karnataka, "Land reforms progress in the state up to the end of November 1980," memorandum from the Revenue Department (Bangalore, 1980).

allowed landlords to escape tenancy legislation in the past. According to the new law, all those who were tenants on the date the law was passed (March 1, 1974) had occupancy rights to that land. While those who were tenants before would not have all the rights of a legal "owner" (e.g., the land could not be sold for the first six years), they nevertheless could no longer be evicted from it. The state would compensate the landlords for their lands, generally at below market prices. And the new "owners" would pay the state small periodic installments in exchange for the land. The new laws also did not allow for any resumption of lands by the landlord for personal cultivation. The nature of the law, especially the elimination of the personal-cultivation loophole, contrasts with much of the tenancy legislation in India. It indicates a seriousness of political intent. In comparison to West Bengal, however, the legislation falls short. We may recall that the onus of proof in West Bengal regarding who is or is not a sharecropper is now on the landlord. In Karnataka it is still the tenants who have to prove their own right to the land. As one might expect, this has proven to be an important problem in the process of implementation.

To facilitate implementation, Urs' regime created special land tribunals. Knowing well that the existing institutional arrangements would not allow the new laws to be implemented, Urs created new, *ad hoc* arrangements. For each of the 175 *taluks* into which the state is divided, one or more tribunals were created. Each tribunal had five members. The chairman was a bureaucrat of the level of Assistant Commissioner and the other four members were political appointees, including a member from the backward classes. Each tribunal would receive applications from tenants, check them for their validity, listen to conflicting evidence (no professional lawyers allowed), make field visits for verification if necessary and arrive at final decisions regarding tenant's occupancy rights. A tribunal's decision could not be appealed against in lower courts, only in the state high court. For all practical purposes the land tribunals were powerful bodies with considerable final authority over the occupancy rights on tenanted lands.

With the laws proclaimed and the tribunals established, applications for occupancy rights on tenanted land flooded in. More than 17 percent of the total owned land, or about 3.8 million acres, was under tenancy in the early 1970s in Karnataka.[33] As Table 4.6 indicates, applications covering all of this (and even more) were filed over the five years. The mere fact that applications covering such a large extent of tenanted land were filed is in and of itself a tribute to the political tilt accomplished by the Urs

33. From Government of India, *National sample survey*, twenty-sixth round, report no. 215. 8 (Controller of Publications: New Delhi, 1971), Table 4. These figures do not correspond with the estimates of the Government of Karnataka. The government chooses

Table 4.6 *Progress of Tenancy Reforms in Karnataka under Devraj Urs, 1975-1980*

	Number	Area involved in millions of acres
1. Applications filed by tenants	800,335	42.7
2. Number of applications dealt with by the end of November 1980	566,595	not known
3. Applications decided in favor of tenants	342,843	1.3
4. Occupancy certificates issued to tenants	134,340	0.5

Source: Government of Karnataka, Revenue Department Memorandum entitled "Land reforms progress in the state up to the end of November 1980" (Bangalore, 1980).

regime. The act of filing for a landlord's land is clearly an act of defiance against the local power structure. How and why this was accomplished without a strong party organization, and thus without any real mobilization from below, has important implications.

What the rush of applications indicates is that laws, when genuinely designed to protect and enhance the interests of lower classes, have important social consequences — they strengthen the social position of the lower classes. Protection from above therefore is far from meaningless. The repeated failure of land reforms in India has led to a widespread feeling that "mere" legislation is not useful — that only actions from below can resolve the land issue. While this remains important, it can just as easily become an alibi for the state authorities. For example, the claim that the necessary land legislation in India is on the books, and the problem is one of implementation, is totally misleading. Though there is a great deal of land legislation on the books, most of it is inadequate and full of loopholes. Legislation, and therefore political leaders, rather than bureaucrats alone, is responsible for the failures. As the case of Karnataka indicates, when legislation is redesigned and loopholes are removed, the political intent of leadership is clear. With indications that state power is backing a segment of the poor, these poor are less helpless than some of the contemporary "organize the poor" literature would lead us to believe.

By the end of Urs' tenure in 1980, about 70 percent of all the applica-

to work with the figures from the agricultural census. Based on "*patwari* records" (the records of village-level administrators), census data as a rule underestimate the extent of tenancy. This in turn allows the government to make exaggerated claims of success regarding its own programs.

tions to procure tenancy land had been processed (Table 4.6). More than 60 percent of the resulting decisions had been in favor of the tenants, and 34 percent of the tenanted land had been legally transferred to former tenants. While only a small proportion had actually received ownership certificates, site visits made it clear that land that came to the tenants through favorable decisions was often being cultivated by them. About one third of the total tenanted land, or about 5 percent of the total cultivated land, had thus changed hands.

The new Congress(I) government, which replaced the Urs government in late 1980, found itself in a dilemma with respect to these land reforms. If the new government continued the programs initiated by Devraj Urs, the resulting political capital would accrue to the opposition, now headed by Urs. By contrast, if the government discontinued the reforms, it would risk losing support due to its "anti-poor" disposition. The Congress(I) rulers thus decided to rush through the programs initiated by Urs, "complete" them, and move on to new programs. This strategy would allow them to claim that they were even more concerned for the poor than was the Urs regime, and yet minimize their involvement in programs initiated by Urs.

By November 1981, about a year after it came to power, the Congress(I) government claimed that tenancy reforms had been completed. Governmental claims of "enormous successes" were met with considerable skepticism,[34] and newspapers were very critical of the land-

Table 4.7 *Progress of Tenancy Reforms in Karnataka up until the "Completion" of the Program, 1975-1981*

	Number	Area involved in millions of acres
1. Applications filed by tenants	813,263	4.60
2. Number of applications dealt with by the end of November 1981	776,658	not known
3. Applications decided in favor of tenants	467,298	1.85
4. Occupancy certificates issued to tenants	305,708	1.03

Source: Government of Karnataka, Revenue Department, "Note on progress achieved under land reform" (November 1, 1981).

34. Interviews with senior officials (one recently retired, one presently employed) of the Government of Karnataka, who wish to remain anonymous, Bangalore, November 10 and 11, 1981.

Table 4.8 *Distribution of Land "Leased In" in Early Seventies, Karnataka*

Land ownership category	Land "leased in"[1]									
	Coastal districts		Eastern districts		Northern districts		Southern districts		Karnataka total	
	in hundreds of acres	% of total leased land	in hundreds of acres	% of total leased land	in hundreds of acres	% of total leased land	in hundreds of acres	% of total leased land	in hundreds of acres	% of total leased land
Landless	1937	38	85	5	1535	7	1138	19	4695	13
Smallholders (0.01 to 2.49 acres)	2242	44	600	35	7082	30	2622	43	12,547	34
Family farmers (2.50 to 9.99 acres)	842	16	545	32	8097	34	1600	26	11,085	30
Landlords (10 acres and above)	104	2	475	28	6952	29	728	12	8259	23

[1] For the definition of coastal, eastern, northern, and southern districts groupings, see Table 4.10 below.
Source: computed from Government of India, *National sample survey*, twenty-sixth round, report no. 215 (Karnataka), vol. II, (1971), table 4 on pp. 94, 120, 146, and 172 respectively.

Table 4.9 *Distribution of Land "Leased Out" in Early Seventies, Karnataka*

Land ownership category	Land "leased out"[1]									
	Coastal districts		Eastern districts		Northern districts		Southern districts		Karnataka total	
	in hundreds of acres	% of total leased land	in hundreds of acres	% of total leased land	in hundreds of acres	% of total leased land	in hundreds of acres	% of total leased land	in hundreds of acres	% of total leased land
Smallholders (0.01 to 2.49 acres)	115.21	12.7	49.9	4.1	669.2	5.4	318.9	10.5	1153.2	6.6
Family farmers (2.50 to 9.99 acres)	313.6	34.7	610.6	49.8	5725.3	46.6	1906.9	63	8556.4	49.1
Landlords (10 acres and above)	475.5	52.6	566	46.1	5893.1	48	801.5	26.5	7736.1	44.3

[1] For the definition of coastal, eastern, northern, and southern districts groupings, see Table 4.10 below.

Source: computed from Government of India, *National sample survey*, twenty-sixth round, report no. 215 (Karnataka), vol. II (1971), table 3 on pp. 93, 119, 145, and 171 respectively.

reform implementation under Gundu Rao.[35] The data released in late 1981 are presented in Table 4.7. It would take another study to assess what lies behind the claimed "accomplishments" of the Congress (I) government and the related data in Table 4.7. For the purposes of this study, therefore, I will assume that (1) land reforms were indeed completed by the end of 1981, and (2) the credit for these reforms goes to the Urs regime. To the extent that these assumptions bias the analysis, the bias will favor the accomplishments of the Urs regime.

As the data in Table 4.7 indicate, 185 million acres of land was legally transferred to tenants during Karnataka's land reforms. This acreage constitutes nearly 50 percent of the land under tenancy in the state during the early 1970s. How does one assess the significance of this tenancy reform? Any assessment must take into account several considerations: Who lost the land? Who received the land? What happened to nearly half the land under tenancy in the early 1970s that was not transferred to the tenants? What have been the socio-economic consequences for the recipients of land? Because direct and hard data on any of these crucial questions is not available, the answers have to be approximated.

Some important data that help estimate who may have lost and received land during the tenancy reforms is presented in Tables 4.8 and 4.9. These tables delineate the distribution of land "leased in" and "leased out" according to landownership categories in Karnataka in the early seventies. The data question the crucial assumption on which tenancy reforms were premised, namely, that big landowners lease out land to the landless or smallholders. The tenancy situation of Karnataka was far more complicated. Over half the land "leased in" in the early 1970s was *not* by the landless and the smallholders, but rather by family farmers and landlords (see Table 4.8, under Karnataka total). Similarly, those who were "leasing out" land were also not predominantly the bigger landlords: more than half the land "leased out" in the early 1970s was by smallholders and family farmers (see Table 4.9, under Karnataka total). While these data do not support a claim that many of the richer farmers actually leased land from the poorer ones, it does suggest that many of those who were leasing in land were already well-off, and many of those leasing out land relatively poor.

What are the likely consequences when tenancy reforms are politically imposed on this pattern of tenancy? It is important to remember that only about half of the land under tenancy in the early 1970s changed hands as a consequence of the land reforms. Is there any reason, then, to believe that the half of the tenancy land that changed hands went from the richer

---

35. Bangalore's *Indian Express* carried periodic district-by-district reports on land reforms throughout 1981. For example, see the issues of October 24-30, 1981.

landowners to the poorer tenants? Certainly no more reason than to believe that many of the small landholders may have lost their lands and many of the already better-off may have gained by the reforms.

In order to understand the tenancy reforms further, one has to go beyond this "formal" evidence and closely analyze the workings of land tribunals. Each tribunal was chaired by a "professional" civil servant of the rank of an Assistant Commissioner. As individuals enjoying considerable authority in the local milieu, the bureaucrats were the most significant members of each tribunal. In addition to the inherited authority of office, the power of government officials was enhanced by several factors. These included a knowledge of administrative and legal regulations, as well as sustained activity due to their role as full-time, salaried employees. The number of times tribunals would meet and the number of cases to be heard were also determined by the civil servants. Most important, the Assistant Commissioners were responsible to higher bureaucrats for fulfilling their quota or for task completion. Momentum for the tenancy reforms was generated in the Chief Minister's office and transmitted through the established bureaucratic hierarchies. The whole program, therefore, had a bureaucratic character that surpassed what one would expect from the inclusion of four political appointees on each tribunal.

Of the political appointees, the local member of the Legislative Assembly was included almost as a rule. A prominent Congressman of scheduled-caste origin was also often a part of the tribunals. The two additional members were of varying backgrounds. It was widely recognized that Devraj Urs had packed the tribunals with his loyal supporters. Proclaiming himself "a man of the poor," Urs argued that his supporters would ensure "popular participation." The reality, however, was somewhat different. The majority of these members did not have very "popular" origins. Of the 8 tribunals in South Kanara and Mandya that I visited and of the 32 appointed members that I interviewed, over 50 percent were of landed origin (owned more than 25 acres of land). Some were extremely rich and powerful local individuals. Most of them had a university-level education. Few, if any, had real commitment to land reforms. A former Divisional Commissioner for the north-eastern districts also argued that most of the tribunals under his jurisdiction were dominated by landlords.[36] In terms of composition, therefore, most tribunals included, and some were dominated by, members of the middle- and upper-rural-class Congressmen loyal to Devraj Urs.

The tribunals served the important political needs of Devraj Urs. For

36. Interview, V. Balsubramanium, Personal Secretary to the Chief Minister of Karnataka, Bangalore, June 15, 1983.

example, each appointed member received 50 rupees per diem for participation on the tribunals. As arbiters of conflict-ridden social situations, moreover, the appointees could use their position to enhance local influence. Tribunal membership was thus coveted for both pecuniary and political reasons. Urs offered the membership to his supporters as favors. Tribunals therefore became one more element in Karnataka's large network of patronage and spoils supporting the Urs machine.

This organizational arrangement provided a steam valve for potential opposition. If the lands of powerful local individuals were threatened, at least some of them, especially those who had personal relationships with tribunal members, could evade the law. Charges of corruption in the local newspapers buttressed the common belief that this was indeed occurring. Opposition to the program, therefore, did not crystallize along class lines. Some members of the landed classes, as suggested by the tenancy data in Tables 4.8 and 4.9, may even have benefited economically from the reforms. Others were involved with implementation and yet others, due to personal association, could minimize their losses. This is not to suggest that significant losses were not incurred by some landowners. Many lost their lands to former tenants. Opposition, however, took a factional rather than a class form. Those close to Urs and Congress (I) often did not lose their lands, while the propertied of opposing factions did not fare well. The latter constituted the bulk of the opposition. Labelling them as "anti-people" and "reactionaries," Urs could simultaneously present himself as a "people's man," without alienating the landed groups that lent him crucial support. And in this lay the political acumen of Devraj Urs. That only half of the tenanted land legally changed hands further bears out the reality of this factional pattern of implementation.

It is important to reiterate the role of the bureaucrats. The civil servants provided an important thrust for whatever success the tenancy reforms have had. This became clear as I observed the workings of the land tribunals. The Assistant Commissioners as the chiefs of the tribunals took the receipts from tenants proving their right to their land, examined the receipts, asked questions of both parties, and after minor consultations with the other members made the decision. The political appointees, by contrast, were quite out of place in legal–bureaucratic decision-making. These members were more like observers than the active decision-making participants they were supposed to be.

Following orders from above, career civil servants provided the momentum for tenancy reforms. In spite of the popular view that bureaucrats act as an obstruction to radical reforms, the professionalism of senior Karnataka bureaucrats needs to be noted. Given a task, they pursued it diligently. This, of course, is not to imply that they did not face

Table 4.10 *Regional Variations in Karnataka's Land Reforms*

Region[1]	Land under tenancy in early seventies (A)[2] (in hundreds of acres)		Land acquired by former tenants (B)[3] (in hundreds of acres)	"Rate of success" (% of B to A)
Coastal	5240	(99.25%)[4]	3138	60
Eastern	1657	(8.19%)	1157	70
Southern	5417	(9.69%)	755	14
Northern	25,772	(18.29%)	7955	31
Karnataka total	38,086	(17.14%)	13,005	34

[1] The districts included in the regions are as follows: coastal (North and South Kanara); eastern (Chickmagalur, Coorg, Hassan,and Shimoga); northern (Belgaum, Bellary, Bidar, Bijapur, Chitradurga, Dharwar, Gulbarga, and Raichur); and southern (Bangalore, Kolar, Mandya, Mysore, and Tumkur).
[2] From Government of India, *National sample survey*, twenty-sixth round, report no. 215 (Karnataka), vol. II (1971), Table 4 on pp. 94, 120, 146, and 172.
[3] From Government of Karnataka, Revenue Department, "Land reforms up to the end of October 1980."
[4] Figures in brackets indicate leased land as a percentage of the total land owned.

obstructions or that the other appointees of the tribunals were powerless. On the contrary, the bureaucrats often complained about political interference. The political appointees sought to influence and obstruct cases important to them, but these deals were generally made out of court. The authority of the bureaucrats in the actual legal proceedings may have been great, but out of court they had to take into account the power of the political figures. Socialized in the Indian legal–administrative system, these government officials understand that laws are meant to apply differentially, so they complied with the wishes of the political appointees. The costs of opposing MLAs (Members of the Legislative Assembly) or others close to Urs were unnecessarily high. As one IAS officer confided:

A lot of bribing went on before the cases came up. One had a clear sense of cases in which other tribunal members had already been influenced. A good Assistant District Magistrate could minimize corruption... but one risked transfer. Most of us learn to compromise... we look the other way.[37]

Ironically, therefore, the momentum towards reforms, as well as the obstructions, originated from the power center. The momentum traveled from top to bottom through the bureaucracy; the obstructions, from bottom to top, through political linkages.

In many cases, the veidence was not clear as to the *bonafides of the tenant applicants. This required a visit by the tribunal members to the vil-*

37. Given the sensitive nature of the subject, the officer wished to remain anonymous. Interview, Bangalore, June 15, 1983.

lages for further investigation. These visits often did not materialize, however, because the work load of the tribunals was heavy, the distances from small *taluk* towns to villages was considerable, and the availability of transportation restricted. The accuracy of decisions thus suffered. Even when the visits were made, rival parties easily mobilized conflicting evidence at the local level. In the absence of personal knowledge and contacts, such problems reduced the efficacy of tribunals as implementing bodies. A more localized organization could possibly have solved these administrative problems, but in the process would have created new ones. Without a strong local party organization, lower-level bureaucrats and landed interests would have indeed created greater obstacles than at the *taluk* level. In other words, decentralization without centralized tools of control would have solved administrative problems only at the expense of strengthening the forces of *status quo*.

Regional variations within Karnataka should also be noted. As Table 4.10 indicates, virtually the entire land in the coastal districts was under tenancy in the early 1970s. This contrasts sharply with the eastern and southern districts, where less than 10 percent of the land owned was out on lease. The tenancy pattern in the coastal districts also resembled the more classical pattern, namely, land was primarily "leased in" by the landless and the smallholders (see Table 4.8, under coastal districts). The rate of success of reforms in the coastal district was, morever, quite high (Table 4.10). This suggests that the two coastal districts, North and South Kanara, with extremely high density of tenancy, indeed experienced redistributive reforms. Because the land under tenancy in the coastal districts constitutes less than 15 percent of the land under tenancy in Karnataka as a whole, these localized redistributive successes do not substantially alter the overall assessment. The reformist performance in these areas nevertheless raises the question: what distinct forces were at work here?

The reformist momentum in the coastal districts is best explained by somewhat unique political circumstances of the area.[38] The major communities of South Kanara, for example, are Brahmin, Bunt, Billawa, and Mogaveer. The Billawas, constituting about 40 percent of the district population, are toddy-tappers by caste. They are the main cultivators in the coastal districts. The bulk of the land is owned by Brahmins and Bunts, but they are not agriculturalists. Over the years, moreover, many of the young of these communities have taken to education and have

38. I have benefited from a number of interviews with individuals familiar with South Kanara. Especially useful were interviews with S. K. Das, former District Commissioner, South Kanara, June 15, 1983; and K.V. Rao, Deputy Director, National Sample Survey, Bangalore, June 11, 1983.

moved out of the rural environment, sometimes even moving up the coast to Bombay. Land owned by these communities thus tended to be mostly "absentee land" given to tenants for cultivation.

Several aspects of this situation were to prove important for reforms. First, an absentee landowner is generally in a weaker position than is a village landlord when it comes to protection of property. Not only is the legitimacy and influence of an absentee landlord weaker, but his capacity to mobilize brute force to defend his interests is also substantially reduced by his absence. And second, the land-owning communities here were not part of the state's dominant castes. As they belonged neither to the Vokkaliga nor to the Lingayat group, it was much easier for Urs to politically isolate the coastal Brahmins and Bunts.

Additionally, there was pressure from below in the coastal districts, which in turn resulted from the greater politicization of the rural population in these areas. As one of the Assistant Commissioners, who chaired a tribunal noted, "The peasants in this area are very shrewd." This shrewdness is a consequence of several unique features of these districts. South Kanara, for example, shares many socio-economic characteristics with the districts of Kerala. Tenancy there has been largely of *moolgani* type — i.e., with permanent, written contracts and based on fixed cash payments. This makes it easier to prove one's legal status as a tenant. The coastal populations are generally more exposed to the forces of commerce. Missionary and other non-governmental organizations, including the left-wing parties, have also been active in the area. They have on more than one occasion provided support for the rural poor. All these factors have created a greater sense of awareness and power among the coastal lower classes. When favorable laws were passed, the tenants of the area, comprising a considerable numerical force, were quick to file their applications, muster the necessary evidence, and press for favorable settlements.

This experience has important analytical implications concerning the political conditions for poverty reform. Successful reform involved actions from both above and below. Favorable tenancy laws reflected a pro-lower-class tilt in state power. A population with a sense of its own power acted upon these laws and contributed to their successful implementation. The political conditions for successful reform in the coastal areas thus appear to be similar to those in West Bengal: a reformist thrust originating from the state, coupled with actions by mobilized lower classes.

The social and political conditions in much of Karnataka differed from those in the coastal districts. These differences can be summarized as follows: tenancy was much less concentrated; land-owning groups were politically powerful; patterns of leasing included many larger landowners "leasing in" land and many smallholders "leasing out" land; and the politicization of lower rural groups had not moved as far as on the coast. Tenancy legislation, therefore, did not have the same redistributive consequences in the bulk of the state as it did in the coastal districts. Taking the state as a unit, then, two conclusions concerning the reforms would be hard to deny. First, as only about half the land under tenancy changed hands, many of those working the other half are no longer tenants; they were in all probability evicted by one method or another. Given the inequities of rural power structures, it would not be unfair to extrapolate that the bulk of those evicted must have been the already weak, namely, the smallholders. And second, of the tenanted land that was transferred to the tenants, only a part went from the rich to the poor. For the rest, given the pattern of tenancy in the early 1970s, some of the already well-off members must have gained and some of the less well-off must have lost.

On balance, then, how does one assess Karnataka's land reforms? In any assessment it is important to re-emphasize that little effort has been made to appropriate and redistribute the "above ceiling" lands. The policies have focused on tenancy reform. These reforms touch a small but not insignificant proportion of the rural poor. While mildly redistributive, tenancy reforms mainly contribute to the emergence of an owner–producer mode of production. Even with reference to this issue, however, the success in Karnataka has been limited.

Political conditions have both facilitated the modest success and obstructed a more meaningful land reform. The driving force behind the reforms was the political needs of a leadership — a leadership determined to oust the older ruling alliance by creating an alternative and broader political base. Hoping to legitimize a populist regime, Urs passed new legislation, created the tribunals, and sustained the pressure from above to implement reforms. An effective bureaucracy, and a population with a sense of its own power in areas with concentrated tenancy, also contributed to the success. Conversely, the patterns of tenancy and the nature of the power structure precluded a concerted attack on rural society. Given that many rich farmers were "leasing in" land and many poorer ones were "leasing out," no blanket legislation aimed at giving land to tenants could have been redistributive. A much more discriminating approach would have in turn required a degree of political organization simply absent in the state.

State organization necessitated a top-heavy reform. Without complementary support from below, such reforms from above are destined to be less than successful. As a loose and amorphous organization with mulbe less than successful. As a loose and amorphous organization with multiple class goals, the Congress party of Karnataka does not really attract a disciplined and ideological following. Because of this Urs consistently had to buy his support. The strategy was to exclude some, but co-opt most, of the social influentials, albeit from different backgrounds, into a large network of patronage. In the absence of a disciplined party, political survival was contingent on avoiding the alienation of the local notables and on including them in such reform institutions as the land tribunals. This precluded the possibility of anything but a modest tenancy reform.

Small-Farmer Program

If the much-publicized land reforms of Karnataka have at best had limited success, the other poverty programs have been of even lesser significance. Neither the small farmers, discussed here, nor the landless laborers, discussed in the next subsection, have benefited much from state intervention. Resources allocated to support these groups have been minuscule, especially when compared to the size of the problem. More importantly, there is no organizational framework in rural Karnataka to strengthen the socio-economic position of the lower classes. Regime rhetoric aside, this reflects the state's larger political reality. The absence of financial and organizational support continues to demonstrate that additional state-initiated poverty reforms are not really on the political agenda.

Karnataka's production policies, like those in most of India, have favored the larger landowners. It is widely recognized that the benefits from subsidized inputs and outputs have not "trickled down." The Urs regime has put foward this criticism itself:

The growth dominated approach has further led to the widening of income inequalities. Redistributive justice could not be realized because whoever had the access and the means was able to increase production. Others remained outside the main stream of development... marginal farmers...and small farmers ...experience difficulties of access to the inputs to improve their productivity ...a change of development policy is imperative.[39]

Following this "imperative," the Urs regime initiated a series of programs aimed at channeling agrarian inputs directly to the smallholders. Prominent among these programs were the schemes initiated by the Small Farmers Development Agency (SFDA). The programs were designed to make the small farmers "economically viable."[40] The idea was to channel

39. *Draft five year plan*, pp. 114 - 15.
40. *Ibid*. p. 122.

credit, irrigation, and "scientific inputs" to the smallholders so that they
have favored access to inputs. While impressive on paper, the results of
the SFDA "on the ground" have been next to negligible.

The resources assigned to the SFDA continue to be extremely small.
There are close to 2 million small- and marginal-farmer families in Karnataka.[41] These add up to about 10 million people and constitute approximately 45 percent of the rural population. At least half of this population
lives in conditions below the poverty line.[42] Less than 2 percent of the
provincial public investment was, however, assigned to the SFDA. Also,
a look at past patterns does not make one optimistic that the benefits of
the more generalized public investment for such needs as irrigation and
crop husbandry will "trickle down" to these groups. Therefore it is not
unreasonable to conclude that programs designed to benefit 45 percent of
the rural population are assigned about 2 percent of the public investment. These investment patterns reflect governmental priorities and it is
not likely that these meager resources can make a noticeable impact on
the small farmers' incomes.

Greater resources can make some difference, but the real problems are
organizational. In order to clarify what is involved here, I will suggest a
simple analogy. From the point of view of social actors, public resources
for social benefit are like extra resources falling from the sky. If some
social actors are tall and others short, the tall ones tend to grab much of
what is coming down. The disposer as well as the receiver of resources
understands this phenomenon. If, for some reason or other, the disposer
wants to ensure that the resources reach the shorter people, he or she has
the following options: eliminate the tall people, make the shorter ones
taller by providing some extra base, and/or stretch out long arms that
hand over resources directly to the short people. The first alternative, the
elimination of tall people, is generally available only in revolutionary settings. The other two approaches are available to reformist states for
accomplishing their egalitarian goals. Redistributive reform from above,
especially in rural settings, is therefore often contingent on the following:
that the base to make the short people tall must be effective; and/or the
arms of the disposer must not only be long enough to reach the short
people directly, but also strong enough to prevent the tall from forcibly
grabbing the resources.

41. Estimate based on the number of small (2.5 — 5 acres) and marginal (below 2.5 acres)
    operational landholdings in Karnataka. See Government of Karnataka, *Agricultural
    census, 1976-77* (State Agricultural Census Commission: Bangalore, 1978) Table 1.
42. Because 50% of the rural population live in conditions below the poverty line, and
    because the landless constitute about a quarter of the rural population, it is not
    unreasonable to extrapolate that the remaining 25% of the rural poor are the marginal
    and the small farmers.

Like all analogies, this one distorts reality. It nevertheless helps clarify some important points. The base that is likely to make the short people tall in the Indian political setting is politicization. Changing conscious-ness, as well as the mobilization and organization of the lower classes, increases their power, enabling them to compete more effectively in the social and political arenas. The function of a "long and strong arm" in turn is likely to be best performed by an ideologically disciplined, radical political party. Only such left-of-center parties can effectively link the dis-poser (the government) to the short recipients (the lower classes) while ensuring that the tall people (the upper classes) do not totally frustrate the reformist attempts.

In the case of West Bengal we noticed the CPM's attempts to simul-taneously provide a politicized social base, build an organizational framework linking the power center to the lower classes, and exclude the propertied from institutional participation. The CPM's experiment is not a total success, yet it stands out as uniquely impressive within the Indian setting. In Karnataka, by contrast, such an organizational structure was missing. The Urs regime neither was capable of making "short people tall," nor had the political and organizational arrangements for handing over resources directly to the "short people." It was thus not likely that public resources, whether little or substantial, would effectively reach the lower rural classes.

In addition to the SFDA, the government has periodically expressed concern regarding the availability of credit for the smallholders. It is widely recognized that neither co-operative lending nor that offered by the commercial banks in Karnataka, as elsewhere in India, tends to reach the small farmers. If the small farmers are to be helped in improving their investments in and incomes from land, how can credit be made available to them? In contrast to the case of West Bengal, the Karnataka govern-ment made no efforts to bargain with the commercial banks. Without an organizational framework, such as the "red *panchayats*" of West Bengal, the Urs regime had nothing to offer to the banks that might induce them to become substantially involved in small rural loans. Co-operatives in Karnataka also continue to be ineffective. As an integral part of Urs' pat-ronage network, co-operative "loans" accrued mainly to larger landown-ers and those associated with the ruling faction.

Some hope was placed in the Farmer Service Societies (FSS). Sup-ported by the World Bank, the FSS are multi-purpose organizations designed to provide credit, inputs, marketing, and other services to the farmers under one organizational umbrella. These are still in the early stages of development. There were only 119 of these societies in Kar-nataka in 1979. Each society had a jurisdiction of about 20 villages. Site visits in the Mandya district revealed that most of the smaller farmers had never even heard of the FSS. Because they were based on the old principle of land as collateral and were run by a combination of government servants and local notables, it is difficult to imagine these organizations making any significant contribution to the lot of the marginal and small farmers.

The retraining of extension workers has been a substantial endeavor in Karnataka. Regime statements have indicated that the retraining may involve a lower-class bias. A close look at these programs, however, revealed a different reality. A senior Agricultural Officer candidly noted, "We have consciously worked with the big and middle farmers. The bigger ones are open to new ideas. That is why production is going up." While further noting the recent attempts to work with the small farmers, the officer also made it clear that there were "no departmental funds especially available for this."[43] In other words, there were no special attempts under way to tilt the agrarian services in favor of the smallholders.

I visited an "elite" center for the training of Agricultural Extension Officers (AEOs). This visit revealed a middle and upper-middle peasant bias in the government's extension services.[44] The center provided intensive training for paddy cultivation to a select group of Extension Officers and "progressive farmers." The latter were larger landowners who were interested in mechanization and, as most instruction was in English, could speak English. The center, established through Indo-Japanese collaboration, was equipped with Japanese power tillers, transplanters, thrashers, and power sprayers.

A good part of the four-month training at this center involved the assembling and dismantling of machinery and the training in its use. The program content, in turn, emphasized the utility of such "progressive" farming techniques as the use of power tillers for "small families with large land." If the "progressive farmers" then wished to invest in machinery, the AEOs could help them secure loans that were readily available from the nationalized banks. That the available machinery was Japanese and being produced in nearby Bangalore was of course no coincidence. The whole arrangement was therefore a clear illustration of a tacit alliance between commercial agriculture, the state, and even representa-

43. Interview, D. R. Dwarkinath, Director of Agriculture, Government of Karnataka, Bangalore, April 22, 1979.
44. The visit was to the Vishwesharaya Canal Farm, Mandya District. Established with Indo-Japanese collaboration in the 1960s, the "farm" now operates as a training and demonstration center. The following account of the center is based on a one-day visit to the farm arranged by the Office of the District Commissioner, Mandya District, Karnataka.

tives of international capitalism. The retraining programs had little to do with introducing a lower-class bias into the extension services.[45]

To summarize, small farmers in Karnataka have hitherto not benefitted and are not likely to benefit significantly from state intervention. The resources allocated for them remain minuscule. Additionally, there has been little attempt to alter the existing patterns of credit flow and extension work. The benefits, therefore, continue to accrue to the larger landowners. Political factors are primarily responsible for this bias. Populist... rhetoric has been easy to espouse; implementing redistributive reform has proven to be much more difficult. To bridge the gap between rhetoric and reality would require the forging of mobilizational and institutional strategies. These have been mostly absent. Regime organization and class constraints in Karnataka have thus precluded the possibility of a decisive attack upon the poverty conditions of smallholders.

Wage and Employment Schemes for the Landless

Thus far I have analyzed poverty policies aimed at improving the lot of those who have access to some land. Tenancy reforms have had some success. The efforts to improve the productivity and incomes of the smallholders have, however, been inconsequential. Now I turn to the issue of landless laborers. Over a quarter of the rural population and about half of the rural poor in Karnataka are landless. Because agrarian employment is limited and radical land redistribution not on the agenda, the only means for systematically buttressing their incomes are higher wages or additional employment. Political attempts to alter these conditions are investigated here.

Over time, agricultural wages in Karnataka have failed to keep up with price increases. Table 4.11 documents the fact that by 1979 the unit wage of landless laborers was about 80 percent of what it was in 1960. Because overall poverty has not increased, wage data in conjunction with the poverty data roughly suggest that expanding employment opportunities have barely allowed the landless laborers to prevent absolute deterioration in their living conditions.

The Urs regime periodically passed legislation to fix the minimum wages for the landless laborers. In 1978 it also went on to make the unlikely claim that due to "vigorous implementation... agricultural wages were enhanced [by] 30 percent."[46] Field visits revealed that this

---

45. To be fair, there are other types of retraining of AEOs also under way. Some of these are supported by the World Bank. I did not get a chance to investigate these other training programs.
46. Urs, *Socio-economic programme for the poor*, p. 7.

Table 4.11 *Actual Wages and Real Wages of Agricultural Laborers in Karnataka, 1960–1979*

Year	Actual wage per day (in rupees)	Wages to be paid as per consumer index number for agricultural labor	Column (2) as % of column (3)
1960	1.66	1.66	100
1961	1.69	1.95	86.7
1962	1.82	1.97	92.7
1963	2.05	2.04	100.4
1964	2.14	2.52	84.9
1965	2.11	2.82	74.8
1966	2.22	3.18	69.8
1967	2.41	3.34	72.1
1968	2.46	3.37	72.9
1969	2.60	3.15	82.5
1970	2.71	3.27	82.8
1971	2.71	3.40	79.7
1972	2.84	3.57	79.5
1973	3.11	4.60	67.6
1974	3.55	5.76	61.6
1979	4.00	5	80

Source: Data for 1960-74 from Bureau of Economics and Statistics, Government of Karnataka "Agricultural wages and their trends in Karnataka " (1975). Data from 1975-8 were not available. The wage data for 1979 were collected during interviews in Mandya district. As wages in Mandya have generally been close to the average wage for the state in the past, it is assumed that they continue to be so. The consumer index number for agricultural laborers for 1979 is taken from Government of Karnataka, *Economic survey* (Government Press: Bangalore, 1978-80).

was not so. Money wages between 1974 and 1979 increased by about 10 percent. As the purchasing power of money continued to decline, real wage increase, if any, was certainly less than even 10 percent. Much of this increase was likely to have resulted from changing economic conditions. There was no evidence to indicate that "vigorous implementation" of the minimum-wage legislation was of consequence for agricultural wages. The regime really has no organizational arrangement to implement wage legislation. It is not likely that a 30 percent wage increment could have resulted from an occasional inspection by bureaucrats, or the landlord-dominated *panchayats*.

Karnataka's rural labor remains unorganized. Congress as the dominant party has made no efforts to unionize the landless. Towards the end of his regime, Urs was still claiming that "during the current year, Farmers and Agricultural Laborers Associations will be organized."[47] In 1981 there was still no move in this direction. Given the fact that Congress has no politicized rural cadres, it is not likely that the mobilization and organisation of rural labor will occur under the leadership of Congress.

47. *Ibid.* p. 7.

This task will have to await the significant entry of the left-of-center parties on the rural Karnataka scene.

Employment-generation schemes have had a little more success. Prominent among these is the Employment Affirmation Scheme (EAS), or what we encountered in West Bengal as the Food for Work Program. These schemes are initiated and sponsored by the center. They have become a convenient mechanism for involving the Indian Central Government in buying up unabsorbed agrarian surplus — unabsorbed due to limited money demand — and turning it into "welfare." Great pains have been taken in Karnataka to make sure that new jobs created by such welfare programs do not put pressure on the existing employment market.[48] Political authorities also benefit because the schemes allow them to act as patronage donors building influence with the receivers.

The implementation of the EAS in Karnataka has not been as effective as that in West Bengal. The major problems have been organizational, resulting in charges of corruption. The Urs regime, with its minimal organizational capacities, resorted to the already-overloaded office of the District Commissioner. Because the schemes are to be operated in selected *taluks*, the administrative authority had to be delegated further down. Effective authority has thus come to rest in the *taluk* committees. These include the Chairman of the Taluk Development Board, the Block Development Officer and the Local Assembly member. The *taluk* committees make decisions regarding the selection and location of projects. They also administer the funds and the grain released for the EAS. As they are staffed by office-holders who are already part of various patronage–corruption networks, it was not likely that the EAS can be administered in the genuine interests of the poor, free of corruption.

My site visits to the EAS projects and discussions in *taluk* towns confirmed that there were charges of corruption. What was surprising was that there was little mention of outright appropriation of public funds for private use. Most corruption occurred in the selection of projects, in who got the resulting contracts, and in who actually got the jobs on the project. For example, in one case there was discussion regarding the building of a "godown" (warehouse) for private use. It was claimed that audit officers were also involved in the cover-up. Such claims were difficult to substantiate, especially because the said "godown" was legally registered as the property of the Taluk Board and thus as public property. In contrast to West Bengal, other projects also failed to reflect any special

---

48. Regime instructions to lower bureaucrats thus go to great lengths to ensure that labor is not taken away from the employers: "It should be ensured that the scheme does not adversely affect the operations and development of agriculture and other rural activities. Particularly, the identification of the slack season should be done carefully." See, Government of Karnataka, *Employment affirmation scheme* (Planning Department: Bangalore, 1978), pp. 27-8.

concern for the members of the lower classes. There were no roads linking the untouchable colonies to main roads. This, of course, did not preclude the landless gaining additional, off-season employment. In general
then, the implementation of the EAS in Karnataka had generated
employment and thus benefited some of the landless of the area. On the
other hand, part of the public resources was being frittered away by corrupt practices, and the selection of projects did not really reflect the needs
of the lower classes.

Conclusion

To summarize and conclude the discussion on Karnataka, I have sought
to analyze the reformist performance of a populist regime. On balance,
Karnataka's poverty reforms have had limited success. Tenancy reforms
in particular have required careful scrutiny. Many of the powerful among
the landed of Karnataka did not lose their lands. As much as 50 percent
of the tenanted land may thus remain under the control of the former
leasing landowners. Given the stringent tenancy laws, one can be sure
that these landowners have found ways to transform their tenancy
arrangements into something resembling managerial or supervisory
farming. Will the turning of former tenants into landless laborers then
contribute to greater equity? No. The results are likely to be the opposite.
With regard to the half of the tenanted land that actually changed hands,
the former tenants were, of course, net gainers. Whether, however, taking lands away from smallholders, or from select large landowners who
are in the political wilderness, really constitutes "egalitarian justice"
remains a debatable case.

Center-sponsored employment schemes have generated additional
incomes. Some of the tenants and the landless laborers are bound to
benefit, even if marginally, from these politically initiated reforms. Conversely, redistribution of "above ceiling" lands has not been touched, and
marginal and small farmers have not gained from regime programs. The
plight of the landless laborers also continues to be serious: despite electoral promises, they remain unorganized; wage legislation is mostly
meaningless; and low wages remain the order of the day. In sum then,
while there has been some success — and this in the face of much of
India's record deserves credit and attention — the gap between Devraj
Urs' claims that "social justice has been translated into reality" and the
reality viewed from the perspective of the lower classes is rather wide.

From an analytical standpoint, more important than the balance sheet
are the regime characteristics facilitating or obstructing poverty reforms.
The limited success resulted from the leadership's need to make true its
claims of a "popular" regime. The Urs regime, therefore, had political

claims of a "popular" regime. The Urs regime, therefore, had political reasons to pursue reforms. Reasons alone, however, never suffice as an explanation of outcomes. Leadership capacity to translate political needs into policy outcomes was crucial. A political arrangement dominated by a strong leader — the followers beholden to the leader for their positions — facilitated coherent and concerted pressure from above. This allowed the pushing-through of some redistributive measures, especially those that did not threaten the existing class structure in any fundamental way. The personal contribution of Devraj Urs was crucial. He played an important role in pressing for new tenancy legislation, in creating the land tribunals, and in then sustaining pressure for ready implementation. A professional bureaucracy and pockets of conscious and mobilized tenant population further aided the process of tenancy reform. A strong populist leadership, helped by some fortuitous circumstances, was thus able to push through limited reforms.

Conversely, the nature of political organization and the class basis of Urs' regime made it impossible to initiate a more thorough reform. The dominant party and the government were little more than a collection of elites from varying backgrounds, bound together in a large patronage network. Party organization was weak and was penetrated by members of landowning classes. There was thus no reformist party to speak of in Karnataka, certainly nothing capable of translating reformist leadership goals into concrete outcomes in the villages. As a consequence, landless laborers could not be organized, institutional arrangements facilitating credit for smallholders could not be designed, and the question of identifying surplus land for appropriation and redistribution could not even be considered. By its very design, therefore, the Urs regime was not capable of undertaking systematic poverty reform.

Both the CPM regime, analyzed in the previous chapter, and the Urs regime have operated within similar social–structural constraints of democratic capitalism. Their reformist performances have varied. In only six years of its existence, the CPM regime has initiated a systematic attack on rural poverty. After nearly a decade of opportunity, the Urs regime had only limited successes to its claim. These varying capacities for reform reflect varying regime types. The Urs regime of course shared some characteristics with the CPM regime in West Bengal — coherent leadership and some ideological commitment to the rural poor. These allowed the Urs regime to push through limited reforms. By contrast to the CPM, however, the Urs regime could neither penetrate the countryside without being co-opted by the landed interests, nor mobilize the lower classes to help implement the reforms from above. The reformist capacities of a patronage-based, populist regime were therefore not as developed as those of a well-organized parliamentary-communist regime.

188

5.1 Map of Uttar Pradesh

5

Uttar Pradesh : Political Fragmentation, Middle-Peasant Dominance, and the Neglect of Reforms

Uttar Pradesh (U.P.) was the crown jewel of the 1977 Janata victory in North India. U.P. is the largest state of India. It is also the heart of the Hindi belt. The political significance of U.P. is manifest in the fact that five of India's six Prime Ministers — Nehru, Shastri, Charan Singh, Indira Gandhi and Rajiv Gandhi — began their political careers in this state. Nothing in early 1977 thus highlighted the rout of Congress(I) better than Janata's whopping 383-seat majority in the 425-seat U.P. Legislative Assembly. While U.P. had been ruled by non-Congress coalitions in earlier periods, this solid majority for a single party appeared to be something new in state politics.

In retrospect, the Janata coalition proved to be short-lived, ruling U.P. for only about three years. Janata's reformist performance during this brief rule is assessed here. Because three years is a rather short time for assessing political performance, the focus in this chapter is on the emerging trends. What was the nature of the Janata regime? And what type of reformist policies were set in motion by this new political force? These questions are analyzed here with the aim of comparing U.P.'s Janata regime with the CPM regime in West Bengal and the Congress(I) regime under Devraj Urs in Karnataka.

I document below the fact that the Janata party neglected poverty reforms: land reforms were excluded from political discussion; the much-publicized "rural tilt" toward marginal and small farmers did not materialize; and "Antyodaya" and other programs for the landless poor remained ineffective. The Janata rulers also turned a blind eye to "caste wars" — a euphemism for the repression of scheduled castes and the poor peasantry by the proprietary castes. On balance, therefore, the emergence of the Janata regime may have been of negative consequence for U.P.'s rural poor.

The neglect of reforms was a consequence of the political and social characteristics of the Janata regime. An analysis of these is the core task of the present chapter. I argue that U.P.'s Janata regime had neither reasons nor the capacity for initiating poverty reforms. The U.P. regime in the late 1970s was an unstable alliance of the erstwhile Lok Dal and Jan Sangh. While both parties drew core support from the middle castes and better-off peasants, they differed considerably in the pattern of their origin, ideology, and organization. These factors, along with issues of personal ambitions, made it difficult for the two parties to achieve a working political consensus. The Janata regime was thus characterized by an unstable coalition on the one hand, and on the other hand by the emergence of the backward and the propertied peasant castes as the dominant political force within the state. Political fragmentation created conditions within which power competition, and not developmental issues, dominated the political agenda. The emergence of land-owning peasantry as politically powerful influenced the policies pursued toward benefiting the privileged in the countryside. U.P.'s rural poor thus did not gain from the Janata phase in U.P.

The Janata Regime

Of the three states compared in this study, U.P. presents the greatest difficulties for generalization. The state has as many people —close to 100 million by now — as a country of the size of Brazil. Moreover, the state's population is quite diverse. This diversity is manifest in a sizable Muslim minority within the Hindu heartland; regionally concentrated caste affiliations; sharp geographical variation among the hills, plains, and swamplands; and regional differences in levels of development. The latter divides the state between a more advanced western half and a relatively underdeveloped eastern part. These distinctions show up in differing levels of per-acre yields, percapita income, literacy, and even degrees of politicization as measured by voter turnout. Western U.P. scores higher on all of these indicators than do the areas of the east.[1]

The size and diversity of the state make a chapter-length study of politics and poverty within it difficult. Both the political and poverty conditions vary considerably. Because I generalize about the political reality of U.P., several caveats ought to be borne in mind. First, the differing degrees of modernization of the western and the eastern halves of the state mask varying political patterns. For example, what looks like middle-peasant support for a political party across the state often has a different basis in the west than in the east; the more commercialized peasantry in the western half increasingly tend to make political demands on economic grounds, while the preferences in the east are still influenced more by such primary group affiliations as caste. Similarly, the support of a party by the poor peasants and the landless laborers reflects dependent political behaviour — dependent on "overlords of varying types — in the

1. See Saraswati Srivastava, "Uttar Pradesh: politics of neglected development," in Iqbal Narain (ed.), *State politics in India*, pp. 323-69.

east, while in the west this support stems from other conditions analyzed below. Such regional diversity can only be touched upon at the level of generality at which this comparative state study is pitched. A more detailed treatment has to be left to U.P. specialists.

A second important caveat is that politics in U.P. often tend to be highly personalistic. Issues of conflict are therefore seldom policy issues; more often than not they have to do with circumstances affecting personal or factional power positions. This is manifest in the continuously shifting alliances, in the high turnover in legislative seats, and in factional politics.[2] It would be easy to overinterpret a political situation of this type in search of patterns that do not exist.

The third and the last caveat prior to discussing the Janata regime is a reminder to readers that, in keeping with the central theme of this study, the task of this chapter is to delineate the nature of a regime and to trace its reformist outcomes. This focus shifts attention away from the other interesting issues of why the Janata regime emerged dominant within U.P. That issue has been splendidly analyzed by others.[3] I will build on their work to link regime type to policy outputs.

The Janata rule in U.P. was characterized by changing leadership, shifting alliances, and endemic instability. This failure of institutionalization reflected in part the nature of the Janata party as a national political force, and in part the political trends integral to U.P. Power competition at the center was often fought out by proxy within U.P. and other states. Personality, as well as factional and social conflict within U.P., in turn both buttressed the centrally generated cleavages and occasionally cut across them. While the sources of conflict and political instability are thus quite complex, the overall consequences are clear. The first Janata government, the Ram Naresh Yadav Ministry, lasted for a little over a year and a half. During this period there were periodic no-confidence motions in the Legislative Assembly; ministries were periodically shuffled, expanded, or contracted; and important individuals switched alliances and parties. The second government, the Banarsidas Ministry, lasted less than a year, when a resurgent Indira Gandhi dismissed it by a presidential decree. The Banarsidas year was no more stable than the year that

2. Paul Brass, *Factional politics in an Indian state: the Congress party in Uttar Pradesh*, (University of California Press: Berkeley, 1965), esp. chs. 3, 9 and 10
3. Paul Brass' work is indispensable here. See his following three articles: "The politicization of the peasantry in a North Indian state: I," *Journal of Peasant Studies*, 7, 4 (July 1980), 395-426; "The politicization of the peasantry in a North Indian state: II," *Journal of Peasant Studies*, 8, 1 (September 1980), 3-36; and "Congress, the Lok Dal, and the middle-peasant castes: an analysis of the 1977 and 1980 parliamentary elections in Uttar Pradesh," *Pacific Affairs*, 54, 1 (spring 1981), 5-41. Also see Pradhan M. Prasad, "Rising middle peasantry in North India," *Economic and Political Weekly*, annual number, 15, 5-7 (1980), 215-19.

preceded it. So bizarre was the overall Janata phase, that it led a commentator to characterize U.P. politics in the following dramatic terms: "If the state administration is a cavernous den of prehistoric dinosaurs, the body politic is Alice's Wonderland. Orwellian doublespeak is the 'lingua franca' and alliances shift like the broken glass patterns in a kaleidoscope."[4]

How does one make sense out of this kaleidoscopic pattern of politics where alliances shift like "broken glass" and governments do not last very long? What are the sources of this governmental instability and what are the developmental consequences for the rural poor?

The Janata party in U.P., as elsewhere, was formed out of disparate parties united in opposition to Indira Gandhi's Congress. The main constituents of the U.P. Janata were the former Bhartiya Lok Dal (BLD) and the Jan Sangh. Of the 383 seats captured by the Janata, 164 belonged to the BLD faction and 103 to the Jan Sangh. The other significant minority factions within the U.P. Janata were the Congress for Democracy (CFD) with 46 seats and the Congress(O) with 32 seats. "Socialists" of various types controlled the remaining 38 seats. Charan Singh's BLD, with its 164 seats, dominated this alliance. Both Ram Naresh Yadav and Banarsidas as Chief Ministers thus belonged to the erstwhile BLD.

As Table 5.1 indicates, the Janata's 1977 victory marked a sizable increase in the support of its constituents over previous elections. Some of this was without doubt a swing-vote against the emergency. And the capacity to match seats with the percentage of votes further reflected successful electoral alliances. As the 1980 election reconfirmed, however, the Janata victory in U.P. was not merely a passing phenomenon. One is tempted to suggest that some fundamental change had taken place in U.P. politics.[5] The former BLD (now Lok Dal) and the Jan Sangh (now the Bhartiya Janata party), taken together, still polled over 50 percent of the popular vote in 1980.[6] Clearly a potential non-Congress alternative has permanently emerged in U.P. politics. Whether this can be converted into majority Assembly seats and stable non-Congress governments in the future is an important but, for this study, a secondary question.

Paul Brass has nicely analyzed this rise of the Janata party in U.P.[7] While some of these issues are further discussed below, the main reasons for Janata's success are clearly brought out by Brass. The Janata party reflected the emergence of middle and rich peasantry — the "backward"

4. See *India Today*, English fortnightly, New Delhi (February 16-28, 1979), 13.
5. The 1985 national election results are just in as this manuscript goes to press. Whether the major electoral gains for the Congress reflect temporary "mood swings" or something more basic remains to be seen.
6. See G.G. Mirchandani, *The people's verdict* (Vikas: New Delhi, 1980).
7. See his three articles referred to in footnote 3 above.

Table 5.1 *Percentage of Votes Polled by the Major Political Parties in Uttar Pradesh*

Party	1952	1957	1962	1967	1971	1977
Congress	53	46	38	33	49	25
Jan Sangh (amalgamated into Janata in 1977)	7	15	18	23	12	—
Bhartiya Kranti Dal (BKD)	(founded 1967, refounded as Bhartiya Lok Dal (BLD) in 1974; amalgamated into Janata in 1977)				13	—
Janata	(founded 1977)					68
Independents	17	16	11	17	9	6

Source: computed from reports of the Election Commission of India.

castes — as the dominant political force in the state. The constituents of the Janata brought together the support of propertied peasantry from various parts of the state: the BLD aggregated the support of such commercial peasant communities as the Jats in western India and Yadavs across the state; the Jan Sangh brought along with it the core support of rich and middle peasants in the Oudh districts; and the former socialist support in the person of Raj Narain had secured the Janata party a base in the cultivating castes of Eastern U.P. The Janata party thus received broad-based support across the state from middle and rich peasants. Why did the middle and rich peasantry support these parties? This issue is really not central to my study. I will nevertheless comment on it briefly below.

Political conflict within the U.P. Janata regime revolved around the accommodation of the Jan Sangh faction under the BLD leadership. This involved primarily a struggle over power and control of patronage, and only secondarily a conflict over the content of public policies. In the early phase, the conflict was temporarily resolved by finding a compromise candidate for the Chief Minister as well as by appointing a few of the Jan Sangh leaders as Cabinet Ministers. This reconciliatory attitude reflected the larger national political trends. Following the victorious post-emergency elections, Janata's euphoria about a "new beginning" sustained a working relationship between Charan Singh and the Jan Sangh at the center. The euphoria was, however, shortlived. As the power conflict at the center hardened, and as issues affecting the relative power balances of the various factions emerged within the state, the reconciliatory accommodation came undone. As one of the important party advisers explained to the author:

The origins of conflict went back to the establishment of the Central Election Panel in late August, 1978. Mr. Charan Singh was not able to place as many of "his" candidates on the panel as he would have liked. When the state election panels were thus formed in October/November of 1978, BLD in U.P. wanted to boycott them. That Yadav fired Jan Sangh ministers in January 1979 does not then seem unrelated.[8]

As the Jan Sangh ministers were fired, the Chief Minister could not muster enough support from the new alliance and the State Government itself came undone.

When a new ruling arrangement emerged in early 1979, it became clear that the BLD had hardened its attitude towards the Jan Sangh. The BLD now formed an alliance with the CFD. A Chief Minister acceptable to both of these factions, namely, Banarsidas, was then chosen. The Banarsidas Ministry excluded all but one prominent member of the Jan Sangh from the Cabinet. While this in part reflected Charan Singh's changed strategy toward the Jan Sangh, it also reflected conflicts within the state. (These are discussed below.) The changed strategy and increased tensions, in turn, had an impact on other states and the national situation. These complex workings of the Janata regime within U.P. can be further untangled by analyzing the leadership, ideology, organization, and social support of the component factions, as well as that of the regime as a whole.

So tangled were U.P. politics with national politics during this period, that it is difficult to locate where the effective leadership power resided. The BLD faction within U.P. seldom made major decisions without consulting its central leader, Charan Singh, or his aides, such as Raj Narain. The Jan Sangh faction was similarly constantly in touch with its national leadership and the CFD with Bahuguna, the National Petroleum Minister and the former Chief Minister of U.P. Aside from interactions within the factions, various U.P. leaders as members of the Janata party periodically consulted with the National President of the party, Chandrashekhar. It is important to note that many of these consultations were about power strategies — who controls which political office with what consequences for the political future of specific factions and individuals — and not about policies. The constant back-and-forth movement of U.P. leaders between Lucknow and Delhi confirmed the fact that few offices in U.P. were assigned without prior consultation with the leaders at the center.

Of all the leaders involved in the U.P. situation, Charan Singh's impact was probably the most significant. Even though he was then in Delhi, he was the unquestioned leader of the BLD faction within Janata. And

8. Interview, Surendra Mohan, Janata party Adviser, Lucknow, June 11, 1979.

because the BLD faction dominated the U.P. government, Charan Singh must have wielded considerable influence in U.P. politics. It is therefore important to highlight some aspects of Charan Singh's leadership style.

Charan Singh is a controversial leader. Loved by *kisans*, especially Jat *kisans* of western India, and derided by his opponents as an opportunistic leader, Mr Singh is the ultimate coalition politician. As far back as 1967, Charan Singh had gained the reputation of being a "fence-sitter" in U.P.'s factional politics.[9] After the 1967 elections, for example, U.P. politics came to be dominated by the intra-Congress party struggles of the C.B. Gupta and the Kamlapati Tripathi factions. Taking advantage of a factionalized situation, Charan Singh made his first of many bids to be the state's Chief Minister. If not made the Chief Minister, he warned, he would withdraw his support from the Congress, leaving the party in a minority position in which it would be unable to form a government. Charan Singh recanted this threat only at the personal urging of Indira Gandhi. This reconciliatory stance, however, lasted only for a few days. Very soon afterwards Charan Singh actually quit the Congress, formed his own party, and joined the main opposition coalition — Samyukta Vidhayak Dal (SVD) — which included the Jan Sangh and the Socialists. This opposition then formed the first non-Congress government in U.P. with Charan Singh as the Chief Minister.

Charan Singh's ministry lasted less than a year. Bickering soon emerged among the coalition partners. Most of the disputes were over assignment of ministerial portfolios and control of other sources of patronage. The Jan Sangh withdrew its support, and presidential rule had to be established. Once again in 1969, when the Congress split, both C. B. Gupta, who had become part of the Congress(O), and Tripathi courted Charan Singh. The condition of Singh's support for either of the competing groups was the position of Chief Minister. Mr Singh, in turn, courted all the possible combinations — including the SVD — that would allow him to head the government. And indeed he finally aligned with Mrs Gandhi's faction, headed by Tripathi, and emerged as U.P.'s Chief Minister once again. But again this was only for a short time. The old disputes reappeared; Tripathi withdrew his support; and presidential rule was decreed. Once again Charan Singh moved away from Congress (I) to join forces with the Jan Sangh and the Socialists.

All this is to highlight that a back-and-forth movement among competing coalitions, irrespective of policy issues, and aimed at maximizing indi-

9. The following account of Charan Singh's role in U.P. politics is based on several interviews in Lucknow and Meerut. Because quite a few people interviewed in U.P. wished to remain anonymous, only some names are mentioned. These interviews were conducted in the summers of 1979 and 1984.

vidual or factional power position, has been the hallmark of Charan Singh's leadership style.[10] Charan Singh is, of course, not alone in this mode of political behavior. Many of India's important leaders act in a similar manner. Charan Singh nevertheless stands out as one of the foremost makers or breakers of coalitions in Indian politics. When pressed in an interview situation to reflect on his leadership style, Charan Singh became philosophical: "Human conduct is highly random. The same person can behave very differently under similar conditions. We are all quite unpredictable."[11] Charan Singh, in other words, did not deny that his leadership style is volatile. He rather explained it away as "human nature." This volatility continued during the Janata experience. Charan Singh's leadership of the BLD thus added an important degree of coalitional instability within the U.P. Janata regime.

U.P.'s Jan Sangh has had considerable experience working with Charan Singh's BLD. While the two have often formed governments as coalition partners, neither party trusted the political motivations of the other. Leaders of both parties blamed each other for being "selfish," "opportunistic," and "without principles."[12] One, and possibly the only, way of resolving U.P.'s leadership issue during the highly factionalized Janata phase was to find "weak" Chief Ministers.

Ram Naresh Yadav, Janata's first Chief Minister, was thus described by his opponents as a "two-rupee *tehsil* court *vakil*" (or a "two-bit lower court lawyer").[13] Yadav was in actuality a small-town lawyer who lacked the qualities of a great leader. He was not a forceful speaker and he had no clear-cut political position and little independent political base. Prior to his ascendance to U.P.'s Chief Ministership, Yadav had actually never

10. This is my own conclusion. A number of U.P. politicians that I interviewed — Kalraj Misra (BJP), Lalji Tandon (former RSS), and Ram Prakash Gupta (former Deputy Chief Minister under Charan Singh's SVD government) — tended to corroborate this interpretation. Those more sympathetic to Charan Singh would, of course, disagree. Mr Rajendra Singh, leader of the opposition in the U.P. Legislative Assembly (summer 1984), who is a senior member of Charan Singh's erstwhile Lok Dal, was among those who suggested that Charan Singh's factional disagreements were over substance of policy. Brass has also argued this position in a scholarly publication. See Paul Brass, "Division in the Congress and the rise of agrarian interests and issues in Uttar Pradesh politics, 1952 to 1977," in John Wood (ed.), *The crisis of state politics in Indira Gandhi's India* (Westview Press: Boulder, Colorado, 1984), pp. 21-52. I have found little public evidence in support of the proposition that Charan Singh has long held a consistent pro-agrarian policy position and that factional conflicts involving Charan Singh were often policy conflicts stemming from these policy preferences.
11. Interview, Charan Singh, New Delhi, August 9, 1984.
12. Interview, Kalraj Misra, General Secretary, U.P. Bharatiya Janata Party, Lucknow, July 12, 1984; and Rajendra Singh (Lok Dal), Leader of the Opposition, U.P. Legislative Assembly, July 17, 1984.
13. These are attributed to Raj Mangal Pande, as quoted in *India Today* (February 16-28, 1979), 15.

won an election.[14] His major qualification in a factionalized political situation was that he had the fewest enemies. As a trusted associate of Raj Narain, who had joined forces with Charan Singh in the early 1970s, he was acceptable to many BLD legislators. Jan Sangh also found him the least threatening of the available options. As a consequence, Yadav became the Chief Minister and survived for a little less than two years. Throughout his brief tenure, however, he faced periodic challenges and eventually lost out because both the Jan Sangh and some of his own faction members withdrew their support.

Banarsidas, the second Janata Chief Minister, did not fare much better. While his tenure was shorter and terminated due to circumstances beyond his control, his brief experience as a leader of the largest Indian state was rather unimpressive. Even though the budget was passed under his tenure, there were no policy innovations. To be fair, we must note that the national and the regional political situation had become very difficult by the early 1980s. With Charan Singh and Jan Sangh at loggerheads nationally, and with Jan Sangh within U.P. excluded from access to high offices, factional struggles were rampant and bare political survival was of the essence.

This leadership situation in U.P. contrasted sharply with those discussed above in the cases of West Bengal and Karnataka. A disciplined party provides a coherent leadership in West Bengal. A strong leader had provided a similar function in Karnataka during the 1970s. The Janata elite, by contrast, was highly fragmented. Weak and factionalized leadership, in turn, created an environment within which power competition dominated the political agenda. Policy concerns were totally relegated to the background. As a thoughtful U.P. politician reflected:

People in Uttar Pradesh are preoccupied with power. Politics here is primarily power politics or politics of coalitions. Real issues are often absent from debate. If there were real issues, minor and personal conflicts would fall in the background. The failure to raise substantial issues is our real failure.[15]

To discuss "politics" in U.P. thus meant to discuss who belonged to which faction, who was on the verge of changing sides, who was gaining favor with whom and how, and who was channeling patronage to whom. That "politics" also has something to do with substantial issues — policies, development, and the public good — was a concept quite alien to U.P.'s

14. I met Ram Naresh Yadav only briefly in Lucknow on July 17, 1984. A number of those interviewed, however, confirmed this general view. Especially relevant were interviews with Ram Prakash Gupta, senior party member, U.P. BJP, Lucknow, July 26, 1984; and Rajendra Singh (same as in footnote 12).

15. From an interview with Ram Prakash Gupta (same as in footnote 14).

political culture. Politics in U.P. was politics of personality and of factional struggles for power, and not politics of substance.

Whether fragmented leadership is a cause or a consequence of politics-without-substance is not important. What is important is that these two traits go hand in hand in U.P. The consequences of this mode of politics appear to be quite profound. When I interviewed senior civil servants in U.P., it was clear that little time was spent thinking about policy issues. Leadership style tended to set a tone within which the civil servants spent most of their time either performing routine administration, or participating in "politics" in the sense of taking direct or indirect sides in the conflicts within the ruling circle.

Many civil servants in the planning and rural-development sections, once comfortable with the interviewer, were more than happy to discuss the political intrigues of the day. No one, however, really thought that land reforms, poverty programs, and other rural problems are issues worthy of conversational interest. This generally reflected a low political priority assigned to developmental concerns within the state. Srivastava is, therefore, quite right in having labelled U.P.'s politics as "politics of neglected development."[16] Politicians mainly fight for power and patronage; bureaucrats seek favors with politicians, protect their positions, and carry out routine administration; and no one debates the government's developmental responsibilities. The political idiom in which a government is conceived of as responsible for social ills, leading to contradictory opinions on what specific role the leaders should play, was mostly missing in U.P.

This is not to suggest that U.P.'s politics lacks an ideological framework. Ideologies exist but either they tend to be without economic and developmental content or, when they have specific economic commitments, these serve the primary purpose of electoral mobilization, and only secondarily relate to policy inputs. Janata's ideological posture can best be understood by first delineating the positions of the BLD and the Jan Sangh, and only then the attempts to amalgamate the two standpoints.

The BLD was formed in 1974 by the merging of the erstwhile Bhartiya Kranti Dal (BKD) and the Samukta Socialist Party (SSP).[17] The BKD itself was Charan Singh's party, formed in the late 1960s from the Jana Congress, a splinter group of a handful of Congress assembly members. The BKD from the beginning was identified as a party of the "backward castes." Charan Singh's deep roots in the Jat community of western U.P.

16. Srivastava, "Uttar Pradesh."
17. See Paul Brass, "Leadership conflict and the disintegration of the Indian socialist movement," *Journal of Commonwealth and Comparative Politics*, 14, 1 (March 1976), 19-41.

(and Haryana) were responsible for this image. In the early years this image primarily conveyed to the electorate a sense that Charan Singh's party, if powerful, would channel patronage to Jats and maybe other non-Brahmin "backward castes." Over the years, however, first the BKD and then the BLD developed an ideological posture favoring the economic interests of the "backward" cultivating castes in general.

It is important to remember that the BLD, like the Jan Sangh discussed below, had matured as parties while in opposition to the dominant Congress. Since the Congress was an aggregating and a national party, opposition parties have had to chip away at wherever there were pockets of dissatisfaction with the Congress. This situation has created a condition within which all opposition parties tend to be less than national parties and have more specific support bases. This specificity is sometimes defined by class or caste support, at other times by regional concentration, and in yet other instances by religious and nationalistic postures.

The BLD's ideological commitments reflected those of its undisputed leader, Charan Singh. As a Jat leader, Charan Singh evokes the image of a son of the soil. The word "Jat" itself in urban India connotes a country hick. Charan Singh's continuing and lasting animosity towards the Nehru family captures the ideological and cultural spirit which had given rise to the BLD:

Nehruji would bring forward all the western educated Brahmins. He never took me seriously because I wore a *dhoti* [loincloth]. I was a Jat and a country fool [my own translation from Hindi] to him. Shrimati [Indira Gandhi] is not that different. Forget the villages, she does not even know what is going on in Delhi. India lives in villages, not in New Delhi.[18]

It is therefore not surprising that a party with Charan Singh as its leader and its origins in "backward" cultivating castes should have sought to counter urban prejudices by developing an anti-urban and anti-industrial character. Arguing against Nehru's commitment to planning and heavy industry, Charan Singh has over the years spoken in favor of "decentralization" and a "rural tilt" in public investments. The latter would consist of greater investments in agriculture and supporting industries; agriculture price supports to alter the "unfair" terms of trade between the city and the countryside; and fertilizers.[19] In an India where the image of a Gandhi has faded, and the country is perceived by some to be dominated by urban sophisticates like the Nehru family, Charan Singh has continued to provide a much-needed *kisan* leadership. Image and economics thus

18. From an interview with Charan Singh (same as in footnote 11).
19. For Charan Singh's critique of Nehru and some of his ideas on development, see Charan Singh, *India's poverty and its solution*, 2nd edn. (Asia Publishing House: New York, 1964).

combined within the BLD to provide a rural alternative to urban and industrial India.

The Jan Sangh, by contrast, was formed in the aftermath of the partition in the early 1950s.[20] Those dissatisfied by the withering of greater India, and therefore with the leaders who presided over this process — Gandhi and Nehru — were among the founders of the Jan Sangh. As a party leader explained: "Our strength from the beginning was based on Hindu sentiment. We held partition as a failure of leadership. We also reacted against the communal conflict [unleashed against the Hindus]."[21] Militant Hindu nationalism was thus at the core of the Jan Sangh party from its inception.

The party was also from the beginning closely associated with a "non-political" and "cultural" organization, the Rashtriya Svayam Sevak Sangh — literally translated as The Association for National Service — the RSS. The RSS, according to a party activist, "was not formally linked to the Sangh. They did, however, have common values." In view of the recent controversies over the role of the RSS, the same activist went on to argue that "it is ridiculous to minimize or deny the link [between the Jan Sangh and the RSS]."[22] Another party member eloquently suggested that the "main goal of the RSS was to change society in accordance with the value of Hindu culture and the Hindu nation, whereas the main goal of the Jan Sangh was to change the government."[23] Emphasizing the "Sanskritik values" of asceticism, physical prowess, pride in the Hindu past, self-denial, and discipline, the RSS attracted many supporters in the urban areas. These generally tended to be the better educated — but better educated in the Hindi medium and therefore often anti-Western in orientation — and concentrated in small business and trading communities.[24] Early support of the Jan Sangh also came from these groups.

As the Jan Sangh, like all parties, has sought a wider electoral base, it has diversified its ideological appeals. It has tried to soften its Hindu nationalism to minimize its perceived threat to the significant Muslim minority of U.P. Moving beyond cultural and social issues, it has also taken positions on economic issues. These positions generally favor free enterprise and lowering of "land ceilings."[25] Jan Sangh's support base in

---

20. For background on the Jan Sangh, especially within U.P., see Angela Sutherland Burger, *Opposition in a dominant-party system, a study of the Jan Sangh, the Praja Socialist Party and the Socialist Party in Uttar Pradesh, India,* Center for South and South Asia Studies (University of California Press: Berkeley, 1969), esp. chs. 5 and 7.
21. From interview with Ram Prakash Gupta (same as in footnote 14).
22. Interview, Lalji Tandon, senior party member, U.P. BJP, Lucknow, July 12, 1984.
23. Interview, Ram Prakash Gupta (same as in footnote 14).
24. Interview, Lalji Tandon (same as in footnote 22).
25. *Ibid.*

U.P., as discussed below, is regionally concentrated and socially more diverse than its ideological appeals would lead one to believe. Its ideology nevertheless emphasizes Hindu nationalism and the interests of the urban and rural propertied classes.

Janata's national leadership needed to reconcile the BLD's and the Jan Sangh's positions, as well as the other ideological postures represented within the ruling coalition. Two significant viewpoints in the national coalition, other than those of the BLD and the Jan Sangh, were the pro-big-industry and puritanical outlook of Desai and his followers on the one hand and, on the other hand, the egalitarian bent of such "socialists" as Fernandez and Chandrashekhar. How does one reconcile such varying ideological postures: state support for commercial agriculture; Hindu nationalism; free enterprise; support of big industry; puritan cultural ethics; and a degree of egalitarianism? The reconciliation proved to be impossible. In the short run, however, the Janata leadership attempted to unify under the banner of "return to Gandhi." A commitment to Gandhism served several purposes for the Janata party: it differentiated what Janata had to offer from that offered in the immediate past by Mrs Gandhi; it allowed the Janata to maintain continuity with the revered memory of Mahatma Gandhi; and it was vague enough to offer something to everyone in the new ruling coalition.

The "return to Gandhi" posture emphasized three elements: decentralization, rural orientation, and a concern for the "small man." These commitments were vague enough to provide a convenient and unified cloak under which factional positions and interests could be pursued — at least temporarily. Decentralization could be interpreted as "less government" and therefore appealed to those concerned with anti-authoritarianism and/or with free enterprise. It also appealed to those attracted to Gandhi's concept of village self-government. A rural orientation could be seen as anti-urban and anti-western-type-modernity, thus appealing to those who wanted to preserve values of traditional India. It also appealed, of course, to those favoring *kisans* and arguing for a "rural tilt" in public policies. The concern for the small man fed on the populist mood generated by Mrs Gandhi. It especially appealed to the socialists. No one in the ruling alliance, however, questioned publicly whether these various goals could ever be accomplished concurrently or whether they had ever been reconciled in any polity even vaguely similar to India.

Charan Singh's BLD was the dominant faction within the U.P. Janata. This faction represented primarily the interests of the middle and the rich peasantry within the ruling coalition. A rural orientation in public policies was therefore emphasized in the state. Because over 85 percent of the regional population lives in the villages, no one could argue against the desirability of a "rural tilt" in public investments. But who would benefit from these investments? The question was kept away from public discussions. Distributional issues along class lines were not discussed in U.P. A politician close to the ruling circles commented on policy-making in the Ram Naresh Yadav Ministry as follows: "The Chief Minister depended mainly on civil servants for policies. The one yardstick with which all policies were judged was: will it benefit the villages? There was really no discussion about who in the villages would benefit. There was no discussion along class lines."[26] Increased public investments in the countryside would thus buttress the profitability of commercial farmers, especially those in the western half of the state, while creating an impression that resources were going to where the majority of the people live — in the villages.

Thus, the ideological posture of the U.P. Janata, while confused, was dominated by certain themes. A concern with "rural tilt" in public investments was matched by a neglect of distributional issues. These interrelated themes were captured by Charan Singh's concern with the *kisans* in general, irrespective of whether they were propertied or propertyless, wealthy or poor. There was also an occasional concern with the "lot of the poor" and with that of the "common man," just as there was lip-service paid to the issue of decentralization of power. These were, however, peripheral themes. They added to the ideological confusion within which a "rural tilt" in public expenditures was the major thrust.

Janata's "rural tilt" differed from the social-democratic position of the CPM in West Bengal and the populist one put forward by Devraj Urs in Karnataka. The contrast with the CPM's position is rather clear. Whereas the CPM has risen to power on a commitment to tilt the political–economic balance toward the lower classes, nothing of the sort was proposed or envisioned by the U.P. Janata. The primary commitment in U.P. was to the land-owning middle peasant castes. The distinction between U.P. Janata's "rural tilt" and Urs' populism is, however, less sharp; it is nevertheless real and important.

First, Urs' commitment to the propertied classes — which included urban and rural upper classes — was more broad-based than that of the U.P. Janata to the middle and rich peasants. This allowed Urs a greater degree of policy flexibility than was available in U.P. Second, Urs' minimal programs for the rural poor stemmed from a clear and explicit populist commitment to them, a commitment quite absent in U.P. The Janata party in U.P. offered broad platitudes to the "poor," but seldom committed itself to land reforms or any other redistributive measures. In

26. Interview, Ram Prakash Gupta (same as in footnote 14).

terms of its posture both toward the propertied and toward the property-less, therefore, the U.P. Janata was more narrowly based than Urs' populist regime in Karnataka. The difference may be only a matter of degree, but such differences are, I will argue below, consequential for policies. In broad terms, then, the U.P. Janata was primarily committed to the middle and upper peasantry, especially to those involved in commercial production, and by the same token, not to the rural poor.

The organizational features of the U.P. Janata and its constituents further reveal clearly the sources of political instability in the area. The former parties, now part of the Janata party, continued to maintain their separate organizational infrastructures. The BLD operated through what is formally a very loose but informally a rather cohesive base. Charan Singh's party does not have an elaborate formal structure. Below the district level, even in Western U.P., it is difficult to find BLD party committees, party offices or dues-paying party members. The Jan Sangh, by contrast, had a relatively well developed party organization. These organizational contrasts require further elaboration.

One important feature of the BLD was that those who supported it thought of it mainly as supporting Charan Singh. Most BLD supporters know of "Thakur Charan Singh" or "Chowdhry Charan Singh." These supporters often had pride in their faces as they talked about "their *chowdhry*," the "leader of *kisans*," now being in power. A senior party member proudly explained that "there are only two individuals in the country with a personal following — Indira Gandhi and Charan Singh."[27] Most village-level party supporters, however, do not know much about the BLD as a party. Charan Singh's party has changed names so many times over the years that most supporters do not identify with the party as an organizational identity. Therefore, to define one's politics in many parts of U.P. is to define whom one will vote for and who is "our" leader. The BLD as a party does not actively recruit members or introduce them to distinct political perspectives and preferences. Organizationally, therefore, the BLD, like the Congress, is more of a mirror of society and less an architect of political beliefs and behavior.

Jan Sangh, by contrast to the BLD, is a tightly organized, disciplined party. Party members acquire that status after a few years of party work. Support groups such as the RSS provide long periods of socialization in party values and discipline.[28] Empirical research on the Jan Sangh has confirmed some of its important features: a considerable number of Jan Sanghis are mobilized through the RSS; most Jan Sanghis tend to be better educated than their counterparts in other parties; and most party sup-

27. Interview Rajendra Singh (same as in footnote 12).
28. Interview Kalraj Misra (same as in footnote 12).

porters have a clear political identity, as is manifest in regular reading of the party periodicals.[29] Those who become party members, moreover, tend to accept party discipline. Factions tend to vote *en masse* in the legislature. With its base in urban traders and shopkeepers; with its "morning exercises" and hymns glorifying health, India, and Hinduism; and with its "brown shirt" drills, the disciplined orientation of the Jan Sangh evokes the interwar fascist parties of Europe in more than a superficial way.

The U.P. Jan Sangh, like the CPM in West Bengal, is much more of a political party than either the Congress or the BLD. It therefore tends to mold political preferences and provide cohesive organization, and it is generally an effective task-performer. Of course, the tasks that the Jan Sangh considers to be important are not the same as those of the other disciplined Indian party — the CPM. These differences, in turn, reflect both the differing party ideologies and varying social support.

What enabled the Janata — mainly a coalition of the BLD and the Jan Sangh — to emerge as the dominant political force within U.P.? The answer requires a brief analysis of the support structure of the BLD and the Jan Sangh within U.P. Paul Brass has described the Janata coalition in U.P. as a coalition of the "middle peasants" and the Congress as a party of the "extremes" — of the upper and the lowest social groups. If correct, this description shifts the burden of analysis to the issue of why the middle peasantry and the upper-middle peasantry have been disaffected from the Congress. Brass' answer, once again, is that this reflects (1) the dissatisfaction of the "backward" castes with the Brahminical elite, who monopolize patronage sources through the Congress; and (2) the policy neglect of the middle peasantry by the respective Congress regimes in the past.[30] While suggestive in important respects, especially in the analysis of the BLD, my own fieldwork in the area leads me to suggest some qualifications of this general interpretation of U.P. politics.

U.P. politics, of course, cannot be fully understood without reference to the underlying caste dynamics. The numerical distribution of castes within the state in recent years is, however, not known. Many analysts thus continue to assume that the last census on the basis of caste — that of 1931 — still provides a good indication of the relative proportions of caste groups within U.P. The figures from the 1931 census are reproduced in Table 5.2.

If these old data still broadly capture the distribution of castes within U.P., they reveal that the elite non-cultivating castes form a considerable minority within U.P. The Brahmins and Thakurs, moreover, own considerable land. Especially after the *zamindari* abolition, U.P. Brahmins

---

29. See Burger, *Opposition in a dominant-party system*, Parts II and IV.
30. See the references to Paul Brass' work in footnote 3.

Table 5.2 _ *Castes in Uttar Pradesh*

Caste category	Name of the caste	% in total population
Elite non-cultivating castes	Brahmins	9.2
	Thakurs	7.2
	Others	3.6
	Total	20
Elite cultivating castes	Jats, Bhumihars and Tyagis	2.1
Intermediate cultivating castes	Yadavs, Kurmis, Koris and others	41.9
Scheduled castes	Chamars and others	21
Muslims	—	15

gained ownership of lands that they had hitherto controlled only as intermediaries.[31] This process of gaining land under the auspices of Congress-supported policies further cemented a relationship between U.P. Brahmins and the Congress party which has lasted to this date. There was virtual unanimity among all those I interviewed concerning the fact that U.P. Brahmins overwhelmingly support the Congress party.

The fact that the Congress party built its support in U.P. through the land-owning, non-cultivating castes set the parameters for future political mobilization in the state. The opposition of elite and intermediate cultivating castes to the Congress–Brahmin alliance eventually crystallized under Charan Singh's leadership. As the Jan Sangh has been a powerful force within U.P., the Muslims have traditionally supported the Congress. Similarly, the Congress has been able to mobilize considerable support from the scheduled castes, based in part on their dependence on elite castes and in part on the "welfare" measures which the Congress has championed. It is this broad pattern which can lead one to characterize the more recent U.P. Congress as a party of extremes — a party supported by Brahmins, Muslims and scheduled castes simultaneously — and the Janata alliance as a party of the middle.

The U.P. Congress is, however, really not best characterized as a party of the extremes. It is better thought of as a broad-based party with declining support in some crucial regions of the state. Several reasons can be cited for why the interpretation of U.P. Congress as a party of extremes is somewhat misleading. First, Brass' own quantitative data suggest that as far as the size of landownership is concerned, "There were no strong

31. How this situation came to be is an interesting story which does not concern us here. It is nicely documented by Imtiaz Ahmed and N.C. Saxena, "Caste, land and political power in Uttar Pradesh," (mimeo) in Frankel and Rao (eds.), *Caste, class and dominance* (forthcoming).

correlations between the Congress vote share in 1977 and any of the individual size categories."[32] The Congress thus continued to receive broad-based support from landholders of all sizes.

Second, the Congress *is* the party of India's "green revolution." It was Mrs Gandhi who was, after all, the chief architect of this new approach to agricultural policies in the late 1960s.[33] If, in spite of this, the Congress has failed to attract the support of U.P. Jats and Yadavs, the reasons for this must lie in factors other than the failure of Congress to provide economic benefits to these groups. As a matter of fact, it could be argued that the political clout of the "backward" cultivating castes has increased precisely because of the economic benefits channeled to them by the Congress. The Congress has, however, tried to balance the interests of the commercial peasantry with those of the urban consumers and the lower castes and classes in the countryside. This broad-based approach has alienated many in the ranks of the middle peasantry, leading them to throw their political weight behind alternative parties — parties promising to be more exclusively for the *kisan*.

The rise of the "backward" cultivating castes or the middle peasantry in U.P. politics is, then, not only a consequence of the past neglect of these groups by the Congress. Though Congress may have neglected these groups systematically in the 1950s, and continued to do so in more recent times as far as patronage was concerned, the economic policies since the latter 1960s have very much been in their favor. This is especially true for Western U.P., where the "green revolution" has progressed the furthest. The commercialized middle peasantry as a political force is then, at least in part, a product of Congress' own creation. The Congress party has released new political forces that it now does not know how to harness for its own benefit.

Another important consideration suggesting that the U.P. Congress is not a party of extremes is the regional concentration of the opposition. Charan Singh's original support was concentrated in U.P.'s western districts; Raj Narain and the former socialists had gained their seats in the eastern parts of the state; and Oudh districts had come under the control of the Jan Sangh. This past pattern indicated that local considerations remained very important for understanding political preferences. Coalition strategies, in turn, often reflected political convenience more than any other consideration. Political patterns determined by local factors and political opportunism, then, are not easily analyzable in terms of their sociological roots. It would be easy to overinterpret such a situation in the search for a social logic of the political process.

32. See Brass, "Politicization of the peasantry, II," p. 30.
33. See Frankel, *India's political economy*, esp. ch. 7.

The BLD's core support came from such elite cultivating castes as the Jats and such intermediate cultivating castes as the Yadavs and the Kurmis.[34] The Jats are concentrated in the western districts. Charan Singh is himself a Jat. Ever since Charan Singh broke away from the Congress, he took the Jat support with him. He has remained the unquestioned leader of the Jat community and has also incorporated those who were formerly in opposition to the Congress and ran as independents.[35] This former alliance of the BKD later merged with an important segment of the Socialist Party to form the BLD. This gave the latter a broader support base. The initial support of Ahirs of eastern U.P. was especially crucial. The Ahirs, or the Yadavs, are a large cultivating caste spread throughout the state. Having gained the support of this caste group in the eastern part of the state in the 1970s, Charan Singh's BLD had also slowly incorporated them. Interviews with MLAs confirmed that there was widespread support for Charan Singh among the Yadavs of eastern U.P.[36] A shared economic situation in this instance at least tended to encourage the political coalition of different castes.

While the Jats, Yadavs, and other cultivating castes provide the BLD's core support, the arithmetic of the Indian situation requires all parties to generate some lower-class support in order to secure electoral majorities. Interviews revealed considerable antipathy among the scheduled castes and other rural poor towards the middle peasantry. In Meerut district, for example, one repeatedly heard complaints from the poor about the "rough and tough" methods used by the Jats to secure compliance. Lower-class political support for the BLD was thus not naturally forthcoming. How did the BLD then secure electoral support from the numerically significant poor? There was considerable discussion in Meerut of the heavy-handed and underhand tactics used by young, enthusiastic Jats to coerce members of the scheduled castes to vote for BLD candidates. These tactics included the "capturing" of voting-booths and the casting of votes for intimidated scheduled-caste members *in absentia*; the performing of dramatic skits highlighting the dire consequences for those who do not vote for Jat supporters; and straightforward threats, bribes, and duplicated or forged ballots.

The Oudh districts remain the stronghold of the Jan Sangh. The Jan Sangh has been primarily a party of Hindu nationalism. The question of which economic groups support the Jan Sangh is therefore not the most

34. See Paul Brass, "Politicization of the peasantry, II."
35. For an analysis of this, see Craig Baxter, "The rise and fall of the Bharatiya Kranti Dal in Uttar Pradesh," in Marguerite Ross Barnett *et al.*, *Electoral politics in the Indian states: party system and cleavages* (Manohar Books: Delhi, 1975).
36. For example, interview, Durga Prasad Misra, MLA (Salempur Constituency, Deoria District), Lucknow, July 12, 1984.

important question one can ask about this party. It would actually be misleading to describe the Jan Sangh primarily in terms of the economic
groups that support it, implying that there is generally an economic
rationale for the support. The core supporters of the party — the hardened urban cadres — are attracted to the party for non-economic
reasons. The supporters are attracted to the Sanskritik, Hindu culture
and to the related antipathy toward both westernization and Muslims.
Rural majorities are in turn generated through a number of strategies.

One strategy had been to incorporate the support of old *zamindars* and
talukdars of Oudh.[37] Although legally abolished, members of the old aris-
tocracy still carry a great deal of authority in local areas. This is especially
true in Oudh. Here commercialization has not proceeded very far, and
the capacity of traditional overlords to sway political opinions, though not
intact, remains of considerable significance. Combining elements of cultural nationalism and traditional authority, therefore, the Jan Sangh had
built itself a powerful base in this rather backward part of U.P.

The Jan Sangh is generally strong in central U.P. It also has pockets of
strength in eastern U.P. The support base is, however, relatively weak in
the western part of the state. A senior party member, who has organized
elections for the Jan Sangh on a number of occasions, explained this pattern:

Our strength increased only where there was leadership affinity with the masses.
This affinity was either due to shared caste or for reasons of personal influence.
In western U.P., for example, urban leadership of the Śangh was in the hands of
the Vaishyas and Kaisthyas. Rural population was, however, Jats and Gujars. We
did not make much inroads. In central and eastern U.P., by contrast, our urban
cadres had rural connections and often shared the caste of rural majorities. It was
in districts like this that we were most successful.[38]

This explanation generally confirms the view that it would be a mistake
to conceive of the support of the Jan Sangh in terms of landownership or
other economic criteria. Urban leadership of the Sangh is drawn to the
party primarily because of its affinity with Hindu nationalism. A mass
base has, in turn, been built through varying local strategies involving
caste and personal loyalties.

The Janata coalition in U.P. was thus mainly a coalition of two quite
different parties. One party, the BLD, derived its support from cultivating, land-owning peasant castes; the other party, the Jan Sangh, was based
on Hindu nationalism with varying patterns of local suport. The Janata
leadership had the unenviable task of carving out a political force with

37. See Burger, *Opposition in a dominant-party system*.
38. From an interview with Ram Prakash Gupta (same as in footnote 14).

these two erstwhile parties as its major constituents. Given the advantage of hindsight, it is clear that the organizational effort failed. The question arises as to whether the failure was inevitable. Or, put differently, what factors were responsible for the failure of consolidation?

The factor most commonly held responsible is simply leadership intransigence, as well as power and personality conflicts within the U.P. ruling circles and within the national Janata coalition. The argument runs that political conflicts at the center spilled over into regional politics and combined with state-level factionalism to create instability. While this remains an important ingredient, and maybe even the decisive one, certain other factors operating within U.P. should also be noted.

The relations of social groups supporting the Jan Sangh and the BLD were often quite hostile. For example, in parts of the Meerut district, the relations of the Jain and the Jat communities have been conflictual. The Jains control trading and markets, while the Jats dominate agriculture production. The Jains generally supported the Congress (O) or the Jan Sangh, and the Jats the BLD. The Jats often complained that Jains charged too much for the goods they sell, manipulated the market to exploit the Jats, charged exorbitant interest rates on loans, and hoarded gold. Jains in turn argued that Jats received all the government favors, including the best jobs, charged high rates for milk, *ghee* (butter fat), and other dairy products, and are now contributing to the escalated prices of wheat flour.

These animosities, born out of the classic conflict of interests between urban and rural commercial groups, often escalated small incidents into "caste wars." For example, a seemingly insignificant incident involving an argument betwen a Jat youth and a Jain sweetseller first grew into a fistfight, then grew into the beating and killing of a young Jat, and finally led to the mobilization of nearly 5000 Jats, who rallied at a Jat college to protest against Jain actions and demand retribution.[39]

This highlights something that comes as no surprise — the fact that there is a real conflict of interest between urban trading groups and rural commercial farmers. If the parties courting these respective groups have, in turn, trouble acting as a unified political force, this again is not difficult to understand. Of course, the conflict of interest is not so antagonistic that it totally precludes the possibility of reconciliation within the framework of a single party. Given the "newness" of the Janata party, however, and the "oldness" of factionalism in the area, local conflicts made it even more difficult for the BLD to act in co-operation with the Jan Sangh.

Uneven organizational development and the electoral strengths of the

39. See Arun Sinha, "Peasant–merchant conflict," *Economic and Political Weekly*, 5, 13 (November 25, 1978), 1929.

Jan Sangh and the BLD within U.P. generated additional pressures against co-operation. The Jan Sangh, as discussed above, had a strong organizational base. The BLD, on the other hand, had the largest number of seats in the legislature. Power competition thus created varying preferences for how the Janata as a whole should proceed.

Jan Sangh favored a membership drive and organizational elections. Given its organizational base and its control over some ministries — and therefore patronage — the Sangh leaders understood well that such a move within U.P. would strengthen them *vis-à-vis* the BLD. For similar reasons, however, the BLD leadership wanted to consolidate its position first, and attend to organizational matters only later. When it became clear to the BLD in late 1978 that, following a national decision, where the BLD was weak, an organizational drive would be undertaken within U.P., the BLD leadership precipitated a political crisis. At this time, Chief Minister Yadav, probably at Charan Singh's behest, fired the Jan Sangh ministers and created a confrontational situation. The BLD leadership must have concluded that the Jan Sangh's capacity to increase its political influence would be greatly reduced without control of ministries and patronage.

Organizational issues and conflicting interests of respective supporters of the Sangh and the BLD thus combined with state-level factionalism and the spill-over effects of the conflict within the Janata leadership in New Delhi. All this made the prospect of the U.P. Janata acting as a cohesive political force impossible. The Janata party in U.P., therefore, had little, if any, organizational structure of its own. Even the attempts to appoint a state-level party committee got bogged down in factional conflicts. Eventually the conflicts were resolved by expanding the size of the committee, as well as by considerable "horse-trading."[40] The centrally sponsored election panel for the state was boycotted by the BLD. Only a few districts had development committees. These committees, moreover, rarely met. In addition, there was no party organization below the district level. Since rural developmental activities can generally be effective only at levels below the district, there was little that Janata could achieve through direct political intervention.

Governmental instability, in part, reflected the minimal party organization. Because there was no party mechanism to impose consensus, internal dissensions, personality conflicts, factional cleavages, and shifting alliances were the order of the day. Additionally, however, and probably more importantly, governmental instability reflected the fact that a rearrangement of the governing order in U.P. was not likely to lead to any major policy changes. The stakes in preserving or altering a given

40. Interview, Surendra Mohan (same as in footnote 8).

government in U.P. were therefore, from the point of view of the legislators, primarily personal or factional. Whether one faction of the Janata was more powerful than the other had little bearing on the policy framework. If there are real policy conflicts involved, or substantial social interests are endangered by temperamental and factional bickering, the stakes involved in political unity are much greater. Because conflicts of this nature did not exist, the political elite could indulge in the pursuit of individual access to office and patronage, even at the risk of bringing down a government of which they were a part.

The Janata regime in U.P., then, had little organizational coherence or penetration. Whatever organization existed belonged to its constituents, especially the Jan Sangh and the Lok Dal as dominant parties. The Jan Sangh is a relatively well-disciplined party. It brings under its fold urban trading groups and national propertied classes sharing the values of Hindu nationalism. The BLD, by contrast, is a loose party aggregating the interests of middle and rich cultivating castes, especially the commercially oriented peasantry of western U.P. Neither the Jan Sangh nor the BLD had any significant lower-class input. The Janata regime in U.P., therefore, could neither penetrate the countryside independently of the propertied peasantry, nor come close to mobilizing the lower castes and classes for reformist ends.

To summarize, the Janata regime in U.P. was characterized by a weak and fragmented leadership. The ideological orientation of the regime brought together vague and often inconsistent goals under one umbrella. The organizational structure was weak and the government unstable. To the extent that ideological and organizational features of the regime are discernable at all, the interests of the middle and the rich peasantry came to dominate state politics. The U.P. Janata regime is thus best characterized as a fragmented regime of shifting alliances through which the better-off *kisans* became politically significant.

Neglect of Reforms

The rural-poverty situation faced by the fragmented Janata regime was serious. Rural poverty in U.P. has over the years hovered around 50 percent.[41] This is approximately the same level as in Karnataka and in India as a whole. It is far below the 65 percent figure of West Bengal. The U.P. figures, however, mask considerable interstate diversity. The eastern and the western halves of the state, in particular, differ sharply. A western district such as Meerut resembles the Haryana and the Punjab pattern of

41. See Ahluwalia, "Rural poverty."

rural poverty. The poverty levels in this part may be as low as 30 percent. By contrast, eastern districts such as Ballia or Deoria resemble Bihar, where more than 60 percent of the rural population lives in conditions below the poverty line.[42]

The patterns of interregional variations within U.P. often lead to the suggestion that if, somehow, the eastern half of the state could be made more like the western half, poverty problems would be ameliorated. On the face of it, this is a powerful argument. If the western half is more "developed" and has less poverty than the east, it follows that more "development" leads to less poverty. Policy implications are that what is desirable is more agricultural growth and "development" in the eastern half. This is a conclusion subscribed to by many policy makers and scholars in U.P.

A closer examination of the problem reveals a complex situation. Two points should be noted. First, the better performance in the western half and the absence of this performance in the east are not unrelated. For example, public investments within U.P. could go either more into building the irrigational base for the east, or into subsidizing the productivity and profitability in the west, which already has access to irrigation. Because successive governments have chosen the latter investment pattern, the backwardness of the eastern half is related to the dynamism of the west. Second, the social–structural complexities of Eastern U.P. — higher tenancy, bonded labor, fragmented landholdings, etc. — reduce the prospects of indirect social engineering aimed at higher growth through the "green revolution" pattern. To achieve growth in the short run therefore, direct agrarian reforms would be necessary to release entreprenurial dynamism. The interregional variations within U.P., therefore, do not lend themselves easily to the argument that poverty in the state can be reduced merely by higher growth rates, especially in the eastern half.

Data on relative inequalities in rural U.P., moreover, suggest that poverty proportions and inequalities have remained mostly unaltered over the last two decades.[43] The relative inequalities in U.P. are about the same as for India as a whole, but are sharper than in West Bengal. This of course reflects patterns of landholdings in the two states (see Table 5.3 for U.P. and Table 3.5 for West Bengal). Close to 30 percent of the cultivated land in U.P. is concentrated in holdings above 10 acres. There are very few really large holdings. The pattern of landownership in U.P., nevertheless, contrasts with that in West Bengal. At the top end of the scale, only 15 percent (in the early 1970s) of the land in West Bengal is in

42. *Ibid*
43. *Ibid*.

Table 5.3 *Distribution of Land in Uttar Pradesh by Size Class of Operational Holdings, 1953-1972*

Size of class operational holdings (in acres)	1953-1954		1960-1961		1971-1972	
	households %	area operated %	households %	area operated %	households %	area operated %
0-1	35.6	2.2	37.2	2.4	39.5	2.8
1-2.5	21	9.9	21.2	10.4	22.2	12.8
2.5-5	20.4	20.4	20.1	20.6	20.5	25.4
5-10	15.4	29.5	14.1	28.1	12.6	29.9
10-25	6.5	26.5	6.1	25	4.8	23.4
25 and above	1.1	11.5	1.2	13.5	0.5	5.6

Source: Government of India, *National sample survey*, eighth round for 1953-4, seventeenth round for 1960-1, and twenty-sixth round for 1971-2.

holdings above 10 acres. In other words, land concentration at the top of the scale is greater in U.P. than in West Bengal, while the intensity of political concerns with land reforms in the two states is the reverse.

The rural poor in U.P., as elsewhere in India, consist of the landless, tenant farmers, and smallholders. The landless in U.P., however, are fewer in proportional terms than in Karnataka or West Bengal. The figure for U.P. is closer to 20 percent while for the other two states it is nearer 30 percent. This in part reflects the absence of commercial penetration in much of U.P. It also reflects the total ineffectiveness of tenancy reforms in the state.

U.P. is one of the few states in India where, over time, area under tenancy has actually increased as a proportion of the total cultivated area (see Table 5.4). Instead of mass tenant evictions, the increasing population pressure here has led landowners to lease out more land — probably on terms improving over time — and collect increased revenues for less work. Given the regional variations, tenancy is probably higher in eastern U.P., while the proportion of the landless is higher in the western half. Any strategy for alleviating rural poverty in U.P. would have to keep these regional variations in mind. While the unionization of the landless for higher wages and small-farmer programs would be most suitable for the western half, tenancy reforms and investment in agrarian infrastructure, such as irrigation, would be needed as a beginning in the eastern parts. The actions and inactions of the Janata regime in these rural developmental spheres are the subject of the following analysis.

Land Reforms

Land reforms in U.P. have only been marginally successful. Until 1973, a landowner could retain 128 acres of land in addition to groves, orchards, and land covered by other exemptions. It is doubtful if landowners in U.P. have ever lost lands of significance due to the "land ceilings" legislation.[44] Most likely, the only lands that changed hands following land reforms were those for which governmental compensations were close to the market value. Even if some lands were expropriated by the government, it is further doubtful that they were redistributed to the landless and remained in their possession. *Gaon sabhas* (village committees), consisting mainly of village notables, were often influential in determining the redistribution of surplus lands. Even by law, up until 1975, the landless laborers did not enjoy a priority on the list of who gets the surplus lands. In addition, the *gaon sabhas* are reputed to be notoriously corrupt in distributing the lands to their favorites rather than to the needy. By the government's own admission, therefore, "The problem of unauthorized occupation of *gaon sabha* land has been disturbing."[45]

With regard to tenancy, sharecropping has been illegal in the state since the 1950s. The fact that, throughout the 1950s and 1960s, tenancy in general, and *batai* (sharecropping) in particular, continued to increase (see Table 5.4), bears testimony to the total irrelevance of tenancy-reform laws in U.P. Other forms of tenancy, especially the arrangement known as *sajhedari* (a form of fixed-cash tenancy), was even recognized as legal until 1974.

Around the mid-1970s, under the prodding of Indira Gandhi, new land-reform laws were put on the books. "Land ceilings" were lowered, many of the exemption clauses removed, *sajhedari* made illegal, and the landless of the scheduled tribes and castes assigned top priority on the list of who gets the surplus lands.[46] This of course reflected the new populist posture of Indira Gandhi. While much of this within U.P. went unimplemented,[47] it did reflect a renewed reformist commitment. In the case of Karnataka, we noted that it took a strong and populist leader, even at

44. For a review of U.P.'s land reforms, see Baljit Singh and Sridhar Misra, *A study of land reforms in Uttar Pradesh*, American edn (East–West Center, University of Hawai Press: Honolulu, 1965).
45. See Government of Uttar Pradesh, "Note showing the legislative measures relating to land reforms in Uttar Pradesh" (Revenue Department memorandum: Lucknow, 1979), p. 6.
46. See Government of Uttar Pradesh, *Land reforms in Uttar Pradesh* (Revenue Department: Lucknow, 1975).
47. For a review of the implementation of Indira Gandhi's twenty-point program in U.P.,

Table 5.4   *Changes in Tenancy in Uttar Pradesh, 1953-1971*

Year	% of cultivated area under tenancy	Area under sharecropping as a % of area under all tenancy
1953-4	11.38	54.17
1960-1	8.06	62.67
1970-1	13.01	81.48

Source: adapted from Pranab Bardhan, "Variations in extent and forms of agricultural tenancy," *Economic and Political Weekly*, 18 (September 11, 1976).

state level, to translate this national reformist momentum into a partial reality. Such political conditions did not exist in U.P. As a consequence, little was done to make tenancy reforms effective. Only about one tenth of the 1 million acres of land, or less than 0.7 percent of the cultivated land in the state, was actually redistributed.[48] The gap between national rhetoric and the reformist reality within U.P., therefore, remained considerable. Nevertheless, the mid-1970s Indira period was certainly the first time in U.P. since the *zamindari* abolition that reform laws that were potentially implementable and of significance were brought onto the books.

The ascension of the Janata regime to power in U.P. put a stop to even this mild renewal of the reformist thrust within the state. This shift is clear in the U.P. *Five year plan* (1978-83), designed under the Janata regime. Five-year plans in India are the documents within which the political elite express their "enlightened concern" for "socialism" and the downtrodden, even if there is no intention of doing anything about it. The U.P. plan also paid lip-service to the cause of the poor. There was, nevertheless, an important difference: land reforms as a means of poverty alleviation were downgraded to the point of being totally insignificant.

In a three-volume document of more than 1500 pages, the subject of land reforms occupied 2½ pages. Even within this, the subject of surplus lands received 3 paragraphs. With regards to this problem, according to the government, "much of the work ... has been completed."[49] In other words, viewed from the perspective of the Janata government, the problem of "above ceiling" lands no longer exists in U.P. Moreover, tenancy

see Dr P.L. Rawat *et al.*, "Levels of achievement in U.P.," (mimeo) (Department of Economics, Lucknow University: Lucknow, 1976).
48. In absolute terms, 116,257 acres of land was alloted. See Government of Uttar Pradesh, *Draft five year plan, 1978-83*, vol II(Planning Department: Lucknow, January 1979), p. 59.
49. *Ibid.*

reforms are not even mentioned as a policy problem. One presumes that since all tenancy is illegal within the state, tenancy is also not a problem. In spite of the fact that about 13 percent of total land (see Table 5.4) and about 20 percent of the rural population in the state is tied up in tenancy arrangements, the official position came to ignore the tenancy issue.

A senior civil servant in the U.P. government recommended that leasing and sharecropping should be made legal and that the names of the sharecroppers should be recorded. The rationale for such a recommendation was that this would legally recognize a widespread practice. This, in turn, if combined with recording of the sharecroppers, would allow some legal protection to the sharecroppers. When this proposal was formally discussed "the ministries were keen to remove the ban on leasing of land but were not interested in bringing the names of the sub-tenants on the official record. The proposal, in toto, was not accepted."[50]

It can thus be argued that the neglect of land reforms was a conscious policy shift. The shift is minimal if one takes the standpoint that it simply recognized the past ineffectiveness of land reforms. At the same time, however, it was an important and qualitative shift. It marked the emergence of land-owning peasantry — middle and rich — as a dominant political force within the state. A weak Congress leadership in the past would proclaim its commitment to land reforms but would not be in a position to force it upon the socially powerful. There was an element of separation between political and social power in this earlier phase of societal change. Of late, this separation has vanished. As landowners have taken to commerce, increased their political significance with their new wealth, and consolidated their strength through such political parties as the BLD and such leaders as Charan Singh, their interests are more consciously expressed through the political process. As a consequence, land reforms came to be eliminated as a policy goal during the U.P. Janata regime.[51]

A comparison between U.P. and Karnataka here is instructive. If anything, commercialization has proceeded further in Karnataka; commercial farmers and the "middle castes" are powerful there as well. Why, then, have land reforms not been eliminated from the policy agenda in Karnataka? In part, they have. That is why land redistribution is increasingly facing benign neglect. For the rest, political factors explain the difference. The Urs regime was more of a "consensual" regime that attempted to accommodate many interests. In this process it was able to eke out

50. The reference here is to N.C. Saxena. He has written about his own experience in Ahmed and Saxena, "Political power in Uttar Pradesh." The quote is to be found on p. 49 of the MS.
51. As Raj Krishna also noted with reference to his discussions on land reforms with members of the Janata Central cabinet, "Charan Singh has no interest in land reforms." Interview, Raj Krishna, New Delhi, May 22, 1979.

some limited reforms for the tenants. Charan Singh's BLD, by contrast, was more narrowly poised on the land-owning, cultivating castes. The dominance of the BLD within the fragmented U.P. Janata then allowed it to diminish the significance of land reforms. As this balance can be altered in the future, land reforms may be proclaimed to be important once again. However, given the organized expression of *kisan* power within U.P., as seen in the BLD, the chances are that land reforms are not likely to re-emerge as a significant goal in the near future.

Small-Farmer Programs

The small amount of resources allocated to the Small Farmer Development Agency (SFDA) schemes in U.P., as well as organizational problems, have combined to make state intervention for the land-holding rural poor ineffective. About 8 million rupees was allocated to SFDA in U.P. in 1979-80. This constituted less than 0.3 percent of the state-level public investment in agriculture and irrigation.[52] By conservative estimates there are at least 4 million rural families of smallholders (including tenants) living in conditions below the poverty line.[53] With government allocations of just 2 rupees per family of five, per year, it will be a long time before public investment can alleviate the rural poverty of small and marginal farmers in U.P.

Just as land reforms were assigned low priority under the Janata regime, the land-holding rural poor were also not high on the governmental agenda. Rhetoric of "*kisan* power" and "rural tilt" aside, much of the agrarian investment and many of the programs were aimed at benefiting the already better-off peasantry. Even in the case of exemption from land revenue, which was publicized as a pro-poor measure, an insider in the government noted: "The real intention of the Janata Government was to abolish the Land Development Tax on medium and large farmers... but in order to project a 'pro-poor' image, appeasement of the poor farmers became a necessity."[54]

The organizational strategies of the Janata further reveal the party's political preference. It is clear to those who are interested in the conditions of the rural poor in contemporary India that politically directed

52. See Government of Uttar Pradesh, *Draft five year plan*, pp. 158-61. The proposed outlay in the plan was close to Rs 10 million. Later this was reduced, as the overall budget was slashed by close to 25 percent at the behest of the Central Government.
53. This estimate is based on the fact that there are about 40 million people living in conditions below the poverty line. As about half of these are landless laborers, the remaining 20 millions are marginal farmers and sharecroppers. Assuming a 5-person family, this gives 4 million households of smallholders below the poverty line.
54. See Ahmed and Saxena, "Political power in Uttar Pradesh."

reform of poverty conditions would have to be preceded by organizational innovations. As discussed in the last chapter, these innovations would have to combine elements of the "long and strong arm" of a pro-lower-class state reaching out into the villages with politicization of the rural poor. Any government that does not undertake such organizational efforts, either through the party or through some *ad hoc* arrangements, reflects a lack of reformist commitment. The Janata regime had no organizational network capable of facilitating pro-lower-class development within U.P. More important, it did not even make a beginning toward this end. The consequences are clear in the haphazard and ineffective pattern of implementation of even the small programs under the SFDA.

The thrust of the SFDA was animal husbandry and credit for smallholders.[55] Providing bullocks or other animals to small and marginal farmers was thought to be of possible utility in raising their incomes. Conducted through the local bureaucracy and the elite-dominated local governments, the implementation was ineffective. In the majority of the cases I visited, recipients of cows, goats or poultry were anything but the rural poor. The local officers and some senior civil servants argued, often convincingly, that the real poor are in no position to maintain the animals.[56]

Whenever animals were given to the poor or marginal farmers, experience confirmed this. Fodder required investment that a poor farmer could not afford. Diseases and medical expenses were also burdensome. And the temptation to sell the animal to make some quick money was great. If the goal of the animal husbandry through SFDA was thus to enhance and sustain higher incomes for even a select few marginal farmers, little of this was being accomplished in the villages. Without a local-level planning organization that concentrates lower-class interests within it — a prospect not too likely without a left-of-center party in control of state power to facilitate and protect such arrangements — such schemes for the marginal farmers are not likely to be successful, even if more money was to be allocated.

Little in terms of institutional credit was also being directed to the marginal landholders. In contrast to West Bengal, the U.P. government did not have its political attention focused on improving the lot of smallholders, and therefore had no innovative schemes or ideas concerning how to channel credit to them. Co-operatives remained entrenched in the corruption–patronage network linking political leaders to local notables. The lower classes got nothing out of them. Commercial banks followed their straightforward policy of land as collateral for loans and were gener-

55. See Government of Uttar Pradesh, *Draft five year plan*, pp. 158-61.
56. Interview, Anand Sarup, Secretary, Planning, Government of Uttar Pradesh, Lucknow, June 11, 1979.

ally accessible only to relatively large landowners. And sharecroppers, by definition, did not qualify because they did not own any land. By the government's own admission therefore, "marginal farmers and landless labourers have generally not benefited from SFDA, mainly because of the rigid procedures and norms of institutional finance."[57] And, it ought to be added, this is due, in turn, to a governmental failure to make the "rigid procedures and norms" less rigid.

Wage and Employment Schemes for the Landless

Actions and the absence of action both reveal governmental priorities. The neglect of reforms in U.P. is clearest when one considers all the actions the Janata government failed to undertake. The lack of action concerning wage and employment conditions affecting the landless agricultural laborers should also be noted. In contrast to Karnataka and West Bengal, the U.P. Janata government made no financial allocations to match the federal grants in kind for the Food for Work Program (FWP). The FWP in U.P. was therefore very limited in scope. Its implementation was even more problematic than in Karnataka. I was not even able to discover FWP-sponsored projects in progress in the districts of Ballia, Jhansi or Meerut. While this may be fortuitous, local-level discussions repeatedly revealed that much of the public money from *gaon sabhas* or *panchayats* was being frittered away in corrupt, non-developmental practices.

The Janata party furthermore made no attempts to organize the landless laborers. On the contrary, the Janata regime often sided with the already powerful landowners in labor–landlord conflicts. For example, with changing conditions in western U.P., the landless laborers have begun to get unionized under various left-of-center leaderships. Landlord–labor conflict is therefore increasingly common. In one of the villages of the Meerut district, Harijan laborers had been allotted house sites under Indira Gandhi's twenty-point program. With the ascension of the Janata regime, local Jats felt strengthened. And there followed attempts to evict the landless laborers from the plots allotted to them. The laborers resisted collectively and sought protection from the police and the bureaucracy. The latter failed to come about and the Harijans lost their pieces of land.

What was true for this one village has been noted by others to have been a more general pattern. N.C. Saxena, a former senior civil servant in U.P., who has also written about his experiences, noted the following:

57. Government of Uttar Pradesh, *Draft five year plan*, p. 160, 1.5.57.

Sometime in 1978, during the Janata regime, it was decided to oust the agriculture labourers from such Gaon Sabha lands where permanent cultivation was not possible or which were being used by the entire village community as pasture or grazing lands. Within six months more than 60,000 cases were filed in the revenue court against the rural poor.[58]

So widespread was the problem of Harijan oppression in U.P., that it led the Janata government to legislate for compensation for the families of murdered heads of the Harijan households.[59] While this reflected a degree of humaneness on the part of the regime, it most of all underlined the total incapacity of the leadership to tilt state power in favor of the landless. The regime was in no position even to prevent the killing of Harijans over issues of class and caste conflict. The party had no village presence independent of the landowners. Bureaucracy and the police often sided with the landlords, local notables, and their powerful political representatives. And the landowners mobilized and hired local thugs to cope with any attempted local-level collective resistance. In the absence of a political force to tilt the power balance toward the landless, a tacit alliance of domination involving the state, the landowners, and local thugs continued to reinforce the socio-economic misery of U.P.'s lower rural classes.

Conclusion

The Janata phase in U.P. was characterized by shifting alliances and political instability. This, of course, was not all that new for U.P. What was new was the concurrent rise in prominence of the BLD within the Janata coalition. Fragmented leadership and the dominant role of a party committed to the landowning peasantry did not bode well for U.P.'s rural poor. Land reforms were eliminated from the policy agenda. In spite of the rhetorical "rural tilt," small and marginal farmers were ignored. Landless Harijans may well have been the worst losers. Not only did the government fail to act on their behalf, but the power of the state was occasionally turned against them to reinforce the already powerful land-owning groups. While many in India and elsewhere had praised the Janata's "new beginning," "decentralization," "rural tilt," and concern for the "small man,"[60] the fact is that, in practice, as far as the problem of attacking rural poverty is concerned, the Janata regime in U.P. was a dismal failure.

58. See Ahmed and Saxena, "Political power in Uttar Pradesh," p. 56.
59. See Arun Sinha, "Uttar Pradesh: mockery of reform," *Economic and Political Weekly*, 13, 51-2 (1978), 2065.
60. For example, see Franda, *India's rural development*.

This failure of reformism in U.P. was a consequence of the political and class characteristics of the Janata regime. The U.P. Janata regime contrasted sharply with the CPM regime in West Bengal. On the leadership dimension, the CPM regime was coherent, while the Janata regime was fragmented. Ideologically, there was a clear commitment to alleviating rural poverty in West Bengal. The situation in U.P. was quite confused. Within the confusion, however, one can discern a commitment to commercial farmers and a concurrent neglect of the lower peasantry. As far as organization is concerned, the CPM and Janata regimes differed in terms both of structure and of membership. As a tightly organized "Leninist" party, the CPM systematically penetrates the countryside without being captured by the land-owning groups. This allows the CPM both to reach the lower classes directly and to mobilize them occasionally to facilitate reformist goals. The Janata regime had no such organisational framework. The party had little rural presence, and what presence it did have rested with the land-owning "middle" castes. Given these contrasting patterns of regime leadership, ideology, and organization, the reformist thrust of the two regimes also varied sharply.

A brief comparison of the U.P. Janata and the Urs regime in Karnataka is also instructive. On the organizational dimension, the two regimes were quite similar — both shared weak organization based on land-owning groups. This put a constraint on the reformist thrusts of both regimes. There were important shades of difference, however, in the ideological orientation of Urs and that of the U.P. Janata leadership. Urs was explicitly committed to the rural poor, while the Janata was not. Even more important was the difference in leadership. Devraj Urs offered a coherent and strong leadership to Karnataka for nearly a decade and this allowed him to take a long-range overview of the political situation. In his calculations, some rewards to the lower classes were perceived to be politically beneficial. His strong leadership was in turn able to push through a modicum of reformism born out of calculations of political necessity.

By contrast, the factionalized situation in U.P. led each faction within the Janata to protect its narrow interests against competitors. As a consequence, governing became impossible. There was no one to take an overview within which even small doses of reforms were considered to be politically wise. The prominent role of the BLD within the factionalized political situation further allowed the interests of the land-owning peasantry to be pursued at the expense of the rural poor. In contrast to the parliamentary–communist regime in West Bengal and the populist regime in Karnataka, a regime based on fragmented leadership and middle-peasant interests in U.P. had neither reasons nor the capacity to undertake poverty reforms. Assessed from the point of view of the poor, and in comparison to the other two state governments analyzed above, the U.P. Janata offered the least prospect of alleviating rural poverty.

6

Conclusion : The State and Reform in Democratic–Capitalist Development

This study has focused on the patterns of state intervention for socio-economic reforms in rural India. Empirical materials have been investigated from a theoretical standpoint emphasizing the state– society interactions within contemporary capitalist development. The study has analyzed the interventionist role of the Indian Central Government and compared the reformist performance of three provincial governments within India, namely, the Communist Government in West Bengal (1977-84) the Congress Government in Karnataka (1974-80), and the Janata Government in Uttar Pradesh (1977-80). Governmental intervention in three policy areas has been studied: land reforms, small-farmer schemes, and wage- and employment-generation projects for the landless. Having presented this material, I now intend to pull together the various strands of the argument, summarize the findings, and draw out the theoretical implications of the study.

The general issue under consideration here has been the political conditions under which developmental reform from above does or does not succeed. The argument suggested by the materials analyzed is that within similar social–structural conditions, differences in regime type are of considerable consequence for the effectiveness of state-initiated redistribution. The analysis of the Indian Central Government's economic role highlights how the perpetuation of poverty in that country has resulted from an increasingly institutionalized pattern of domination involving an alliance between a loosely organized nationalist elite and entrepreneurial classes. The range of redistributive choices available within this larger constraint of democratic capitalism emerges from the comparative analysis of Indian regional materials. A well organized, parliamentary–communist regime in West Bengal has successfully initiated redistributive programs. By contrast, a populist leadership in Karnataka had limited success in implementing social reforms and a factionalized government dominated by commercial-peasant interests in Uttar Pradesh had no success in that endeavor.

Comparative analysis of Indian materials suggests that regime characteristics — leadership, ideology, and organization — and the class basis of the regime in power are the major variables explaining variations in redistributive outcomes. Regime characteristics and the nature of the social support are helpful in defining why some regimes have both reasons and the capacity to pursue reforms, why others have neither, and why yet others may have reasons but not the capacity to carry through redistributive programs.

As far as capacities are concerned, a left-of-center regime, headed by a tightly organized ideological party, can penetrate the rural society without being co-opted by the propertied groups. This facilitates a degree of separation between political and social power, making state intervention possible for social reforms. Conversely, multi-class regimes with loose organization and diffuse ideology are not successful at reformist intervention. Regime types and related policies — and not only the levels of development or patterns of international dependency — are therefore important for understanding the stubbornness of poverty and the occasional attacks on it within a Third World setting.

This argument has important implications for understanding the issues of poverty and inequality in India as well as in other comparable cases. These implications need to be delineated in some detail.

The State and Poverty in India

Three decades of democratically planned development have failed to alleviate India's rural poverty. While the relative inequalities have not increased, the standard of living of the lower rural groups has also not improved. Why? Why has even the worst of rural poverty not been mitigated? Neither the "liberal" nor the "Marxist" world views provide a satisfactory answer to this question. I have therefore interpreted the Indian situation by emphasizing the twin and interrelated impacts of political organization and social structure.

From one standpoint, often labelled a "liberal standpoint,"[1] the problem of India's lower-class poverty is a long-range problem. It can only be solved over a considerable time period. With more "development," according to this perspective, comes sustained economic growth and, it is hoped, democratic politics. Some combination then of continuing growth and the spread of democracy facilitates a degree of social leveling and some raising of the economic base. As a consequence, the economic situation of the lower classes improves. Reinforced by the historical experiences of Western democracies, this perspective has a powerful hold on the scholarly imagination.

I have found this perspective less than satisfactory for the interpreta-

---

1. Although such labels are useful, they can also be highly misleading. I put them in quotation-marks to highlight my ambivalence in using them.

tion of the Indian situation for several reasons. First, a cursory glance at the conditions of the lower classes in developmental communist states (e.g., China and Cuba) suggests that the problem of poverty is related as much to socio-political conditions as it is to levels of economic development.[2] Secondly, there is little evidence in India's experience — including that of Punjab — to suggest that, over time, growth "trickles down."[3] Thirdly, it is difficult to support the view, on logical or on empirical grounds, that over time, democratic politics automatically reduce socio-economic inequalities.[4] And lastly, a "liberal" perspective on Indian poverty relegates any solution to a far-off, indefinite future. Both on normative and on explanatory grounds, therefore, this particular "liberal" position on lower-class poverty in India is not satisfactory.

A straightforward Marxist position also does not suffice for the Indian situation. While class constraints on state intervention have been significant, it is difficult to substantiate historically a view of Indian politics as being molded directly by the propertied social classes. As argued above, the Congress, first as a nationalist movement and later as a party-regime, cannot be conceptualized as a mere reflection of rising new classes within India. The Congress was first and foremost a political movement. It ended up serving the interests of the propertied classes. To interpret this outcome through borrowed historical glasses can, however, be misleading.

For Marxist scholars, as for the liberal ones, historical experiences, to paraphrase Marx, "weigh like a nightmare on the brain of the living." Any regime serving "bourgeois interests" becomes identified analytically as a "bourgeois regime." Going by historical parallels, if the outcomes are similar and have historical parallels, Marxist scholars often assume that the causes are also similar. This common fallacy in logic — "affirming the consequent" — stems from the superimposition of theories based on limited historical data upon cases that may or may not be similar.

India's capitalist development at the time of independence was miniscule. Historically, therefore, the Congress faced first the problem of how to create capitalism, and only second, how to protect and preserve it. Capitalist forces represented such a small proportion of the economy at this historical juncture that it does not seem reasonable to assign to them political capacities significant enough to mold India's pattern of socio-

2. This is not to suggest that the communist model of development does not incur other types of significant human costs for its population. For an interesting discussion on the "costs" of various models of development, see Berger, *Pyramids of sacrifice*, ch. 5.
3. See Bardhan, "Poverty and 'trickle-down.'" as
4. I have developed this argument in chapter 1 as well as in "Democracy and inequality in India's development." Also see Dahl, "Pluralism revisited"; and Maravall, "The limits of reformism."

economic change. While the die for the Indian model of development was indeed cast by the Congress, and while this increasingly capitalist model of development is responsible for the perpetuation of India's rural poverty, the case that Congress itself merely reflected dominant capitalist interests cannot be sustained empirically.

The failure to alleviate rural poverty has, then, also been rooted in the weakness of India's political organizations. The organized political capacity to confront the propertied groups in India has been minimal. This political weakness is, in turn, not merely a function of the omnipotence of the propertied groups. It is in part related to it, but it is also independent of it. The institutional patterns that India has inherited and evolved stem from a complex interaction of colonial influences, the ·actions of the commercial classes, and the political traditions — cultural and structural — of India. The resulting political structures have been suited for certain goals and not others.

The Congress party as the hub of the new Indian state thus highlighted both the strengths and the weaknesses of India's political arrangements. As a political organization, Congress was loose and amorphous. It had left-of-center affinities but no clear-cut ideology, its membership was open, and it had little or no internal control structure to bring a measure of political discipline to its membership and following. Many have celebrated the consensual and democratic nature of such an organization. And there is no need to underemphasize the contributions of such an arrangement historically to a mass nationalist movement and later to the creation of a relatively stable democratic polity. What needs to be emphasized also, however, is that these arrangements have been totally unsuited for utilizing the quintessential political resource — legitimate compulsion — as a tool of social reform.

The propertied classes in India could have been tamed. Right after independence the propertied were significant but not all that strong. The urban industrial and commercial groups controlled a very small fraction of the economy. The landed classes were in retreat. Not only had they lost their colonial patrons, but nationalism as a force could have been utilized against them to implement land reforms. Moreover, the propertied groups as a whole were not very well organized. A measure of political forcefulness could have created a more egalitarian pattern of development. A reformed social order was, in other words, not totally impossible; it would have required some use of compulsion from above. Such compulsion could have, in turn, been generated only by a state apparatus controlled through strong leaders, a clear-cut ideology, and a well-disciplined, tightly organized political party incorporating the interests of the lower classes. The failure, then, to translate "socialist" ideological commitments into a strong left-of-center regime capable of redistributive intervention is India's great political failure.

In the absence of a strong left-of-center regime, there was only one alternative to stimulate economic change politically within the framework of democratic capitalism. This was to provide economic incentives to those in a position to generate economic growth. Out of these circumstances evolved a developmental alliance between the Congress regime and India's entrepreneurial classes, an alliance that has molded the shape of India's development. The consequences were first manifest in the pattern of heavy industrial development. Later they became even clearer in the adoption of the "green revolution" strategy. This arrangement has achieved several important goals: maintenance of democracy, a modicum of industrial development, and self-sufficiency in food for India. These impressive achievements need to be acknowledged. The tragic consequences have, however, also been evident in the fact that the living conditions of nearly 40 percent of India's poor have not been affected.

These broad patterns of state-class interactions in India mask considerable diversity. The interaction of varying political organizations with the social structure, resulting in different redistributive outcomes, has thus been brought out in the core empirical chapters with reference to comparative regional·Indian experiences. A well organized, parliamentary–communist regime in West Bengal has initiated systematic social reforms. The fragmented, middle-peasant-dominated regime in U.P., by contrast, has totally failed in its reformist initiatives. Karnataka represents an in-between case. A strong leader, presiding over a populist political arrangement, has had limited success in channeling resources to some select members of the lower rural classes. What political–sociological conditions explain these variations?

To restate in a summarized form, the case of West Bengal suggests four political conditions, or four features of the regime in power, help explain the existence of some political capacity to reform the social order from above. First, the CPM rule in West Bengal has a coherent and stable leadership. This allows for the clarification of goals, the arrangement of priorities, and then sustained pressure from above for goal completion. Second, the CPM has a clear pro-lower-class ideology. This ideological position gave the CPM leaders, once they were democratically elected, a degree of legitimate authority to pursue goals beneficial for the rural poor. Third, in spite of being a communist party, the CPM has clarified the limits of its redistributive intent. All democratically elected parties in a private-enterprise economy, even if communist in name, must set these limits. Predictability is essential for the functioning of a capitalist economy. And last, and most important, the organizational arrangement of the CPM regime allows it to penetrate the countryside without being captured by the propertied groups. In part because of the democratic–centralist nature of the party organization, and in part because of the carefully reorganized local government, the CPM can now reach the lower peasantry without landlord mediation. This allows the regime to channel some developmental resources directly to the rural poor, as well as to mobilize them occasionally for fulfilling reformist goals. These regime features, then, explain the relative reformist capacities of the CPM regime.

Both ideologically and organizationally, the CPM has sought to exclude the propertied from political governance, while allowing them to maintain their social power. The CPM experiment is now eight years old; the extent of its continued success will hinge on its capacity to survive and sustain its reformist thrust. Irrespective of its long-term prospects, however, the analytical point is clear: reformism requires institutionalization of pro-lower-class goals within the state structures. The case of the CPM in India's Bengal highlights the political features that have the potential to allow such institutionalization to take place. The CPM regime in West Bengal, therefore, comes closest to what a successful, left-of-center, reformist regime within the Indian context of a developmental–capitalist state is likely to resemble.

The cases of U.P. and Karnataka buttress the above argument. The Janata regime in U.P., in contrast to the situation in West Bengal, was characterized by a fragmented leadership, confused ideology, and little or no organizational base. As a coalitional regime, the dominant interests represented within it were those of middle and rich peasants. It is of little surprise not only that nothing was achieved in the interests of the rural poor, but that their case may even have received a further setback under this political arrangement. The Urs regime in Karnataka, however, had limited reformist success. Coherent leadership and populist ideology facilitated a modicum of reform. The organizational base, however, was weak and the propertied classes penetrated the ruling groups. The reformist thrust thus remained limited.

The three provincial governments examined functioned within similar social–structural constraints. They were all elected democratically, and the economy in all of these areas is increasingly capitalist — wage labor, money as a basis of exchange, and commodity production — with some significant pockets of pre-capitalist formations. In spite of these similar constraints, the regime types within them and the developmental performance of the regimes vary. This suggests that an overemphasis on socio-economic determinism in political analysis can distort the Indian situation and other empirical realities. Regimes with differing ideologies, organizational forms, and underlying coalitions can and do come to power in similar social settings. Furthermore, because these regimes have significant policy consequences, they represent more than a mere rearrangement of the "superstructure;" they represent varying political capacities to facilitate redistribution within capitalist development.

To suggest that there is scope for redistributive political intervention within capitalist development is not necessarily to suggest — or even imply — that redistributive outcomes are likely in India in the near future. The jump from an analytic assertion to a predictive one is highly problematic. Several mediating conditions must be noted before the predictive and prescriptive implications of this analytic study are made clear.

While I have sought to delineate the redistributive consequences of regional regime variations, this focus presupposes that redistributive efforts are constrained within India's democratic–capitalist model of development. A number of factors are responsible for this. First, India's dominant political institutions are penetrated and increasingly controlled by propertied classes, especially the entrepreneurial classes. Even when propertied classes do not control the political process, political organizations — especially the political parties — are too weak to confront and control the upper classes. Owing to either direct control by dominant classes or the *de facto* dependence of regime authorities on the propertied classes, the state–capitalist alliance is now firmly in place in India.

Even when forces representing groups other than the upper classes come to dominate the political scene, they are constrained by the very nature of the developmental–capitalist arrangement. These forces can discourage privately initiated economic growth only at the risk of undermining their own popularity and legitimacy. Regime policies, therefore, must tacitly support the entrepreneurial classes. And finally, given the framework of electoral politics, no ruling party in India can afford to alienate the politically significant middle classes in the cities and the countryside. Regime authorities must therefore make policy concessions — price supports for agriculture, subsidized agrarian inputs, low taxation on luxuries, essential urban services, etc. — catering to middle-income groups. In sum, left-of-center regimes are either not likely to emerge within India's developmental–capitalist framework or, if they do, are likely to be effective only under rare political conditions.

The rare political conditions facilitating incremental redistributive intervention bear reiterating. Well-organized, left-of-center regimes, if they win elections and come to power, concentrate redistributive goals as legitimate goals within the state apparatus. This gives the leadership a mandate and therefore reasons to pursue reforms. If ideologically and organizationally cohesive, moreover, such regimes can exclude the propertied from direct participation in the governing process. This creates a degree of separation between social and political power, making the pursuit of reformist policies possible.

The implementation of these policies further requires organizational capacity, especially a well-developed party, capable of penetrating society without being captured by the propertied classes. Well-organized left-of-center parties in power are then the crucial variable facilitating a modicum of redistribution within the framework of democracy and capitalism. Such parties not only concentrate reformist goals in the political process, but are also capable of pursuing them effectively. Of course, such parties constantly face the danger of being undermined both from the right (too socialist) and from the left (not socialist enough). Nevertheless, parties such as the CPM in India also possess the unique capacity to appease the propertied, while generating controlled mobilization of the lower classes. A CPM-type of regime, therefore, may well represent a singularly unique formation facilitating the pursuit of some egalitarian goals within India's democratic–capitalist developmental model.

On balance, then, what is being argued is that only rare regime types are capable of facilitating reforms within the seriously constrained Indian political economy. Are such regimes likely to come to power in Indian states other than West Bengal, or maybe even nationally? While intuitively the prospects seem remote, it would require a study quite different than the one presented here — a study that focused on the determinants rather than on the consequences of state forms and patterns of intervention — to answer this question satisfactorily. This study has focused on the policy consequences of regime types. This focus allows one to infer conclusions relating regimes to development outcomes, but not those concerning conditions giving rise to varying regime types. An investigation of the former does not shed light on the latter issue. In India, as elsewhere, one must eschew the widespread functional analytical tendency which holds that specific regime types emerge because they are capable of solving important social problems.

More specifically, this study suggests that barring the ascension of well-organized left-of-center regimes in other Indian states, the prospects of alleviating rural poverty by deliberate state intervention will remain slight. As long as the regional political alternatives in India are offered by parties such as the Congress (I), Janata, or its former constituents (mainly the Lok Dal and the Jan Sangh) under new party labels, the reformist thrust will remain limited. Only the CPM or similar parties capable of generating a disciplined left-of-center regime will have the capacity to push through policies benefiting the lower rural classes.

From a perspective that holds the alleviation of India's rural poverty as an important goal, the installation of CPM-led regimes in at least the poorest of the Indian states – say, in addition to West Bengal and Tripura, such states as Bihar and Orissa – would be a desirable direction for political change. It is possible to imagine a scenario in the near future in which some states in India pursue the Punjab-type of rapid growth model, while others come to be ruled by redistributive left-of-center regimes. Varying political–economic arrangements in different states may well be the most suitable "model" for India in the near future. Whatever the probability of such arrangements emerging in India, it is clear that short-term alleviation of mass poverty in the poorest of the Indian states will remain contingent upon political intervention being directed by disciplined left-of-center regimes.

Democracy and Reform in Capitalist Develpment

Examination of the Indian materials highlights the significance of disciplined, left-of-center regimes as agents of redistributive capitalist development. The existence of such party-regimes makes it probable that an ideological position reflecting a commitment to incremental redistribution can be imposed upon competing social forces: with radical elements of the lower classes wanting more redistribution, and with the propertied wanting less. The focus on a party of this nature is what distinguishes the argument here from the more commonly held "left–liberal" perspective.

The left-liberal position, while also sympathetic to goals of redistribution, often finds distasteful the prospect of well-disciplined parties utilizing a measure of compulsion for social reform. Committed to "pluralism," many left-liberals support goals of "organizing the poor." However, the prospect of rule by a party organized along "Leninist" lines and calling itself communist, even though reconciled to existence within the framework of democratic capitalism, often causes uneasiness. I have suggested here that organizing the poor really does not shift the class basis of political power. What does shift the class basis is not merely the degree of organization of various classes, but also the institutionalization of lower-class goals within the state. In the case of India, this has only been facilitated by a well-disciplined, left-of-center party in power. Parties aggregating lower-class interests, calling themselves communist, or by another name, but reconciled to parliamentarianism and private-property economies, may then offer the best hope — to the extent that there is hope — for reconciling growth with distribution within the context of democratic capitalism.

A cursory look at two cases other than that of India reinforces the plausibility of this argument. First, the brief and tragic experiment of Salvador Allende in Chile. Allende attempted to bring about social reform within a democratic–capitalist, Third World setting and failed. The experience therefore speaks to the ideas developed above regarding the political conditions for reformist success. Why did Allende's experiment fail? As Brian Lovemen explained,

Whatever the full extent of United States complicity in the tragedy of September 1973... the most critical factor of all in the failure of the Allende administration was bad politics. Bad politics... the sprouting of revolutionary rhetoric without the force to impose a revolutionary program... produced a politico-economic crisis.[5]

Underlying these "bad politics" were regime conditions. Allende "headed a precarious multi-party coalition lacking both internal cohesiveness and underlying agreement on the pace and character of change to be implemented."[6] Fragmented political structure, in other words, did not facilitate the development of a coherent reform program. Workers had to be satisfied, so wages were raised.[7] The entrepreneurial classes could not be appeased, so production fell. As the gap between supply and demand increased, inflation became rampant, shortages of goods occurred, and many elements of the middle and even lower classes became alienated.[8] "Bad politics," or the ideological and political fragmentation within the Unidad Popular government, was responsible for a lot of these failures.

Fragmentation "prevented conciliation and compromise with the Christian Democrats, the small shopkeepers, the truckers, the beneficiaries of the Frei agrarian reform — in short, with all the elements of the middle strata, working class, and peasantry who had nothing to lose and much to gain by an attack on economic monopolies and foreign corporations."[9] As Allende lost political support, the armed forces, the corporations, and the American involvement combined to "impose upon Chile a regime of coercion, intolerance and brutality unequalled since the era of conquest."[10]

Chile's experience under Allende, therefore, supports my overall argu-

5. See Loveman, *Chile*.
6. *Ibid*. p. 333.
7. For a persuasive argument suggesting the fallacy of short-term "consumption boom" as a redistributive strategy, see David Lehman, "The political economy of Armageddon: Chile, 1970-73." *Journal of Development Economics*, 5, 2 (June 1978), 107-23.
8. See Alex Nove, "The political economy of the Allende regime," in Philip O'Brien (ed.), *Allende's Chile* (Praeger: New York, 1976), pp. 74-6.
9. Loveman, *Chile*, p. 348.
10. *Ibid*. p. 348.

ment in certain important ways. Most significantly, it highlights the necessity of a well-organized reform party in control of state power. In the absence of such a party, the fragmented nature of Allende's coalition regime was at the root of many of his problems. Because the workers could not be kept in the party fold, incremental reforms were bypassed and immediate wage benefits granted to sustain their support. That this in turn contributed to inflation and economic troubles is beyond doubt. As coherent reform ideology did not exist, the revolutionary utterances, whether sincere or not, created considerable economic uncertainty. That investment and production fell is hardly surprising. As economic problems got worse, again in the absence of an organized, ideologically based core of support, short-term problems became impossible to handle. Political support dwindled as a response to economic problems. And finally, in the absence of an organized party, it became difficult to confront the onslaught of the counter-revolutionary forces. While none of this is to suggest that Allende's experiment would have succeeded had it been based on a well-organized, disciplined political party, it does imply that the absence of such a party made the reformist experiment in Chile relatively vulnerable to failure.

Another "social-democratic" development experiment which has recently begun — and one that may have better results than did Chile — is Zimbabwe under Mugabe. While the experiment is in its early stages, some of the features are of interest. According to Michael Bratton, the Zimbabwe experiment leads to a general question: "Is it possible to use the power of the state in a capitalist society to create an egalitarian and democratic pattern of development?"[11] Because this is precisely the issue under discussion here, the case of Zimbabwe indeed bears on the major propositions developed above.

Since coming to power, Robert Mugabe and his relatively well organized Zimbabwe African National Union (Patriotic Front) or ZANU(PF) has sought to restructure the state and society in Zimbabwe. The goals have been moderate and the results seemingly satisfactory. The developmental aim of the ZANU(PF) government is to build a "socialist, democratic, and egalitarian" Zimbabwe. While the initial task of consolidating state power was a formidable one, "the new government made considerable progress in consolidating its hold on power"[12] during the early years in office. This newly gained state power is now slowly but surely being used to initiate a democratic–socialist pattern of development. For one thing, the government is committed to restoring production. To appease the propertied, therefore, the government has clearly

11. See Bratton, "Development in Zimbabwe," p. 475.
12. *Ibid*. p. 453.

indicated that it will encourage foreign and domestic private capital in Zimbabwe.[13] Western governments have been pleased with these concessions and, in contrast to Chile, much-needed foreign support has been forthcoming. On the other hand, "a great deal of progressive social legislation has been rapidly introduced, which has put concrete benefits in the hands of the majority of the population."[14] While the real test of reformist capacities will come when land redistribution is attempted or efforts made to implement minimum-wage legislation, the fact is that a promising beginning has been made. What accounts for the "balanced reformist thrust" in Zimbabwe?

Underlying the balanced beginnings of reform in Zimbabwe is of course the Mugabe regime itself. While the nature of the Mugabe regime is a complex issue involving the interactions of several historical factors, the regime features that facilitate a reformist thrust are clear. The regime is based on a relatively cohesive political organization, the ZANU(PF). Organized along democratic–centralist lines, the dominant party facilitates ideological cohesion and concentrates political power. While this is not to suggest the absence of factionalism within ZANU(PF), it has been held in check by Mugabe himself.[15] As Bratton notes, "A policy process is emerging in which ZANU(PF) is clearly the main force." He also suggests that, "Policy decisions emanate almost exclusively from the Central Committee of the dominant party."[16]

Recent trends have suggested that decision-making pluralism in Zimbabwe may be in jeopardy. There are also indications that the regime may not be serious about some of its redistributive commitments. These trends may create a situation in the future whereby Zimbabwe would not really qualify as a democratic–socialist experiment of sorts. As it is, however, in contrast to the coalitional fragmented situation in Allende's Chile, the cohesiveness of the Mugabe regime has allowed it to initiate a balanced beginning. Judging and balancing the various constraints, a competent and organized leadership has been able to impose a mildly redistributive policy on those who would like radical redistribution as well as on those who would rather be living in the past. Revolutionary rhetoric and inflation causing sudden wage hikes are thus not necessary for sustaining coalitional support in Zimbabwe. Regime cohesion and an aura of predictability, moreover, appease the propertied. And yet, in spite of

---

13. Mugabe government's economic policy is outlined in, Government of the Republic of Zimbabwe, *Growth with equality: an economic policy statement* (Salisbury, 1981).
14. Bratton, "Development in Zimbabwe," pp. 431-2.
15. For a discussion of the role of Robert Mugabe, see Xan Smiley, "Zimbabwe, southern Africa and the rise of Robert Mugabe," *Foreign Affairs* (summer 1980), 1060-83
16. Bratton, "Development in Zimbabwe," p. 451.

these compromises, an organized and relatively consolidated regime, committed to development with redistribution, has initiated policies that appear to approximate to leadership goals.

A cursory attention to Allende's Chile and Zimbabwe under Mugabe, then, has two important implications. The first is a qualification on the argument developed above. In the cases of both Chile and Zimbabwe, international constraints on the redistributive thrust have been more significant than those encountered in the case of India. Stemming in part from the theoretical orientation of this study, in part from India's large size and its somewhat unusual "self-reliant" policy posture, and in part from the comparative regional focus of the analysis here, this study may have given too little attention to international determinants of developmental processes. One who attempts to extend the argument of this study to other cases would have to keep this limitation in mind.

By the same token — and this is the second implication — the review of Allende's Chile and Zimbabwe under Mugabe suggests that the argument developed above with reference to India has wider applicability. If development with distribution is the goal for a capitalist Third World country, an organized and disciplined left-of-center regime is necessary to accomplish it. If there is no consolidated left-of-center regime, there will be no "growth with distribution." The further focus on the significance of an ideologically and organizationally cohesive party helps us understand both the failures in Chile and the smooth beginning in Zimbabwe. A reform-oriented, disciplined party at the helm, then, appears to be an essential ingredient for the success of reformist development.

Disciplined left-of-center parties are rare in the contemporary Third World. The existence and evolution of such parties presupposes the "freedom of association" or a modicum of political democracy. The dominant political configurations in much of the Third World, however, are anything but democratic. As a matter of fact, the road to authoritarianism in many Third World cases has been paved precisely by failed reform experiences. Reformist regimes alienate the upper classes, often fail to deliver meaningful reforms in the short run and thus fail to gain the support of the lower classes. And if they are not based on a well-organized party, these regimes create political fragmentation, thus inviting military or other authoritarian interventions. Brazil in 1964, Ghana after Nkrumah, the Philippines prior to Marcos, and Chile in 1973 readily come to mind.

Do failures of reformism suggest that left-of-center arrangements are not viable for India or other Third World countries? On the contrary, the failures simply highlight the inability of most Third World countries to develop political–economic arrangements that are capable of long-term institutionalization and capable of facilitating steadily rising standards of living for their populations. The alternatives to reformism (e.g., authoritarian–exclusionary models of development, such as Brazil from 1964 to 1984) face their own problems: regime institutionalization remains a core dilemma; highly skewed income distribution becomes a constraint on overall money demand and therefore on growth; societal factionalization penetrates regime institutions and threatens to politicize the supposedly apolitical rulers; and financing of the economy with foreign money — once considered the basis of high growth rates — itself becomes a constraint as debt-servicing generates formidable growth constraints. Even sustaining high growth rates — once thought to be a unique contribution of authoritarian–exclusionary regimes—becomes problematic. Many authoritarian–exclusionary regimes, therefore, do not offer long-term solutions to the multi-faceted problems of Third World countries; they themselves have a tendency to move towards the nationalist–reformist models of capitalist development.

Just as failures of reformism have often led to authoritarianism, so the inherent limitations of authoritarian–exclusionary regimes push them towards more democratic–inclusionary directions. Is this see-saw in the contemporary capitalist Third World inevitable? Quite possibly! If it is to be avoided, however, and stable political arrangements are to be designed to facilitate economic growth with redistribution, then the empirical materials analyzed above suggest some possible directions for action.

The analysis undertaken in this study suggests that regimes controlled by disciplined left-of-center parties offer a rare opportunity for reconciling growth with redistribution within the frame of a democratic–capitalist development. Therefore, for those concerned with the question, "What is to be done in the Third World?" the focus of this study shifts the attention away from some of the more standard panaceas of development, namely, foreign aid, trade, investment, new policies, or even the concerns of a new international economic order. While none of these issues is unimportant, their effective translation into redistributive development presupposes the existence of suitable regime organization. This primacy of political conditions in the contemporary Third World has been lost in the recent debates between liberal and neo-Marxist scholars. Its recognition suggests that one of the more important long-term tasks facing India and other capitalist Third World countries is the organization and sustained development of viable left-of-center political parties.

Appendix I

On the Political Relevance of Social Classes in a Developmental Setting

I have used the concept of social class throughout this study but have not formally defined it. Because the study is concerned primarily with the role of the state in society, I did not feel the need to formalize my use of class as a concept within the main text; that would have detracted from the central concern with political issues. Class as a concept is nevertheless a controversial and a much abused one.[1] This appendix briefly elaborates on my understanding of social class in a developmental setting and, in an abstract fashion, outlines how social classes became politically significant forces.

Following Marx, three questions can be raised concerning the organization of production in a Third World society: who owns the means of production? Who controls the decisions on production? And who has primary access to the fruits of production? To the extent that the means of production are owned by some and not by others and to the extent that the owners control both the decisions on and the fruits of production, the production system is organized on class lines. In other words, if the division in the ownership of production forms a parallel and reinforcing hierarchy to the division of labor and the patterns of exchange, then the production system generates cleavages along which social actors are interlocked into class relations. Those at the top of this class hierarchy enjoy, at minimum, a disproportionate access to the wealth of society. In most of these cases, however, the upper classes are not only relatively wealthy, but also enjoy high status and considerable political power.

Class structures within the Third World vary widely. It is clear that some of the agriculture, services, and domestic/foreign-owned industry in the Third World are organized along the classical capitalist lines of commodity production for profit and wage labor. The conceptualization of social classes in other sections of the economy requires sensitivity. The concurrent existence of varying arrangements for "surplus appropriation" in pre-capitalist agriculture (tenancy, sharecropping, bonded labor, etc.), the owner–operator peasantry, the "marginals" and unemployed in the cities, the public-sector employees, and the independent professionals all add complexity to the class structure. A general conceptualization of this forces one to use such broad categories as the "upper," the "middle," and the "lower" classes, while leaving further specification for the empirical context.

---

1. While the concept of social class is used often, very little has been written on it in the context of developing countries. For one of the rare book-length treatments of the subject, see Rodolfo Stavenhagen, *Social classes in agrarian societies*, trans. Judy Adler Hellman (Doubleday, Anchor Books: Garden City, N.Y., 1975).

How do these class interests become salient for our understanding of political intervention for societal transformation, that is, how do regimes and social classes interact in the process of deliberate development? Before I proceed with this central question, two common objections claiming that social structures in the Third World are not class structures need to be dealt with. The first objection is that "class" definitions categorize social actors who share common "economic situations." Social class, in this view, points to a probable criterion along which class actors may associate so as to wage a political struggle to enhance their economic interests. The concept of class, therefore, if at all useful, is so only in "modern" societies where the "public" and the "private" realms have been differentiated. Only in "modern capitalist" formations, the objection would continue, does it make sense to conceptualize individuals as class individuals with common economic interests associating as "citizens" to gain political leverage. These conditions do not hold in the Third World countries. A considerable part of the Third World populace remains entrenched in the "traditional" rural milieu. These social formations are characterized by the fusion of the status, economic, and power realms. Social actors in these settings do not associate "politically" to influence their "private" interests. According to this viewpoint, therefore, it is not very useful to conceptualize Third World social actors as class actors.[2]

The second related objection stems from the view that "developing" societies consist of many heterogeneous, somewhat isolated, and self-sufficient social units on which a legal unity of a "nation–state" has been imposed. From this perspective, tribes, castes, and villages are all seen as localized units that do not belong to a "national community" because their loyalties are "primordial" rather than "national." And since the political significance of classes stems primarily from their "interest association" at the "national level," the absence of such associational behavior is from this vantage-point seen as evidence for the minimal utility of applying the concept of class to the analysis of developing societies. If social actors do not act politically as class actors, how can the concept of class be a useful one for the study of state–society interactions?[3]

Inspired by Weber's critique of Marx, one sees that both of these objections to class analysis in the "pre-modern" settings fail to grasp the distinction between structure and behavior. The concept of class is structural, while these objections stem from a primary concern with behavior; that is, from a concern with the "meaning" of social action or with the social–psychological underpinnings of concrete behavior. The concept of class structure, like any structural formulation in social–scientific analysis, attempts to grasp the positional relationships generated by the differential distribution of objectively identifiable resources; in this case, economic ones. The objections stated above would have validity only if the for-

2. This argument has on occasion been put forward even by those who are otherwise sympathetic to the use of social class in more modern contexts. For example, see Anthony Giddens, *The class structure of the advanced societies* (Harper Touchbooks: New York, 1973), esp. p. 84.

3. *Ibid*. p. 84. For a development of this argument with specific reference to India, see Frykenberg's introduction to R.E. Frykenberg (ed.), *Land tenure and peasant in South Asia* (Orient Longman: New Delhi, 1977), pp. 12-13.

mulation tended to assume that predictable behavior follows from the objective positions in the social structure. However, no such claim is made here. Structures do not determine behavior; they constrain and thus influence behavior. In a sense, this problem of relating objectively conceived structural patterns to social behavior highlights what is problematic in both Marxist and Weberian analyses. Marxist analysis tends to assume too close a relationship between structure and behavior, or attributes the gap to "false consciousness." On the other hand, Weberian analysis, partly as a response to this problem, tends to abandon the concern with structure in favor of the more immediate determinants of behavior, namely, culture. The position taken here holds that, while a prior conceptualization of class structure is indispensable, it is the task of empirical analysis to delineate how the structural and the cultural variables combine to determine patterns of consciousness and action.

Thus the focus on the ownership and control patterns in the production and distribution system allows one to conceptualize the social structures of many of the Third World countries as class structures. Whether the social classes pursue their interests in a conscious and cohesive manner is primarily an empirical issue, which has little bearing on whether a society has classes or not. The constraints on political action generated by class structure manifest themselves through various social mechanisms of which class-conscious behavior is only one. (These will be discussed below.) Furthermore, the focus on class structure highlights the fact that even if the loyalty structures in many Third World countries are highly fragmented, the structures of surplus generation and distribution are not. If one could observe what happens to the "value" created by a sharecropper in a remote village of some Third World country, one could without doubt discover a portion of it being appropriated by the landlord, and then a further portion becoming part of the larger national economy in the form of the landlord's consumption, savings, and investment. In this sense, the system of creation and distribution of the society's wealth forms not a fragmented structure, but rather an integrated one. And it is this integrated class structure that, in turn, constrains and conditions the workings of political power in social life.

How does the class structure condition the developmental role of the regime, or how are class interests translated into identifiable influences on the political process? While this is also primarily an issue for empirical analysis, four mechanisms linking class to politics can be specified in a general way. These are: conscious class action, patterned but discrete class behavior, the anticipation of class constraints by the political elite, and institutional internalization. Of these four, conscious class action — social classes acting politically in a more or less organized fashion to further their currently perceived class interests — is the most readily understood mechanism, because it is the most dramatic and the most widely discussed by proponents and critics of "class analysis" alike. In the countries of the Third World, however, this mode of class-based political behavior is often limited to the dominant classes in the more capitalist sectors of the economy. Because social classes are often not very well organized, there is considerable room for the regime authorities to mediate and structure social change. What conditions prompt social classes to pursue their interests in a conscious and organized manner, and what conditions in other instances lead to the absence of this action, are questions for empirical research.

The mode of class behavior that is more prevalent in the Third World, especially among the upper classes, is the individually discrete pursuit of economic interests. Because the pursuits of those sharing similar economic positions tend to be similar, these actions constitute a discernable pattern. Cumulatively, these discrete but patterned actions have the consequence of systematically translating class interests into a political force. For example, the landed groups of a Third World country, even if not very class conscious or well organized, can frustrate the attempts of the political authorities to implement land redistribution by various discrete but similar actions aimed at preserving their individual economic interests. In the aggregate, these actions can add a landed-class bias to the political process that leads to the inability of the state to act against the landed interests. This inability, of course, reflects both the power of the landed classes and the weakness of Third World capitalist states to utilize compulsion as a tool of reform. Nevertheless, if the landed elite are consciously organized to preserve or enhance their economic interests, their activities represent class-conscious action; if they pursue their interests individually and thus cumulatively introduce a class bias to the political process, their actions exemplify patterned but discrete class behavior.

Even if classes do not actively pursue their interests, the political elite may choose to serve the interests of one particular class because of anticipated class constraints, that is, from a valid or invalid belief held by the elite that their actions must take account of the class constraints existing in society. Because political leaders are socialized in the process of acting politically, they acquire a sense — and the more successful ones acquire a fairly accurate sense — of which actions are rewarded and which actions are punished by specific social groups. Following these learned perceptions of the social constraints of political action, leaders often choose to direct the role of the state in a manner that elicits the support of significant social actors.

Lastly, as a consequence of any of these three mechanisms for translating class interests into political variables, the political institutions of a society may, in time, internalize dominant class interests. If this happens, the institutional internalization becomes another mechanism for generating and sustaining the "automatic" support of the dominant interests. This process of the institutionalization of class interests can occur at any of the various levels — ideological, party, governmental, bureaucratic, etc. — through which the inputs to the political process are converted into outputs. Because political institutions in Third World countries are often not well established, such means of class domination are not widely prevalent. Elements of it are, however, occasionally present. For example, at the ideological level, the various socialization agencies of a society (religious, educational, informational, etc.) may, after a period of active participation and control by elements of the upper class, come to automatically generate and sustain value systems that support class domination. The resulting political culture may then view in a positive light such values as efficiency, cohesiveness, acceptance of the *status quo*, or incremental change, and may attach negative sanctions to all modes of behavior leading to class conflict or holistic change. Similarly, political parties, governmental arrangements, and bureaucratic structures can also internalize class interests. As a consequence, the range of acceptable political values and actions usually buttresses dominant interests.

Class forces thus condition regime intervention through one or more of the four mechanisms discussed. What is important to reiterate at this point, however, is that class constraints do not determine the political process; they condition it. While this is mainly an analytical assertion, from an empirical perspective also, Third World class relations are structured in a manner that enhances a regime's maneuverability in society. These characteristics deserve to be stressed. First, Third World class structures are fragmented and are seldom dominated by a single class capable of imposing hegemonic rule in the Gramscian sense. Organized and cohesive regimes are then well positioned to mediate and structure social relations. Second, the transition from pre-capitalist to capitalist class relations is a problematic phase from the standpoint of surplus accumulation and social order. Social institutions stabilizing pre-capitalist class structures erode with the penetration of capitalism. The problem of creating a new capitalist social order, then, is how to get the many to value new arrangements that primarily serve the few. An inherently conflictual process, it has often been.euphemistically interpreted as "demand overload" or as the gap between "differentiation and integration."[4] Under these conditions, the propertied tend to exchange their right to rule for the right to make money. The political authorities, in turn, having gained these rights, develop their own modes of controlling society as a means of preserving and enhancing their interests. Regime structures, then, themselves become a force molding social relations. In sum, Third World conditions of class fragmentation and rapid change weaken class capacities to control the political process, while enhancing regime willingness and capacity to structure social relations.

4. For example see Huntington, *Political order*; and Smelser, "Mechanisms of change."

Appendix II
Does Agriculture Growth Really
"Trickle-down" in India?

Montek Ahluwalia concluded in an important article on India's rural development that "there is evidence of some 'trickle down' associated with agriculture
growth."[1] The purpose of this appendix is to argue that the data presented by
Ahluwalia can be interpreted in ways that would not support this conclusion.

Ahluwalia's general conclusion rests on his two specific prior conclusions: (1)
Indian data do not indicate a trend increase in the incidence of rural poverty, and
(2) the incidence of rural poverty is inversely related to agriculture performance,
indicating that faster growth might have led to a reduced incidence of poverty.
Both of these conclusions are debatable. The first of the two is somewhat more
convincing because it is well supported; it nevertheless requires qualification. The
second conclusion does not flow readily from the data presented.

Ahluwalia's data on the incidence of rural poverty in India do not disagree with
the conclusion arrived at by Bardhan:[2] from 1960 to 1968 there was a steady
increase in the percentage of the rural population living below the poverty line.
The time series data for these years only reconfirm this finding. The interesting
issue then arises as to what has been happening to poverty since the late 1960s.
Ahluwalia provides data for three more years, namely, 1968-9, 1970-1, and 1973-
4. These years do not fit into the trend discerned by Bardhan. On the contrary,
the trend appears to be reversed. However, does this amount, as Ahluwalia
would have it, to a negation of the earlier evidence? It is possible to interpret the
data in a somewhat different way. The data set is consistent with the argument
that the 1960s marked the beginning of a trend toward an increase in the proportion of the population living below the poverty line. The figures from the early
1970s cast doubt on whether this trend is continuing. As a consequence, we must
await further evidence from the 1970s to make conclusions about whether the
trend begun in the 1960s has continued into the 1970s or not.

If Ahluwalia's trend data are moderately useful, in that they suggest the time-
bound validity of the earlier findings, his attempt to derive explanatory conclusions from correlational data is at least simplistic, if not incorrect. There is no
doubt about the validity of the inverse "fit" that he discovers between the agriculture growth data and the data on the incidence of poverty. This may be interesting, but what does this fit mean? Does it really suggest, as it does to Ahluwalia,
that higher agriculture growth in itself could have or can reduce the incidence of
rural poverty? Or does it indicate something considerably less revealing, namely,

---

1. Ahluwalia, "Rural poverty," p. 320
2. Bardhan, "The incidence of rural poverty in the sixties."

242

that good monsoons mitigate the worst of rural poverty in India? I would argue that the level of aggregation of Ahluwalia's data does not lend itself to any general conclusions relating agriculture growth to rural poverty.

In attempting to relate agriculture growth to the incidence of rural poverty, the critical issue is one of the pattern of growth rather than of growth *per se*. The variations in growth can be weather-related or policy-related. It can be reasoned that the consequences of the two types of growth for the rural poor will not necessarily be similar. This would especially be true if the policy is consciously aimed, as it has been in India for the recent past, at subsidizing the profitability of the medium and rich farmers.[3] It can be argued that such a policy-stimulated growth is less likely to "trickle-down" to the poorest, while the weather-induced growth indeed tends to mitigate the worst of rural poverty.

The shortage of rainfall in India is especially problematic for the rural poor. Small farmers often do not have access to sources of reliable irrigation. The absence of adequate rainfall must also result in shortage of work availability and therefore in lower wages for the landless. That Ahluwalia's data should then indicate an inverse relationship between the incidence of poverty and weather-related variations in agricultural output is not surprising. What is important to note, however, are the reasons why the poorest are better off in the good years. Suitable monsoons probably benefit the poorest directly by providing higher output per acre for the small farmers, and by raising labor demand and thus the availability of work or wages for the landless. An argument for a "trickle-down" resulting from weather-induced growth can therefore be sustained on both logical and empirical grounds.

In contrast to this, it is not at all clear whether a similar "trickle-down" is associated with the growth resulting from the "green revolution" policies.[4] There is little unambiguous data demonstrating that the growth in output in the "green revolution" areas of India had been accompanied by higher output per acre for the small farmers or increments in the availability of work or increments in the real wages for the landless. While real wages may well have undergone some improvement, the situation is unclear with regard to the overall availability of work over time. Only direct empirical evidence of this nature can finally substantiate a general case relating agriculture growth to rural poverty. Furthermore, it is well known that such factors as a shortage of credit for small farmers, labor-displacing technology, and the eviction of tenants may be neutralizing any potential "trickle-down" gains. On both empirical and logical grounds, then, the case for a "trickle-down" associated with the "green revolution" can at best be weak.

Ahluwalia's macro-data do not allow us to distinguish between the consequences of varying patterns of growth. In other words, while it can be reasoned as

---

3. In India this has been done not only by channeling the subsidized inputs to the better-off farmers, but also by providing price supports to the producers. The latter action, by contributing to inflation, may well hurt the poor, who are after all net consumers, even more than the skewed distribution of publically supported agrarian inputs.
4. For a recent argument suggesting that the evidence is a lot more mixed than Ahluwalia makes it out to be, see Bardhan, "Poverty and 'trickle-down'."

to why the distributional consequences of rain-fed agricultural growth would be beneficial for the rural poor, the same does not necessarily follow for policy-stimulated growth. Ahluwalia ignores this issue and as a result arrives at conclusions that are more general than his data warrant.

The variations in the output at the all-India level, as Ahluwalia himself notes, are "dominated by weather fluctuations."[5] It is these data that have an inverse relationship with the poverty data. The data that primarily reflect the consequences of policy-stimulated growth are those from Punjab and Haryana. These data, again as Ahluwalia himself notes, "do not support the hypothesis that improved agricultural performance will help reduce the incidence of poverty."[6] If any conclusion is then supported by Ahluwalia's data, it is not the one he derives. Rather, it is the one that emerges by contrasting the Punjab and Haryana data with the all-India data: growth generated by the adequate availability of moisture may tend to reduce the incidence of poverty, while the consequences of the "green revolution" for poverty remain, at minimum, unclear. It should be obvious that the policy implications of this conclusion would be somewhat different from those derived from a belief in the "trickle-down" associated with growth-oriented strategies in general.

5. Ahluwalia, "Rural Poverty," p. 325.

6. *Ibid*. p. 315. Ahluwalia suggests that the "immigration" of labor from the outside of the Punjab and Haryana may be responsible for depressing the "trickle-down" gains here. While this argument may have some validity, it needs to be balanced against the following facts. A considerable portion of this immigration is to the urban areas, where the labor force from U.P. and Bihar has moved into the service sector: rickshaw-drivers, street hawkers etc. Rural Punjab, like most rural communities, remains inhospitable to "outsiders." The Punjabi farmer is furthermore, following the cultural prejudices of the area, generally reluctant to hire this new labor force, as he doubts its productivity. The effective contribution of immigrant labor in rural Punjab must therefore remain an open issue until confirmed one way or the other by empirical work. Also, if "in-migration" is indeed so significant in neutralizing the gains in Punjab, why does "out-migration" not show up in reducing poverty levels in other states?

Bibliography

Adelman, I., and Robinson, S. *Income distribution policy in developing countries: a case study of Korea.* Stanford, California: Stanford University Press, 1978.

Ahluwalia, Montek. "Rural poverty and agricultural performance in India," *Journal of Development Studies*, 14, 3 (April 1978), 289-324.

Ahmed, Imtiaz, and Saxena, N.C. "Caste, land and political power in Uttar Pradesh," in Frankel and Rao (eds.), forthcoming.

Alavi, Hamza. "Peasants and revolution," in Gough and Sharma (eds.), 291-337.

"The state in post-colonial societies," *New Left Review*, 74 (July–August 1972), 59-82.

Apter, David. *The politics of modernization.* Chicago: the University of Chicago Press, 1965.

Bakhru, Mira. "Distribution of welfare: people's housing scheme in Karnataka," *Economic and Political Weekly*, 19, 10 (1984), 427-36, and 19, 11 (1984), 473-80.

Bandyopadhyaya, Nripen. "Operation Barga and land reforms perspective in West Bengal: a discursive review," *Economic and Political Weekly* (Review of Agriculture), 16, 25-6 (1981), A38-A42.

Bardhan, P.K. "India," in Chenery *et al.,* pp. 255-62.

"On the incidence of poverty in rural India in the sixties," in Bardhan and Srinivasan (eds.), 264-80.

"Poverty and 'trickle-down' in rural India: a quantitative analysis," in a forthcoming volume of essays in honor of Dharm Veera, ed. John Mellor.

Bardhan, Pranab, and Rudra, Ashok. "Labour, employment and wages in agriculture: results of a survey in West Bengal, 1979," *Economic and Political Weekly*, 15, 45-6 (1980), 1943-9.

Bardhan, P.K., and Srinivasan, T.N. (eds.). *Poverty and income distribution in India.* Calcutta: Statistical Publishing Society, 1974.

Baxter, Craig. "The rise and fall of the Bharatiya Kranti Dal in Uttar Pradesh," in Marguerite Ross Barnett *et al., Electoral politics in the Indian states: party system and cleavages.* New Delhi: Manohar Books, 1975.

Bell, C.L.G. "The political framework," in Chenery *et al.,* pp. 52-72

Bendix, Reinhard. *Max Weber: an intellectual portrait.* New York: Anchor Books, Doubleday and Company, 1962.

Nation-building and citizenship: studies of our changing social order. Enlarged edn. Berkeley: University of California Press, 1977.

Bhambri, C.P. *Bureaucracy and politics in India.* Delhi: Vikas Publications, 1971.

Berger, Peter. *Pyramids of sacrifice: political ethics and social change*. New York: Doubleday, 1976.

Beteille, André. *Inequality among men*. Oxford: Basil Blackwell, 1977.

    Inequality and social change. New Delhi: Oxford University Press,1972.

Bienen, Henry. "Armed forces and national modernization: continuing the debate," *Comparative Politics*, 16, 1 (October 1983), 1-16.

    Tanzania: party transformation and economic development. Princeton, New Jersey: Princeton University Press, 1967.

Boyce, James K. "Agricultural growth in West Bengal, 1949-50 to 1980-81: a review of the evidence," *Economic and Political Weekly* (Review of Agriculture), 19, 13 (1984), A9-A16.

Brass, Paul. "Congress, the Lok Dal and the middle-peasant castes: an analysis of the 1977 and 1980 parliamentary elections in Uttar Pradesh," *Pacific Affairs*, 54, 1 (spring 1981), 5-41.

    "Division in the Congress and the rise of agrarian interests and issues in Uttar Pradesh politics, 1952 to 1977," in John Wood (ed.), *State Politics in Contemporary India: Crisis or Continuity?*. Westview Press: Boulder, Colorado, 1984, pp. 21-52.

    Factional politics in an Indian state: the Congress Party in Uttar Pradesh. Berkeley: University of California Press, 1965.

    "Leadership conflict and the disintegration of the Indian socialist movement: personal ambition, power and policy," *Journal of Commonwealth and Comparative Politics*, 14, 1 (March 1976), 19-41.

    "The politicization of the peasantry in a North Indian state: I and II," *Journal of Peasant Studies*, 7, 4 (July 1980), 395-426, and 8, 1 (September 1980), 3-36.

Bratton, Michael. "Development in Zimbabwe: strategy and tactics," *Journal of Modern African Studies*, 19, 3 (September 1981), 447-75.

Brecher, Michael. *Nehru: a political biography*. New York: Oxford University Press, 1959.

Burger, Angela Sutherland. *Opposition in a dominant-party system: a study of the Jan Sangh, the Praja Socialist Party and the Socialist Party in Uttar Pradesh, India*. Center for South and South Asia Studies. Berkeley: University of California Press, 1969.

Byres, Terry J. "The dialectic of India's green revolution," *South Asian Review*, 5, 2 (January 1972), 99-116.

Byres, Terry J., and Crow, Ben. *The green revolution in India*. The Open University Press, 1983.

The Calcutta Gazette, West Bengal Act XXXIV. Calcutta (February 3, 1978).

Cardoso, Fernando. "Associated-dependent development: theoretical and practical implications," in Alfred Stepan (ed.), *Authoritarian Brazil: origins, policies and future*. New Haven: Yale University Press, 1973, 142-78.

Cardoso, Fernando, and Faletto, Enzo. *Dependency and development in Latin America*, trans. Marjory Mattingly Urquidi. Berkeley: University of California Press, 1979.

Carnoy, Martin. *The state and political theory*. Princeton, New Jersey: Princeton University Press, 1984.

Chenery, Hollis *et al.*, *Redistribution with growth*. London: Oxford University Press, 1974.

Coleman, James. "The resurrection of political economy," in Norman Uphoff and Warren F. Ilchman (eds.), *The political economy of development: theoretical and empirical contributions*. Berkeley and Los Angeles: University of California Press, 1973, 30–9.

Collier, David (ed.). *The new authoritarianism in Latin America*. Princeton, New Jersey: Princeton University Press, 1979.

Communist Party of India (Marxist), (Resolution of the Central Committee), *On certain agrarian issues*. New Delhi, March 1976.

    Political resolution, adopted at the tenth Congress. Jullundur, April 2-8, 1978.

    (Resolution of the Central Committee), *Tasks on the kisan front*. New Delhi, March 1976.

Dahl, Robert "Pluralism revisited," *Comparative Politics*, 10, 2 (January 1978), 191-203.

Dandekar, V.M., and Rath, N. "Poverty in India: dimensions and trends," *Economic and Political Weekly*, 6, 1 (1971), 25-48 and 6, 2 (1971), 106-46.

Dasgupta, Biplab. "Sharecropping in West Bengal: from independence to Operation Barga," *Economic and Political Weekly* (Review of Agriculture), 19, 26 (1984), A85-A96.

Dasgupta, Jyotindra. *Authority, priority and human development*. New Delhi: Oxford University Press, 1981.

    "The Janata phase: the reorganization and redirection in Indian politics," *Asian Survey*, 19, 4 (April 1979), 390-403.

Dasgupta, Pramode. Speech to the silver jubilee celebration of the Kisan Sabha, reported in *Ganashakti* (February 10, 1979).

Deccan Herald, English daily. Bangalore (January 4, 1979).

Desai, A.R. *Social background of Indian nationalism*, 4th edn. Bombay: Popular Prakashan, 1966.

Dutt, Kalyan. "Operation Barga: gains and constraints," *Economic and Political Weekly* (Review of Agriculture), 16, 25-6 (1981), A58-A60.

Eckstein, Harry. "On the 'science' of the state," in Graubard (ed.), 1-20.

Epstein, Trude Scarlett. *South India: yesterday, today and tomorrow*. London: Macmillan, 1973.

Evans, Peter. *Dependent development: the alliance of multinational, state and local capital in Brazil*. Princeton, New Jersey: Princeton University Press, 1979.

Evans, Peter, Rueschemeyer, Dietrich, and Skocpol, Theda (eds.). *Bringing the state back in*. New York: Cambridge University Press, 1985.

Finkle, Jason L., and Gable, Richard W. (eds.) *Political development and social change*, 2nd edn. New York: John Wiley and Sons, Inc., 1971.

Ford Foundation. *Report on the agricultural situation in India*. New York, 1959.

Franda, Marcus. *India's rural development: an assessment of alternatives*, published in association with the American Universities Field Staff. Bloomington, Indiana: Indiana University Press, 1980.

Organizational alternatives in India's rural development. New Delhi: Wiley Eastern Limited, 1979.

Radical politics in West Bengal, Studies in communism, revisionism and revolution, 16. Cambridge, Massachusetts: MIT Press, 1971.

"Rural development, Bengali marxist style," *American Universities Field Staff Reports*, Asia, 15, (1978).

Frankel, Francine. "Compulsion and social change," *World Politics*, 30, 2 (January 1978), 215-40.

India's political economy, 1947-1977. Princeton, New Jersey: Princeton University Press, 1978.

Frankel, Francine, and Rao, M.S.A. (eds.). *Caste, class and dominance: patterns of politico-economic change in modern India*, forthcoming.

Frykenberg, R.E. (ed.). *Land tenure and peasant in South Asia*. New Delhi: Orient Longman, 1977.

Gandhi, Mohandas K. *An autobiography: the story of my experiments with truth*, trans. from original in Gujarati by Mahadev Desai. Ahmedabad: Navjivan Publishing House, 1957.

Gay, Peter. *The dilemma of democratic socialism*, 1st edn New York: Collier Books, 1962.

Ghosh, Ratan. "Agrarian programme of left front government," *Economic and Political Weekly* (Review of Agriculture), 16, 25-6 (1981), A49-A55.

Giddens, Anthony. *The class structure of the advanced societies*. New York: Harper Torchbooks, 1973.

Gough, Kathleen, and Sharma, Hari (eds.). *Imperialism and revolution in South Asia*. New York: Monthly Review Press, 1973.

Government of India. *Draft five year plan, 1978-83.* Planning Commission: New Delhi, 1978.

Draft fourth five year plan. Planning Commission: New Delhi, 1967.

First five year plan. Planning Commission: New Delhi, 1953.

Fourth five year plan. Planning Commission: New Delhi, 1969.

National sample survey, twenty-sixth round, report no. 215.8. Controller of Publications: New Delhi, 1974.

Progress of land reform. Planning Commission: New Delhi, 1963.

Report of the Lok Sabha Committee on the draft fourth five year plan (Agriculture and rural economy). New Delhi, 1966.

Report of the National Commission on agriculture, 15 vols. Ministry of Agriculture and Irrigation: New Delhi, 1976.

Second five year plan. Planning Commission: New Delhi, 1954

Third five year plan. Planning Commission: New Delhi, 1960.

Government of Karnataka. *Agricultural census*, 1976-77. State Agricultural Census Commission: Bangalore, 1978.

Draft five year plan, 1978-83. Planning Department: Bangalore, 1978.

Employment affirmation scheme. Planning Department: Bangalore, 1978.

Report of the Karnataka backward classes commission. Bangalore, November 1975.

"Land reforms progress in the state up to the end of November 1980," memorandum from the Revenue Department. Bangalore, 1980.

Government of the Republic of Zimbabwe. *Growth with equality: an economic policy statement*. Salisbury, 1981

Government of Uttar Pradesh. *Draft five year plan, 1978-83*, vol. II. Planning Department: Lucknow, January 1979.

    Land reforms in Uttar Pradesh. Revenue Department: Lucknow, 1975.

    "Note showing the legislative measures relating to land reforms in Uttar Pradesh," Revenue Department memorandum: Lucknow, 1979.

Government of West Bengal. *Economic review, 1978-79, statistical appendix*, Calcutta, 1979.

    Guidelines for bank financing to share-croppers and patta holders. Calcutta, 1983.

    Guidelines for the settlement of harvesting disputes — protection of bargardars and assignees of vested land. Office of the Board of Revenue: Calcutta, 1978.

    Land reforms in West Bengal, a statistical report. Land Revenue Department: Calcutta, 1981.

    Land reforms in West Bengal, statistical report VII. Board of Revenue: Calcutta, 1982

    National rural employment programme in West Bengal. Development and Planning Department: Calcutta, 1982.

Graubard, Stephen R. (ed.). *The state*. New York: W.W. Norton and Company, Inc., 1979.

Griffin, Keith. *The political economy of agrarian change: an essay on the green revolution*, 1st edn Cambridge, Massachusetts: Harvard University Press, 1974.

Hamilton, Nora. *The limits of state autonomy: post-revolutionary Mexico*. Princeton, New Jersey: Princeton University Press, 1982

Hanson, A.H. *The process of planning: a study of India's five year plans, 1950-1964*. London: Oxford University Press, 1966.

Hebsur, R.K. "Karnataka," *Seminar*, 278 (August 1978), 21-6.

Heginbotham, Stanley. *Cultures in conflict: The four faces of Indian Bureaucracy*. New York: Columbia University Press, 1975.

Hindustan Times, English daily (September 3, 1966).

Hiro, Dilip. *Inside India today*. New York: Monthly Review Press, 1976.

Hirschman, Albert. *Journeys toward progress: studies of economic policy-making in Latin America*. New York: Twentieth Century Fund, 1963.

Huntington, Samuel. *Political order in changing societies*. New Haven, Connecticut: Yale University Press, 1968.

Hutchins, Francis. *India's revolution: Gandhi and the Quit India movement*. Cambridge, Massachusetts: Harvard University Press, 1973.

IBRD. *Economic situation and prospect of India*. Washington, DC, 1979.

    World development report, 1981. New York: Oxford University Press, 1981.

India Today, English fortnightly. New Delhi (February 16-28, 1979).

Indian Finance, "Wooing business to West Bengal" (September 10, 1977).

Kalecki, Michael. *Selected essays on the economic growth of the socialist and the mixed economy*. Cambridge: Cambridge University Press, 1972.

Khasnabis, Ratan. "Operation Barga: limits to social democratic regime," *Economic and Political Weekly* .(Review of Agriculture) 16, 25-6 (1981), A43-A48.

Khusro, A.N. "New emphasis on agriculture," *Times of India* (March 8, 1979).

Kohli, Atul. "Democracy, economic growth, and inequality in India's development," *World Politics,* 32, 4 (July 1980), 623-38.

"From elite radicalism to democratic consolidation: the rise of reform communism in West Bengal," in Frankel and Rao (eds.), forthcoming.

"Karnataka's land reforms: a model for India?," *The Journal of Commonwealth and Comparative Politics*, 20, 3 (November 1982), 309-28.

"Parliamentary communism and agrarian reform," *Asian Survey*, 23, 7 (July 1983), 783-809.

"The state, economic growth and income-distribution in the Third World," paper presented to the International Studies Association meetings. East Lansing, Michigan, November 3-5, 1983.

Kohli, Atul, Altfeld, Michael F., Lotfian, Saideh, and Mardon, Russell. "Inequality in the Third World: an assessment of competing explanations," *Comparative Political Studies*, 17, 3 (October 1984) 283-318.

Kothari, Rajni. *Politics in India*. Boston: Little, Brown and Company, 1970.

Krishna, Raj. "The next phase in rural development," *Voluntary Action*, 20, 7 (July 1978), 38.

Lehman, David. "The political economy of Armageddon: Chile, 1970-73," *Journal of Development Economics*, 5, 2 (June 1978), 107-23.

Lipton, Michael. "Strategy for agriculture: urban bias and rural planning," in Paul Streeten and Michael Lipton (eds.), *The crisis of Indian planning: economic planning in the 1960's*. London: Oxford University Press, 1968, 83-147.

Why poor people stay poor: urban bias in world development. Cambridge, Massachusetts: Harvard University Press, 1977.

Loveman, Brian. *Chile: the legacy of hispanic capitalism*. New York: Oxford University Press, 1979.

Lowenthal, Richard. "The nature of underdevelopment and the role of the state," in Richard Lowenthal (ed.), *Model or ally? the communist powers and the developing countries*. New York: Oxford University Press, 1976, 11-46.

Majumdar, R.C. *History of the freedom movement in India*, 3 vols. Calcutta: Firma K.L. Mukhopadhyay, 1962-3.

Manor, James. "Karnataka: caste, stratum and politics in a cohesive society," in Frankel and Rao (eds.), forthcoming.

Political change in an Indian state, Mysore 1915-55. Australian National University Monographs on South Asia, 2. Columbia: South Asia Books, 1978.

"Pragmatic progressives in regional politics: the case of Devraj Urs," *Economic and Political Weekly* (annual number), 15, 5-6 (1980), 201-13.

"Structural changes in Karnataka politics," *Economic and Political Weekly*, 12, 44 (1977), 1865-9.

Maravall, Jose M. "The limits of reformism," *British Journal of Sociology*, 30, 3

(September 1979), 267-90.

Mellor, John. *The new economics of growth: a strategy for India and the developing world*, a Twentieth Century Fund study. Ithaca, New York: Cornell University Press, 1976.

Minhas, B.S. *Planning and the poor*. New Delhi: S. Chand and Company Ltd, 1974.

"Rural poverty, land distribution and development strategy: facts," in Bardhan and Srinivasan (eds.), 252-63.

Mirchandani, G.G. *The people's verdict*. New Delhi: Vikas, 1980.

Misra, B.B. *The Indian middle classes: their growth in modern times*. New York: Oxford University Press, 1961.

Montgomery, John D. "Allocation of authority in land reform programs: a comparative study of administrative progress and output," *Administrative Science Quarterly*, 17, 1 (March 1972), 62-75.

Moore, Barrington, Jr. *Social origins of dictatorship and democracy: lord and peasant in the making of the modern world*. Boston: Beacon Press, 1966.

Myrdal, Gunnar. *Asian drama: an enquiry into the poverty of nations*, a Twentieth Century Fund study. 3 vols. New York: Pantheon, 1968.

Narain, Iqbal (ed.). *State politics in India*. Meerut: Meenakshi Prakashan, 1976.

Nataraj, V.K., and Nataraj, Lalitha. "Limits of populism: Devraj Urs and Karnataka politics," *Economic and Political Weekly*, 17, 37 (1982); 1503-6.

Nayar, Baldev Raj. *The modernization imperative and Indian planning*. New Delhi: Vikas, 1972.

Nehru, Jawaharlal. *The discovery of India*, Anchor books edn New York: Doubleday, 1960.

Nordlinger, Eric. *On the autonomy of the democratic state*. Cambridge, Massachusetts: Harvard University Press,1981.

Nove, Alec. "The political economy of the Allende regime," in Philip O'Brien (ed.), *Allende's Chile*. New York: Praeger, 1976, 51-78.

O'Donnell, Guillermo. *Modernization and bureaucratic authoritarianism: studies in South American politics*, Politics of Modernization series, 9. Berkeley: University of California Press, 1973.

Offe, Claus. "Political authority and class structure," *International Journal of Sociology*, 2, 1 (1972), 73-108.

Strukturprobleme des kapitalistischen Staates: aufsatze zur politischen Soziologie, edn Suhrkamp 549. Frankfurt: Suhrkamp, 1972

Overstreet, Gene, and Windmiller, Marshall. *Communism in India*. Berkeley: University of California Press, 1959.

Pani, Narendra. "Reforms to pre-empt change: land legislation in Karnataka." Indian Institute of Management typescript: Bangalore, 1981.

Parameshwara, N., and Rayappa, P.H. "Collective and distributive land reforms in Karnataka." Paper presented at a symposium on land reforms. Bangalore, March 18, 1982.

Patil-Okaly, B.B. "Karnataka: politics of one party dominance," in Narain (ed.), pp. 129-45.

People's Democracy, "West Bengal budget breaks new ground" (March 11, 1979), 6.

Poulantzas, Nicos. *State, power and socialism*, verso edn, trans. from the French by Patrick Camiller. New York: Schocken Books, 1980.

Prasad, Pradhan M. "Rising middle peasantry in north India," *Economic and Political Weekly* (annual number), 15, 5-7 (1980), 215-19.

Raj, K.N. "The politics and economics of intermediate regimes," *Economic and Political Weekly*, 8, 27 (1973), 1189-98.

Rajan, M.A.S. "Working of land tribunals of Karnataka." Paper presented during a symposium on land reforms. Bangalore, March 18, 1982.

Rajapurohit, A.J. "Land reforms and changing agrarian structures in Karnataka." Paper presented during a symposium on land reforms. Bangalore, March 18, 1982.

Rawat, P.L., *et al.* "Levels of achievement in U.P." Mimeo, Department of Economics, Lucknow University: Lucknow, 1976.

Roy, Ajit. "West Bengal panchayat elections: class mobilization without class struggle," *Economic and Political Weekly*, 18, 26 (1983), 1141.

Rudolph, Lloyd I., and Rudolph, Susanne Hoeber. *The modernity of tradition: political development in India.* Chicago: the University of Chicago Press, 1967.

Rudra, Ashok. "One step forward, two steps backward," *Economic and Political Weekly* (Review of Agriculture), 16, 25-6 (1981), A61-A68.

Satyapriya, V.S., and Erappa, S. "Land reforms in Karnataka: some field evidence." Paper presented during a symposium on land reforms. Bangalore, March 18, 1982.

Scott, James. "Patron-client politics and political change in south-east Asia," *American Political Science Review*, 66, 1 (March 2, 1972), 91-113.

Sen Gupta, Bhabhani, *Communism in Indian politics.* New York: Columbia University Press, 1972.

   CPI-M: promises, prospects, problems. New Delhi: Young Asia Publications, 1979.

   "Pramode Das Gupta: party builder in eastern India," *Perspective*, Calcutta (April 1978).

Sengupta, Sunil. "West Bengal land reforms and the agrarian scene," *Economic and Political Weekly* (Review of Agriculture), 16, 25-6 (1981), A69-A75.

Sharma, Hari. "The green revolution in India: prelude to a red one," in Gough and Sharma (eds.), 77-102.

Singh, Baljit, and Mishra, Sridhar, *A study of land reforms in Uttar Pradesh*, American edn. Honolulu: East–West Center, University of Hawai Press, 1965.

Singh, Charan. *India's poverty and its solution*, 2nd edn. New York: Asia Publishing House, 1964.

Sinha, Arun. "Peasant–merchant conflict," *Economic and Political Weekly*, 5, 13 (November 25, 1978), 1929.

   "Uttar Pradesh: mockery of reform," *Economic and Political Weekly*, 13, 51-2 (1978), 2065 and 2067.

Sitaramayya, P.B. *The nationalist movement in India.* Bombay National Information and Publications, 1950.

Skidmore, Thomas, *Politics in Brazil, 1930-1964: an experiment in democracy.*

New York: Oxford University Press, 1967.

Skocpol, Theda. *States and social revolutions: a comparative analysis of France, Russia and China*. Cambridge–New York: Cambridge University Press, 1979.

Smelser, Neil. "Mechanisms of change and adjustment to change," in Bert F. Hoselitz and Wilbert E. Moore (eds.), *Industrialization and society*. The Hague: UNESCO and Mouton, 1963, 32-54.

Smiley, Xan. "Zimbabwe: Southern Africa and the rise of Robert Mugabe," *Foreign Affairs* (summer 1980), 1060-83.

Smith, Tony. "The underdevelopment of development literature," *World Politics*, 31, 2 (January 1979), 247-88.

Snodgrass, Donald R. *Inequality and economic development in Malaysia*. Kuala Lumpur: Oxford University Press, 1980.

Spear, Percival. *A history of India*, Pelican original, vol. II. Baltimore: Penguin Books, 1965.

Srinivas, M.N. "The social system of a Mysore village," in McKim Marriott (ed.), *Village India, studies in the little community*. Chicago: University of Chicago Press, 1955, 1-35.

Srinivas, M.N., and Panini, M.N. "Politics and society in Karnataka," *Economic and Political Weekly*, 19, 2 (1984), 69-75.

Srivastava, Saraswati. "Uttar Pradesh: Politics of neglected development," in Narain (ed.), 323-69.

Stavenhagen, Rodolfo. *Social classes in agrarian societies*, trans. Judy Adler Hellman. Garden City, New York: Doubleday Books, Anchor Press, 1975.

Stepan, Alfred. *The state and society: Peru in comparative perspective*. Princeton, New Jersey: Princeton University Press, 1978.

Thimmaiah, G., and Aziz, Abdul. "The political economy of land reforms in Karnataka, a South Indian state," *Asian Survey*, 23, 7 (July 1983), 810-29.

Thorner, Daniel, and Thorner, Alice. *Land and labor in India*. Bombay–New York: Asia Publishing House, 1962.

Times of India, English daily (August 21, 1966).

Times of India, English daily (February 28, 1979).

Urs, Devraj. Inaugural speech at the seminar on land reforms in Karnataka. Asian Institute for Rural Development: Bangalore, November 1978.

   Socio-economic programme for the poor: some policy imperatives. Office of the Chief Minister: Karnataka, April 1978.

Vermeer, E.B. "Income differentials in rural China," *China Quarterly*, 89 (March 1982), 1-33.

   "Social welfare provisions and the limits of inequality in contemporary China," *Asian Survey*, 19, 9 (September 1979), 856-80.

Waterbury, John. *The Egypt of Nasser and Sadat: the political economy of two regimes*. Princeton, New Jersey: Princeton University Press, 1983.

Weiner, Myron. *Party building in a new nation: the Indian National Congress*. Chicago: the University of Chicago Press, 1967.

World Bank, The. *The assault on world poverty: problems of rural development, education and health*. Baltimore: Johns Hopkins University Press, 1975.

Wright, Erik Olin, Gold, D.A., and Lo, C.Y.H. "Recent developments in Marxist theories of the capitalist state," *Monthly Review, 27, 5* (October 1975), 29-43 and 27, 6 (November 1975), 36-51.

INDEX

Adelman, I., 37, 37n, 245
agricultural growth: in India, and
    rural poverty, 12-13, 242-4; in West
    Bengal, 120; in Karnataka, and rural
    poverty, 161-5
Ahluwalia, Montek, 2n, 34n, 82, 82n, 83,
    83n, 84n, 118n, 161n, 162n, 211, 242-4,
    245
Ahmed, Imtiaz, 205n, 216n, 217n, 220n,
    245
Alavi, Hamza, 18, 18n, 20n, 131n, 245
Allende, Salvador, 34, 232-5
Amnesty International, 108n
Angola, 32, 33
Apter, David, 17, 17n, 245
authoritarian–dependent regime: defined,
    35; and economic development, 35-6
Aziz, Abdul, 152n, 165n

Bahuguna, 194
Bakhru, Mira, 165n, 245
Balasubramanium, V., 151n, 173n
Banarsidas, 191, 192, 197
Bandyopadhyay, D., 124n, 125n, 127n,
    134n, 135
Bandyopadhyaya, Nripen, 95n, 245
Bangladesh, 32
Bardhan, Pranab K., 2n, 34n, 83, 84n,
    119n, 142n, 164n, 214n, 225n, 242, 242n,
    243n, 245, 250
Barnett, Marguerite Ross, 207n, 245
Basu, Jyoti, 97, 97n, 101n
Basu, Sajal, 130n
Basvalingappa, 156
Bell, C.L.G., 3n, 245
Bendix, Reinhard, 18, 18n, 22n, 245
Berger, Peter, 38n, 225n, 246
Beteille, Andre, 148n, 246
Bhambri, C. P., 63n, 245
Bhartiya Janata Party (BJP), 91, 192;
    see also Jan Sangh
Bhartiya Kranti Dal (BKD), 198, 207
Bhartiya Lok Dal (BLD), 91, 230; in
    U.P., ideology of, 199-200, as a Janata
    faction, 191-7, 200, 208-11, and land

reforms, 216-17, organization of, 203,
    211, social support, 207, 209-11
Bienen, Henry, 17n, 246
Bihar, 104, 231, 244
Boyce, James K., 120n, 246
Brahmins in U.P. politics, 204-9
Brass, Paul, 191n, 192, 196n, 198n, 204,
    204n, 205, 206n, 207n, 246
Bratton, Michael, 32n, 233, 233n, 234n, 246
Brazil, 35, 190, 235-6
Brecher, Michael, 57n, 246
Burger Angela Sutherland, 200n, 204n,
    208, 246
Byres, Terry J., 73n, 246

Cardoso, Fernando, 17, 17n, 20n, 246
Carnoy, Martin, 16n, 247
caste: in Karnataka, Brahmins, 152, and
    class, 148-54, dominant castes, 145,
    148-54, 160, in South Kanara, 176-7; in
    U.P., "backward" castes, 198-9, role in
    politics, 204-9; in West Bengal politics,
    104
Champaran, 53
Chandrashekhar, S., 194, 201
Chenery, Holis, 2n, 3n, 245, 247
Chile, 34, 35, 232-5
China, 38, 41, 59, 225
Chowdhry, Binoy, 97, 97n, 104, 106, 121,
    121n, 122n, 123, 124n, 135n
Coleman, James, 1n, 247
Collier, David, 15n, 247
Communist Party of India (CPI), in West
    Bengal, 107, 108
Communist Party of India, Marxist
    (CPM), in West Bengal: compared
    with U.P. Janata, 9-11, 221, 227-31;
    compared with Urs regime, 9-11, 187-8,
    227-31; electoral strength, 107-8;
    ideology, 98-102; leadership, 96-8;
    organization, 102-7; and *panchayats*,
    108-17; party membership, 102-3; and
    poverty reforms, 117-43; relations
    with *Kisan Sabha* 105-7
Congress for Democracy (CFD), 192, 194

255

CAMBRIDGE SOUTH ASIAN STUDIES

These monographs are published by the Syndics of Cambridge University Press in association with the Cambridge Centre for South Asian Studies. The following books have been published in this series:

1 S. Gopal: *British Policy in India, 1858–1905*
2 J. A. B. Palmer: *The Mutiny Outbreak at Meerut in 1857*
3 Ashin Das Gupta: *Malabar in Asian Trade, 1740–1800*
4 Gananath Obeyesekere: *Land Tenure in Village Ceylon: A Sociological and Historical Study*
5 H. L. Erdman: *The Swatantra Party and Indian Conservatism*
6 S. N. Mukherjee: *Sir William Jones: A Study in Eighteenth-Century British Attitudes to India*
7 Abdul Majed Khan: *The Transition in Bengal, 1756–1775: A Study of Saiyid Muhammad Reza Khan*
8 Radhe Shyam Rungta: *The Rise of Business Corporations in India, 1851-1900*
9 Pamela Nightingale: *Trade and Empire in Western India, 1784–1806*
10 Amiya Kumar Bagchi: *Private Investment in India 1900–1939*
11 Judith M. Brown: *Gandhi's Rise to Power: Indian Politics 1915–1922*
12 Mary C. Carras: *The Dynamics of Indian Political Factions: A Study of District Councils in the State of Maharashtra*
13 P. Hardy: *The Muslims of British India*
14 Gordon Johnson: *Provincial Politics and Indian Nationalism: Bombay and the Indian National Congress, 1880 to 1915*
15 Marguerite S. Robinson: *Political Structure in a Changing Sinhalese Village*
16 Francis Robinson: *Separatism among Indian Muslims: The Politics of the United Provinces' Muslims, 1860–1923*
17 Christopher John Baker: *The Politics of South India, 1920–1937*
18 D. A. Washbrook: *The Emergence of Provincial Politics: The Madras Presidency, 1870–1920*
19 Deepak Nayyar: *India's Exports and Export Policies in the 1960s*
20 Mark Holmström: *South Indian Factory Workers: Their Life and Their World*
21 S. Ambirajan: *Classical Political Economy and British Policy in India*
22 M. Mufakhrul Ismal: *Bengal Agriculture 1920–1946: A Quantitative Study*
23 Eric Stokes: *The Peasant and the Raj: Studies in Agrarian Society and Peasant Rebellion in Colonial India*

262